Risk Assessment for Juvenile Violent Offending

This volume is the result of an EU project involving two different European countries (Italy and Cyprus) on risk and needs assessment for juvenile violent offenders. The book is based on a longitudinal database of juveniles who have committed violent crimes and who have been followed up after six months to measure their recidivism rate.

The aim of this book is to provide practitioners who are dealing with juvenile (violent) offenders with scientifically based theories and knowledge derived from results about risk assessment. In particular it shows how a newly developed and tested instrument/approach, the EARN (European Assessment of Risk and Needs), works and how it can be used to help practitioners.

Recidivism of violence in juveniles is based on several risk factors and is reduced on the basis of protective factors. Juvenile justice systems in Europe tend to approach the juvenile who has committed a crime not only from a sanction point of view but more as an opportunity for the juvenile, his or her family and the social context in general to reduce the risk of recidivism.

This book will be of interest to researchers, students, social workers, police officers and lawyers.

Anna Costanza Baldry is Associate Professor of Social Psychology at the Second University of Naples. Her major research interests are violence against women, and bullying and cyber bullying. She has led several national and international funded projects on intimate partner violence, femicide, risk assessment and, in addition to over 50 published journal articles and book chapters on criminological and psychological topics, she has published ten books, monographs and government publications.

Andreas Kapardis is Professor of Legal Psychology and Chairman of the Law Department, University of Cyprus. He holds a PhD in Criminology from the University of Cambridge. His main research and teaching interests lie in criminology, criminal justice, psychology and law, and penology, and he has published extensively internationally. He has represented Cyprus on various committees abroad and is currently a member of the Crime Prevention Council in Cyprus and has been Vice-Chairman of the Cyprus Parole Board.

Risk Assessment for Juvenile Violent Offending

Edited by
Anna Costanza Baldry
and Andreas Kapardis

Routledge
Taylor & Francis Group
LONDON AND NEW YORK

First edition published 2013
by Routledge

This edition published 2013
by Routledge
2 Park Square, Milton Park, Abingdon, Oxon, OX14 4RN

Simultaneously published in the USA and Canada
by Routledge
711 Third Avenue, New York, NY 10017

Routledge is an imprint of the Taylor & Francis Group, an informa business

British Library Cataloguing in Publication Data
A catalogue record for this book is available from the British Library

Library of Congress Cataloging-in-Publication Data
Baldry, Anna C.
Risk assessment for juvenile violent offenders / Anna Costanza Baldry and Andreas Kapardis.
p. cm.
Includes bibliographical references and index.
1. Juvenile delinquency–Europe. 2. Juvenile delinquency–Italy. 3. Juvenile delinquency–Cyprus. 4. Juvenile justice, Administration of–Europe. 5. Juvenile justice, Administration of–Italy. 6. Juvenile justice, Administration of–Cyprus. I. Kapardis, Andreas. II. Title.
HV9144.A5B356 2013
364.36094—dc23 2012028247

ISBN: 978–1–84392–822–5 (hbk)
ISBN: 978–0–415–66274–1 (pbk)
ISBN: 978–0–203–10277–0 (ebk)

Typeset in Times New Roman by
Swales & Willis Ltd, Exeter, Devon

Contents

Illustrations

Figures

Tables

Notes on contributors

Anna Costanza Baldry is Associate Professor of Social Psychology at the Second University of Naples. Her major research interests are violence against women, and bullying and cyber bullying. She has led several national and international funded projects on intimate partner violence, femicide, risk assessment and, in addition to over 50 published journal articles and book chapters on criminological and psychological topics, she has published ten books, monographs and government publications. She is a UN and NATO consultant and trainer on gender-based violence.

Raymond R. Corrado is Full-Professor in the School of Criminology and the Department of Psychology at Simon Fraser University and Visiting Fellow at Clare Hall College and the Institute of Criminology, University of Cambridge. He is a founding member of the Mental Health, Law, and Policy Institute at Simon Fraser University, Co-Director of the BC Centre for Social Responsibility and recently was the Director of the Centre for Addictions Research British Columbia, SFU Site. He has co-authored five edited books as well as having published over 100 articles and book chapters on a wide variety of policy issues including juvenile justice, violent young offenders, mental health, adolescent psychopathy, Aboriginal victimization, and terrorism. Currently he is working on a number of research projects involving gaming issues, Aboriginal issues, and incarcerated serious and violent young offenders.

David P. Farrington, OBE is Emeritus Professor of Psychological Criminology and Leverhulme Trust Emeritus Fellow at the Institute of Criminology, University of Cambridge. His major research interest is in developmental criminology, and he is Director of the Cambridge Study in Delinquent Development, which is a prospective longitudinal survey of London males aged 8 to 56. In addition to hundreds of published journal articles and book chapters on criminological and psychological topics, he has published 91 books, monographs and government publications.

Chiara Giacomantonio has been a police officer in the Italian Department of Public Security, Ministry of Interior since 2000. She has a university degree in law and one in public administration science. Since 2005 she has been the chief of a Unit of the Central Operational Service of the Italian State Police with the task of monitoring criminal phenomena in which women and children are involved both as victims and perpetrators of crimes. She has represented the Italian Ministry of Interior at conferences and on committees both in Italy and abroad (*inter alia*, UN, OSCE, EU). She is also involved in ongoing training of State Police personnel in matters of domestic violence, missing children, child abuse and juvenile offenders.

Andreas Kapardis is Professor of Legal Psychology and Chairman of the Law Department, University of Cyprus. He holds a PhD in Criminology from the University of Cambridge and his main research and teaching interests lie in criminology, criminal justice, psychology and law, and penology. For many years he taught in Australia before taking up his position at the University of Cyprus. Among other things, he has researched a broad range of offenders (including juveniles), criminal justice issues and psycho-legal questions in various countries, and his work has been published extensively internationally. He has represented Cyprus on various committees abroad and is currently a member of the Crime Prevention Council in Cyprus and has been Vice-Chairman of the Cyprus Parole Board.

Stefano Maccioni is a lawyer specializing in criminal procedure. He was a member of the Italian Ministerial Commission on the protection of victims of crime and in 2006 founded the forensic association 'Avvocati&Avvocati'. He has published several books and articles on victims' rights, medical responsibility and social implication in the lawyer's practice.

Adrienne Peters is a doctoral student at Simon Fraser University. Her research interests include: young offenders; mental health and serious and violent young offending; young offender treatment, programming and rehabilitation; and the Canadian Youth Criminal Justice Act and young offender policies. Her doctoral research is on specialized interventions for serious young offenders in custody and in the community.

Cesare Porcaro is a psychologist and honorary judge in juvenile courts in Naples. His main research interests are violence against women and youths at risk. He worked as a junior researcher in several European projects coordinated by Professor Anna Baldry.

George Poyiadjis is a school psychologist, working as a private practitioner. His main research interests are evidence-based interventions applied in schools, and family counselling. He has worked as a postgraduate assistant in many University of Cyprus research programmes.

Gilda Scardaccione is Associate Professor of Social Psychology at Chieti/Pescara University 'G. D'annunzio'. She has been an honorary judge for over ten years in juvenile courts in Rome. Her major research interests are victims of crime, juvenile delinquency and restorative justice. She has published more than 80 journal articles and book chapters in Italy on criminological and psychological topics.

Foreword

A great deal has been learned, over many years and in several different countries, about the most important risk factors for offending and violence (see e.g. Farrington, 2012; Farrington et al., 2012). These include individual factors such as high impulsiveness or low intelligence, family factors such as disrupted families or poor supervision, and socio-economic factors such as low family income and large family size. These risk factors are often similarly important in different Western industrialized countries such as the US and the UK (e.g. Farrington and Loeber, 1999).

Knowledge about risk factors has often been used to construct risk assessment instruments that predict future offending. For example, in Toronto, Canada, Leena Augimeri and her colleagues developed the EARL-20B (see Augimeri et al., 2010). Boys aged 6–11 who were referred by the police for engaging in antisocial behaviour were scored on 20 risk factors such as impulsivity, antisocial attitudes, household circumstances (e.g. low family income) and caregiver continuity. Each item was scored 0 (does not apply), 1 (partially applies), or 2 (fully applies). The scores were used in implementing interventions such as Stop Now and Plan (SNAP: see Augimeri et al., 2011). This type of instrument is useful and useable by practitioners because it is relatively short and simple. This is an excellent example of evidence-based practice.

A number of very useful risk assessment instruments for juvenile delinquents have been developed and used widely in North America, including the SAVRY and YLS/CMI (see Hoge et al., 2012). In addition, several effective interventions for juvenile delinquents have been developed and tested in North America (mainly), including multisystemic therapy (MST), functional family therapy (FFT), cognitive-behavioural therapy (CBT) and multidimensional treatment foster care (MTFC: see Welsh et al., 2012). It is extremely important to develop and test risk assessment instruments and effective interventions for juvenile delinquents in other settings, and especially in Europe.

With this background, it is easy to welcome this excellent book edited by Anna Costanza Baldry and Andreas Kapardis. Their main aim is to develop and test a new risk/needs assessment instrument, in Italy and Cyprus, called EARN (the European Assessment of Risks and Needs). The main aim of this instrument is to predict recidivism among juvenile violent offenders. EARN, containing 32 items, is inspired by the Cracow Instrument (see Corrado, 2002) but goes beyond it by including some protective factors as well as risk factors. It is a more positive message to strengthen protective factors rather than to reduce risk factors. Commendably, the effectiveness of EARN in reducing recidivism is experimentally tested in Italy (see Chapter 7). This book really pushes back the frontiers of knowledge about risk/needs assessment in Europe.

This is a great start! I really hope that Anna and Andreas will follow up by investigating whether EARN works better with boys or girls, with different aged children, or at different stages of the juvenile justice system (including arrest). It would be extremely valuable to carry out randomized experiments to evaluate EARN and to conduct cost–benefit analyses of its use. I wonder what types of recidivism are predicted best, and whether the instrument can be used repeatedly to assess treatment progress? It would also be useful to specify in more detail how the scores map onto different types of interventions and to what extent EARN is useful in other countries.

Anna Costanza Baldry, Andreas Kapardis, Ray Corrado and their colleagues should be warmly congratulated for greatly advancing knowledge about risk/needs assessment in European countries. This book should be essential reading for scholars and practitioners in such areas as criminology, juvenile justice, psychology, sociology, education, social work, policing and risk assessment.

David P. Farrington
Emeritus Professor of Psychological Criminology
University of Cambridge

References

Augimeri, L. K., Enebrink, P., Walsh, M. M. and Jiang, D. (2010). Gender-specific childhood risk assessment tools: Early Assessment Risk Lists for Boys (EARL-20B) and Girls (EARL-21G). In R. K. Otto and K. S. Douglas (eds) *Handbook of Violence Risk Assessment.* New York: Routledge (pp. 43–62).

Augimeri, L. K., Walsh, M. M. and Slater, N. (2011). Rolling out SNAP, an evidence-based intervention: A summary of implementation, evaluation and research. *International Journal of Child, Youth and Family Studies,* 2, 330–52.

Corrado, R. R. (2002). An introduction to the Risk/Needs Case Management Instrument for children and youth at risk for violence: The Cracow instrument. In R. R. Corrado, R. Roesch, S. D. Hart and J. K. Gierowski (eds) *Multi-Problem Violent Youth: A Foundation for Comparative Research on Needs, Interventions and Outcomes.* Amsterdam, Netherlands: IOS Press (pp. 295–301).

Farrington, D. P. (2012). Predictors of violent young offenders. In B. C. Feld and D. M. Bishop (eds) *The Oxford Handbook on Juvenile Crime and Juvenile Justice.* Oxford: Oxford University Press (pp. 146–71).

Farrington, D. P. and Loeber, R. (1999). Transatlantic replicability of risk factors in the development of delinquency. In P. Cohen, C. Slomkowski and L. N. Robins (eds) *Historical and Geographical Influences on Psychopathology.* Mahwah, NJ: Lawrence Erlbaum (pp. 299–329).

Farrington, D. P., Loeber, R. and Ttofi, M. M. (2012). Risk and protective factors for offending. In B. C. Welsh and D. P. Farrington (eds) *The Oxford Handbook of Crime Prevention.* Oxford: Oxford University Press (pp. 46–69).

Hoge, R. D., Vincent, G. M. and Guy, L. S. (2012). Prediction and risk/needs assessments. In R. Loeber and D. P. Farrington (eds) *From Juvenile Delinquency to Adult Crime: Criminal Careers, Justice Policy and Prevention*. Oxford: Oxford University Press (pp. 150–83).

Welsh, B. C., Lipsey, M. W., Rivara, F. P., Hawkins, J. D., Aos, S. and Hollis-Peel, M. (2012). Promoting change, changing lives: Effective prevention and intervention to reduce serious offending. In R. Loeber and D. P. Farrington (eds) *From Juvenile Delinquency to Adult Crime: Criminal Careers, Justice Policy and Prevention*. Oxford: Oxford University Press (pp. 245–77).

1 The juvenile young violent offender

From bullying to delinquency

A. C. Baldry and A. Kapardis

This book is the outcome of "The EARN in JVO project" that was developed, conducted and implemented in Italy and Cyprus, with the supervision and support of the Institute of Criminology (David P. Farrington and Friedrich Loesel) and Raymond Corrado from Simon Fraser University in Vancouver, British Columbia, Canada.

The project was conducted over a period of two years and covered several activities. This book puts together some of these experiences and outcomes that derived from that project, as well as offering some broader contribution on *risk assessment* and *risk management* approaches and their rationale in the field of juvenile delinquency.

Thanks to this project, we developed and validated the so-called EARN tool, the "European Assessment of Risks and Needs" for juvenile violent offenders, by identifying risk factors and needs associated with juveniles who committed crimes.

This approach is not new and it was developed and implemented by Corrado, Roesch, Hart and Gieroswski (2002); the EARN is a derivation from the so-called "Cracow Instrument" since it is tailored for those professionals working directly with juveniles: social workers, educators, law enforcement and psychologists, to screen out the risk factors belonging to different domains (e.g. family, individual, environmental). This helps understand which are the most problematic characteristics or areas in a given individual that might explain his violent behaviour and the risk of recidivism and actual recidivism. Law enforcement and social workers in charge of offenders need to have an advanced scientific structured method to learn how to manage risks/needs and set up provisions following the onset of peer violence (Corrado, 2002).

To prevent recidivism we should not only focus on *problematic areas* that lead juveniles to commit a crime, but, given the peculiarities of the age group under consideration and the legal provision foreseen by most EU and non-EU criminal legislation with regard juvenile delinquency, the EARN approach focuses also on *needs*.

A juvenile who commits a crime, is not *only* a "criminal": he or she is someone who by breaching the law is also communicating to experts, professionals, family and society that the reasons that lead to that (those) illegal action(s) are multiple, complex, dynamic and not static. A juvenile who has committed a crime can step back from a criminal career: most offenders desist and only a few of them will go on committing crime in adulthood (Farrington, 2006).

If we were able to allocate resources for services that are tailored on the risk factors, but also on the *need* of that adolescent, we might even save more money because they are better spent. To be able to know which are the *critical areas* that can be addressed, for each individual who commits a crime, we should think in terms of treatment by addressing specific risks and needs, and empowering the so-called *protective factors*: the personal, relational and contextual resources each juvenile has to reduce the recidivism rate.

This project involved as ultimate beneficiaries, juveniles; as far as the target is concerned, the professionals involved in the project who dealt with juveniles are: police, social workers, educators, psychologists, and juvenile judges. The interventions and the assessment were based on the outcome from the EARN screening, by identifying which areas from the EARN resulted in "weak", needing special attention.

Most studies on early identification of risk factors in juvenile violence have focused on bullying in school (Olweus, 1993; Baldry, 2003; Smith et al., 1999) and are cross-sectional in nature. Loeber et al. (1998) have conducted the most extensive investigation of risk factors for multiple problematic boys by taking into account a wide range of risk factors, showing that it is possible to identify risk factors that, if present, increase the risk of violence.

We were interested in risk factors of recidivism for those juveniles who have already committed violent acts and who are at most risk of recidivism and determine the positive impact of tailored intervention by focusing also on their needs, especially according to whether they have been victims themselves. The same approach was used by the UK longitudinal study, conducted originally by West and Farrington (1973), followed up to two generations by Farrington (2002).

Offending violent behaviour in juveniles is related to several risk factors (Corrado et al., 2002). Research has demonstrated a number of factors that put youth at higher risk of involvement in violence and recidivism (Aguliar, 2011). A systematic translation of this body of research into practice was still pending, especially in Mediterranean EU countries. Research on peer violence has focused mainly on bullying at school and less on violent criminal behaviour among peers (even murder) and risk/need factors related to it. Canada and other English-speaking countries (UK) have adopted a conceptual framework to assess risk/need factors by focusing on management strategies (Loeber and Farrington, 2001). A structured risk/need approach to identify and manage factors related to violence was needed also in Mediterranean countries such as Italy and Cyprus, where public and social concern about criminal violent behaviour, especially among peers, is a high concern. This needed to be tested first as a pilot in some parts of Italy, given its geographical extension and, with regard to Cyprus, in the free areas of the Republic of Cyprus. The EARN approach has proved to be a new method for social workers and law enforcement to have a shared common language/understanding to address peer violent juvenile offenders, not general offending, and provide them with a tailored intervention to reduce recidivism. For this reason, a longitudinal experimental prospective study was chosen and adopted to establish the effectiveness of intervention, and is presented in this book (Chapters 5, 6 and 7).

Special attention in this project was initially devoted to those violent offenders who are/were also victimised at home, because they were raised in families with Intimate Partner Violence (IPV). In this regard, intervention delivered to the experimental group involved juveniles by enhancing relational empathic perspective skills and resiliency, and increasing victim-oriented, stimulated, empathic responses through, e.g. mediation. Structured scientific methods are a viable way to prove efficacy.

Juvenile delinquency is explained by a plethora of risk factors, one of these being bullying in school (Augimeri et al., 2011; Farrington and Ttofi, 2011). Bullying per se is not a crime, though some bullying behaviours are already consisting of criminal actions (e.g. stealing peers' goods, offending others' reputations, hitting). What characterises bullying is its reiteration, the imbalance of power between the victim and the bully, and the intention of harming (Farrington, 1993).

Longitudinal research has indicated that bullying can persist over time (Aguliar, 2011; Farrington, 1993, 2011). According to the study conducted by Yates and Smith (1989) almost 70% of all children who bullied "this term" did so also in the previous one. More persistent behaviours were found by Olweus (1978) over the period of one year both in relation to bullying others and being bullied. Stephenson and Smith (1989) found that 89% of bullies started bullying at least the previous year and 72% of victims were also victimised the previous year. Farrington (1993) found it helpful to apply to bullying the concept of "career" used for criminal behaviour, and bullying as a "stepping stone" to further violence (Winkel and Baldry, 1997). Farrington (2011), looking up to the second generation of youth taking part in the Cambridge Study, confirms the persistency of bullying as a strong precursor of deliquency further in adulthood. In this regard, he defines a criminal career as a "longitudinal sequence of offences. It has a beginning (onset), an end (desistance), and a career length in between (duration). Only a certain proportion of the population (prevalence) has a criminal career and commits offences. During their careers, offenders commit their offences at a certain rate (frequency) and they may accelerate, decelerate, and have periods of remission" (Farrington, 1993: 398). According to Farrington (1993, 2011), the same definitions can be applied to the bullying career that could provide a better approach to understand and to assist in intervening to reduce the duration of bullying or even prevent its onset. Bullying may, in fact, escalate into more serious criminal acts (Farrington, 1993; Le Blanc and Loeber, 1993; see also Baldry and Farrington, 2000; Farrington and Ttofi, 2011). From the original studies by Olweus (1991) it emerged that up to 60% of bullies were eventually convicted of criminal offences by the time they were 24. To reduce the duration of bullying and prevent it from turning into a criminal career, it is important to intervene at an early stage (Menard and Huizinga, 1994).The best way to develop long-term prevention strategies would be by adopting a career approach based on the identification of risk and protective factors but by addressing the needs of the individual. Rigby and Cox (1996) identified the importance of determining how many bullies engage in other forms of delinquent behaviour while still at school. Their study in fact shows that there is a strong association between bullying and the identification of delinquent behaviour. The recent meta-analysis conducted by Ttofi, Farrington, Lösel and Loeber (2011: 86) indicated that "school bullying is a unique childhood risk factor for later offending and that the bullying perpetration increases the probability of adverse outcomes later in life", stressing once more that even if we can not refer to causal effects, bullying and its persistency over years strongly leads to later offending.

This is why the most effective responses to youth being involved in criminal behaviours, is to promote and enhance education systems (Nance and Novy, 2011). Failures of educational systems to identify early risk factors and tackle them, by reinforcing the socially proactive capabilities of the individual, is the best response also for those juveniles who have already committed a crime.

In this regard the chapters presented in this book describe on one side the different justice systems in Italy and in Cyprus with regard to juvenile delinquency (Chapters 3, 4 and 5). Chapters 7 and 8 respectively describe the adaptation and use and outcomes of the EARN project in Italy and Cyprus by stressing also the limitations besides a positive impact of the justice treatment system for juvenile offenders. Chapter 2 is systematic overview of what consitutes risk factors in juveniles and how this approach is needed to design and implement intervention and prevention strategies. Chapter 5 is a thorough overview of community-based intervention programmes for released incarcerated serious and violent young offenders, for the best understanding of what might constitute for societies effective intervention programmes for so-called "violent offenders".

We would like to acknowledge the European Union, Daphne programme, Funded Project for the support of the JLS/2006/DAP/-1/121/Y30-CE-0123316/00-95 project.

References

Aguliar, J. P. (2011). Developmental pathways and life trajectories of delinquency. In D. W. Springer and A. Roberts (eds) *Juvenile Justice and Delinquency* (pp. 189–202). Sudbury, MA: Jones & Bartlett.

Augimeri, L. K., Walsh, M., Liddon, A. D., and Dassinger, C. R. (2011). From risk identification to risk management: A comprehensive strategy for young children engaged in antisocial behavior. In D. W. Springer and A. Roberts (eds), *Juvenile Justice and Delinquency* (pp. 117–140). Sudbury, MA: Jones and Bartlett.

Baldry, A. C. (2003). Bullying in schools and exposure to domestic violence. *Child Abuse and Neglect*, 27, 713–32.

Baldry, A.C. and Farrington, D.P. (2000). Bullies and delinquents: personal characteristics and parental styles. *Journal of Community Applied Social Psychology*, 10, 17–31.

Corrado, R. R. (2002). An introduction to the risk/needs case management instrument for children and youth at risk for violence: The Cracow instrument. In R. R. Corrado, R. Roesch, S. D. Hart, and J. K. Gierowski (eds), *Multi-Problem Violent Youth: A Foundation for Comparative Research on Needs, Interventions and Outcomes.* Amsterdam, Netherlands: IOS Press (pp. 295–301).

Corrado, R., Roesch, R., Hart, S. and Gierowski, J. (2002). *Multi-Problem Violent Youth: A Foundation for Comparative Research on Needs, Interventions and Outcomes.* Amsterdam, Netherlands: IOS Press.

Farrington, D. P. (1993). Understanding and preventing bullying. In M. Tonry (ed.) *Crime and Justice*, vol. 17. Chicago: University of Chicago Press (pp. 381–458).

Farrington, D. P. (2002). Criminology. *Criminal Behaviour and Mental Health*, 12, S10–S16.

Farrington, D. P. (2006). Origins of violent behaviour over the life span. In D. J. Flannery, A. T. Vaszonyi and I. Waldman (eds) *The Cambridge Handbook of Violent Behaviour*. Cambridge: Cambridge University Press.

Farrington, D. and Ttofi, M. M. (2011). Bullying as a predictor of offending, violence and later life outcomes. *Journal of Criminal Behavior and Mental Health*, 21, 90–8.

Le Blanc, M. and Loeber, R. (1993). Precursors, causes, and the development of criminal offending. In Dale F. Hay and Adrian Angold (eds) *Precursors and Causes in Development and Psychopathology*. New York: Wiley.

Loeber, R., Farrington, D. P., Stouthamer-Loeber, M., and Van Kammen, W.B. (eds) (1998). *Antisocial Behavior and Mental Health Problems: Explanatory Factors in Childhood and Adolescence*. Mahwah, NJ: Erlbaum.

Loeber, R. and Farrington, D.P. (eds) (2001). *Child Delinquents: Development, Intervention and Service Needs.* Thousand Oaks, California: Sage.

Menard, S. and Huizinga, D. (1994). Changes in conventional attitudes and delinquent behavior in adolescence. *Youth and Society*, 26, 23–53.

Nance, D. and Novy, F. A. (2011). The power of education in juvenile justice. In A. R. Roberts and D. W. Springer (eds), *Juvenile Delinquency and Juvenile Justice: Policies, Programs and Intervention Strategies*. Sudbury, MA: Jones and Bartlett Publishers.

Olweus, D. (1978). *Aggression in the Schools: Bullies and Whipping Boys*. Washington, DC: Hemisphere.

Olweus D. (1991). Bully/victim problems among school children: basic facts and effects of a school based intervention program. In D. Pepler and K. H. Rubin (eds) *The Development and Treatment of Childhood Aggression* (pp. 411–48). Mahwah, NJ: Lawrence Erlbaum Associates Inc.

Olweus, D. (1993). *Bullying at School: What We Know and What We Can Do*. Cambridge, MA: Blackwell.

Rigby, K. and Cox, I. (1996). The contribution of bullying at school and low self-esteem to acts of delinquency among Australian teenagers. *Personality Individual Differences,* 21, 609–12.

Smith, P. K., Morita, Y., Junger-Tas, J., Olweus, D. Catalano, R., Slee, P. (eds) (1999). *The Nature of School Bullying: A Cross-National Perspective*. London and New York: Routledge.

Stephenson, P. and Smith, D. (1989). Bullying in the junior school. In D. P. Tattum and D. A. Lane (eds), *Bullying in Schools*. Stoke-on-Trent: Trentham.

Ttofi, M. M., Farrington, D. P., Lösel, F. and Loeber, R. (2011). The predictive efficiency of school bullying versus later offending: A systematic/meta-analytic review of longitudinal studies. *Criminal Behaviour and Mental Health*, 21, 80–9.

West, D. J. and Farrington D. P. (1973). *Who Becomes Delinquent?* London: Heinemann.

Winkel, F. W. and Baldry, A. C. (1997). An application of the Scared Straight principle in early intervention programming: Three studies on activating the other's perspective in pre-adolescents' perceptions of a stepping-stone behaviour. *Issues in Criminological and Legal Psychology*, 26, 3–15.

Yates, C. and Smith, P. K. (1989). Bullying in two English comprehensive schools. In E. M. Roland (ed.), *Bullying: An International Perspective* (pp. 22–34). London: David Fulton.

2 Risk factors for serious and violent young offenders and risk assessment

R. Corrado

When Professors Ron Roesch, Steve Hart, and I began our initial discussions about the need to develop a risk/needs management instrument to assist practitioners responsible for diagnosing and providing case plans for children and youth at risk for serious violent behaviours, we knew that such an instrument would be enormously complex, and, therefore, there would be major obstacles in not only devising such an ambitious instrument but also validating it, let alone convincing governments to implement it. However, we all had been involved for over 20 years with researching mental health and criminal laws for both youth and adults, and with participating in the discussions and debates about how to devise effective policies to reduce the likelihood that multi-problem youth and adults would become entrenched in often tragic criminal lifestyles and imprisonment. In Canada and the United States, it had become evident that the deinstitutionalization of the mentally ill movement that took place in earnest in the 1970s had the unintended consequence of the criminal justice system and incarceration becoming the most pervasive policy option in responding to mentally ill, aggressive, and violent offenders, even minor ones.

In addition, it became evident in our advisory work with government ministries and agencies and in our research that there were few integrated programs to address the wide range of problems or risks that virtually ensured that multi-problem offenders, especially youth, would end up incarcerated for long periods of their youth and into their adulthood. Most distressing was the common response from senior government officials that there were inherent political and bureaucratic obstacles to integrated multi-ministerial programs. For example, there is a deep-seated reluctance of school officials under the Ministry of Education to share information on their most troubled students with social workers under the Ministry of Social Services, with the police under the Ministry of the Solicitor General, and with family doctors under the Ministry of Health. Each ministry has services for multi-problem youth, yet it is extremely difficult to share relevant information across ministries for individual case planning often because of confidentiality rules, time and personnel resources, and perceived differences in ideological values among the disparate ministries. In other words, only in rare circumstances were treatment intervention case plans based on complete information of an offender's full range of risk and protective factors. In addition to sharing information limits, case planners routinely face the challenge of incomplete information, especially acute for the earliest age stages beginning with pregnancy/birth or perinatal and then infancy. Another concern involves ethical issues focused on the fear that sharing extremely sensitive personal information could seriously increase the likelihood of the negative official labeling of already highly disadvantaged families by the varied group of officials with access to a centralized data instrument bank yet without the professional expertise to interpret it validly. An additional concern was that too many officials would have access to the confidential data, thereby increasing the possibilities that some of this information could become public. Still, we believed that it was vitally important to create an experimental risk management instrument for aggressive and violent multi-problem children and youth despite these fundamental practical political, bureaucratic, and ethical challenges. Our major justification was that research on risk factors, preventive factors, and related treatment intervention programs had progressed dramatically, and there was desperate need to provide professionals with an instrument that would enhance their ability to design and implement more effective case planning for highly vulnerable multi-problem children and youth.

There were several other inherent challenges in developing a complex risk management instrument. First, primarily through the Mental Health, Law, and Policy Institute at Simon Fraser University, we had considerable experience with our colleagues who developed short risk violence assessment instruments for spousal abuse, sexual aggression and pre-trial detention risk for self harm and/or violent behaviour. These instruments, typically, consisted of 20 interview items that could be administered reliably by trained personel in a short time period, that is, approximately less than 1 hour. Even such narrowly focused risk instruments required an exhaustive review of an extensive theoretical and empirical literature to identify the minimum number of risk factors that could be validly utilized largely by criminal justice and mental health professionals. The essential prerequisites for these professionals considering the use of these risk instruments are the ease of training, short time needed, and minimum resource costs. Instruments that required additional information from institutional files and interviews with other staff, professionals in other departments, and ministries, as well as family and friends, invariably added substantial time and cost to the process. In other words, a lengthy and complex instrument simply would be resisted. Second, it was clearly evident by the mid-1990s that persistent aggressive and violent behaviour was both evident in only a small percentage of children, youth, and young adults and that it varied highly across age stages. Most importantly, while levels of aggression and violence were most pervasive among 2- to 3-year-old toddlers, the levels dropped dramatically in the remaining childhood stages, began to increase in adolescence, peaked at 15 to 16 years old, and then declined in late adolescence and early adulthood with another major reduction in the mid-20s. In addition, males overwhelmingly engaged in these behaviours. Certain social contexts predominated, including schools and public spaces (e.g., parks, malls, and transit). The most extreme context was socially disorganized neighbourhoods with concentrated economic disadvantage where youth and adult gangs were entrenched. Third, developmental theories of delinquency and criminality had become prominent largely because of several large-scale cohort studies conducted first in the United States and England followed by Canada, Sweden, and New Zealand. All of these cohort studies confirmed that risk factors appeared in different developmental periods and that early prevention and intervention strategies appeared the most effective.

Given these fundamental obstacles or challenges to creating a risk management instrument, we believed the most efficacious approach was to assemble a multinational team of experts from the various academic disciplines that had been involved in identifying the key risk factors for aggressive and violent children and youth and related intervention strategies to reduce these risks. We also assumed that the eventual Cracow Instrument would be experimental and require a long period of validation projects, most likely section by section rather than in its entirety and in different national contexts (Corrado, 2011).

The Cracow Instrument

The Cracow Instrument (CI) was presented in Odgers et al. (2002). The structure of this instrument consists of five age-based developmental stages: perinatal (pregnancy/birth), early childhood, middle/late childhood, and adolescence. Distinctive risk factors for violence are identified for each stage. These are also divided into individual risk factors (e.g., low birth weight and high reactive temperament) and environmental risk factors (e.g., teenage single mother/social assistance dependent family and socially disorganized/economic disadvantaged neighbourhood) (see Table 2.1 for a more exhaustive list of the risk domains). This is consistent with the developmental theories that have emerged in recent years to explain youth delinquency and violence at different periods in life and with different intensities (Kazemian and Le Blanc, 2004; Loeber et al., 2008; Thornberry, 2005). These theories generally recognize five distinct developmental stages including birth, preschool, elementary school, middle/secondary school, and early adulthood (Farrington, 2005; Loeber and Hay, 1997; Lösel and Bender, 2006).

A recent study conducted on a sample of 100, mixed-gendered preschoolers in Vancouver, Canada, utilizing the Cracow Instrument found that the use of such a comprehensive instrument is valuable, particularly when examining pre/perinatal risk/needs (Lussier et al., 2011). The research found that highly aggressive children presented with many of the individual and familial risk/needs factors identified by the Cracow. For example, children coming from a family with poor parenting practices combined with a criminogenic environment were more likely to be highly physically aggressive than those children who were not (Lussier et al., 2011). Based on this study, as well as other research done in the area of developmental stages and violence/aggression (Broidy et al., 2003; Côté et al., 2006; Farrington, 2005; Loeber, Slot, and Stouthamer-Loeber, 2008; Lösel and Bender, 2006; Thornberry and Krohn, 2005; Tremblay et al., 1999; Tremblay and Nagin, 2005; Tremblay et al., 2004), there is strong support for the use of multidisciplinary risk tools to assess a young person's risk for aggression. By being able to determine this at an early stage, practitioners can implement interventions in the early stages of development

Table 2.1 Domains of risk/need factors on the CRACOW

Domains of risk/need factors	*Severity/intensity*	*Risk/need sub-factors*
1. Pre/perinatal section	Low-level Mid-level High-level	Maternal substance use Pregnancy related complications Birth related complications Low birth weight Premature birth
2. Socio-economic situation section	Low-level Mid-level High-level	Low occupational status Low family income Poor parental education Familial adversities (e.g., single mother, large family size, high residential mobility) Economic dependency
3. Family environment section	Low-level Mid-level High-level	Parent's mental health problems Parent's antisocial behaviours Parent's criminal history Intimate partner violence Poor familial support Parental antisocial attitudes
4. Psychological functioning section	Low-level Mid-level High-level	Low verbal IQ Callousness Negative emotionality Daring/risk taking Attention deficits Hyperactivity
5. Parenting skills section	Low-level Mid-level High-level	Hostile parenting Lack of consistent discipline Lack of positive involvement Inadequate norms/rules

and provide support for the specific stage in combination with the identified risks. With the plethora of support and encouragement for early intervention, this evidence should not be overlooked (Cullen et al., 1998; Hosking and Walsh, 2010).

While there has been enormous progress in identifying risk and protective factors for aggression and violence largely based on the developmental theoretical perspective both in psychology, health sciences, and criminology, several challenges have emerged regarding, first, genetic/epigenetic/brain research and, second, in understanding distinctive sets of risk/protective factors, that is, separate pathways to aggression and violence including different onset periods including early childhood, late childhood, and adolescence. A general theme that has emerged from the recent risk/protective factors' research has been the elaboration of the understanding of already identified risk factors, as well as the finding of new risks within the general categories of the CI. Most typically, these new risks have been found within the perinatal and early childhood stages (Agin, 2010; Caspi et al., 2002; DeLisi and Vaughn, 2011; Haberstick et al., 2005; Lussier et al., 2011; Tremblay and Japel, 2003). Before discussing the implications of these new risks for identifying distinctive treatment pathway strategies, it is important to review several examples of the individual risk factors.

Patterns of risk factors: old ones revisited and new risks

In the original construction of the CI a central theme was the importance of healthy fetal development, early maternal bonding, early childhood/mother healthiness, and early positive infancy/childhood learning opportunities. Another focus was the identification of family and neighbourhood risk and protective factors again, especially during pregnancy, infancy, and early childhood. The most influential theoretical and empirical basis for these CI foci was the now classic contributions of the Canadian scholar Richard Tremblay. His central thesis is: infants typically are driven by genetically determined physiological determinants such as motor control, language attainment, temperament, and learning capacities to be physically aggressive, albeit in differing degrees, up to approximately the age period of 2 to 3 years and that then it is the parenting styles that socialize their toddlers either toward prosocial alternatives to immediate fulfilment wants or the reinforcement of antisocial physical aggression in attaining their needs such as attention, control of toys, and dominating social interactions with peers, older children, and adults. Moffitt and her colleagues, in particular, Kim-Cohen et al. (2006), subsequently added a specific set of new risk factors – the presence of the Monoamine oxidase A (MAOA) genetic polymorphism and early childhood trauma – that explained a substantial amount of the variation in the relationship between early childhood physical aggression and similar aggression in adulthood (late 20s). While their empirical research about this relationship has continued to be the subject of an empirical debate, primarily because their results have not been replicated consistently in subsequent studies, on balance, of the issues raised, the Kim-Cohen et al. (2006) set of risk factors, at least tentatively, has been accepted as important.

More recent genetic research summarized by DeLisi and Vaughn (2011) has further revealed the importance of genetic propensity of certain genetic polymorphisms or mutations that are related to the presence of aggression, violence, and certain personality traits such as impulsivity and executive function deficits also associated with aggression and violence (discussed below in detail). While there are indications also, but non-definitive, that traits (such as those just mentioned) of certain phenotypes or personality types (most importantly, psychopathic) likely have a genetic basis, there is a growing consensus that temperament is genetically based, though subject to some degree of environmental modification, especially in later childhood, adolescence and adulthood (DeLisi and Vaughn, 2011; Kagan, 1994, 2010). And further, that the extreme high reactive and low reactive temperament types are both associated with early onset aggression and even aggression in subsequent developmental stages – especially in the absence of certain personality traits, high IQ, strong executive functions, appropriate parental discipline, prosocial peers and prosocial/structured activities (for the low reactive temperament types) and prosocial but less structured (and, therefore, typically, less stress inducing) for the high reactive temperament type in home, leisure, and school environments.

In effect, the research on how environmental protective factors appear to mediate the relationship between temperament types and aggression/violence suggests both the importance of identifying these types and then considering the profile of individual risk and protective factors and, very importantly, family risk and protective factors, along with community risk and protective factors for case management planning based on a distinctive temperament-based developmental pathway to aggression and violence. This pathway and other pathways are outlined in Figures 2.1 to 2.5.

Whether personality disorders are either simply and primarily inherited, primarily environmental or a combination of "nature and nurture", as mentioned above, is not yet evident. Nonetheless, there is the continuing debate about whether childhood and adolescent disorders are too pervasive and too general to be sufficient risk factors to inform case management decisions. Another key theoretical/conceptual and case management issue is the extent to which the adult personality disorders, in particular the Axis II, Cluster B, dramatic, emotional or erratic disorders, including Histrionic, Narcissistic, Borderline, and Antisocial, and, subsumed under the last category , Psychopathic Personality Disorder (PPD), can be extended down into adolescence and even into childhood. There is substantial evidence suggesting that PPD is a valid category for adolescents despite continuing concerns that the antisocial behavioural facet is most strongly predictive of aggression and violent recidivism (Vincent et al., 2003; Corrado et al., 2005; Salekin and Lynam, 2010). In reaction to the longstanding theoretical/conceptual/empirical debates about the concept of psychopathy and its various measurement instruments, Cooke et al. (2005) introduced their Comprehensive Assessment of Psychopathy Personality Disorder (CAPP) construct and measurement instrument. The CAPP is a much broader conceptualization of psychopathy and is based primarily on a clinical perspective and usage. In effect, if subsequently and sufficiently validated, the CAPP is designed for clinical diagnosis and possibly case management purposes. Also, the CAPP currently has been the subject of validation studies regarding adolescent samples. Preliminary results have suggested that it has potential regarding an institutional sample of serious and violent incarcerated young offenders (Dawson, McCuish, Hart, and Corrado, 2012). While the CI does not have the indicators for this broader range of personality disorders, their inclusion in case management planning, nonetheless, might be considered as, arguably, the more narrow range of distinctive personality-based childhood/adolescent disorders have been a traditional risk management consideration.

Another risk factor that was not well understood in the original CI is whether government programs that place children in care or foster families is a protective or a risk factor for future aggression and violence. The assumption was that it was a protective factor for the obvious reason that the child or youth was being removed from an abusive family context (whether the form of this abuse was neglect, emotional, physical, or sexual) and then placed into a protective, that is, supportive or rehabilitative, family context. However, this original assumption was not supported by research primarily because there was evidence that multiple childcare or foster placements was associated with much higher likelihood of involvement in youth criminal justice and sentences to youth custody. Why the later negative relationship was found has been the subject of a growing debate about the shortcomings of childcare programs especially with regard to children and youth from highly vulnerable or historically marginalized ethnic groups such as Aboriginals in Australia and North America, Maori in New Zealand, and Roma in Europe. One hypothesis is that too frequently children and youth placed in care do not undergo adequate risk/protective factor assessments, and then they are placed with foster families that lack the capability to respond positively to the needs of these foster care youth. These youth eventually are rejected by their foster families, placed in another foster family until these youth experience continual rejection and then turn to antisocial peers, dropping out of school, resorting to street-kid lifestyles involving, drug and alcohol abuse, property crime, drug trafficking, sex trade and informal gang membership to survive. Initial, though necessarily tentative, research has suggested further that children with certain risk factors, including fetal alcohol spectrum disorder (FASD), autism spectrum disorder, oppositional defiant disorder (ODD) and conduct disorder (CD) increase the likelihood of multiple childcare placements and subsequent persistent criminality into adulthood (Corrado and Freedman, 2011).

An important risk factor related to childcare placement is childhood trauma associated with abuse. Why trauma has been a traditional risk factor for aggression and violence for certain children and youth and not others, possibly the majority, has not been well understood. Typically, the most common trauma outcome has been internally directed or self-harm traits, especially evident in later childhood and adolescence. Post-traumatic stress disorder (PTSD), for example, is one of the extreme reactions to trauma. PTSD is associated with other directed aggression and violence especially evident among young adults returning from war zones such as Iraq and Afghanistan and child soldiers forcibly recruited into long and excessively brutal and even genocidal civil wars such as in coastal central African countries. Arguably, however, undetected infant and early childhood trauma (up to ages 4 to 5) is far more prevalent than both reported abuse cases and the egregious PTSD cases associated with war. The obvious reason for unreported, undetected early abuse is the inability of these victims to remember or verbalize their abuse experiences to a responsible older person. However, during the last decade, brain research has suggested that infant and early childhood can be associated with fundamental changes in brain-based endocrinology, most importantly, elevated levels of cortisol and epinephrine, both excitatory hormones associated with aggression. The inability to recall the traumatic abuse experience is not only a risk factor in itself for future aggression and violence, but also increases the difficulty of providing the appropriate treatment programming typically available to traditional PTSD or lesser trauma victimization types. Nonetheless, this research suggests that the CI likely should consider including a "likelihood of trauma based on family history of abuse" risk factor (Corrado and Freedman, 2011).

More recent research on criminal trajectories has specified late adolescent onset criminality (Lacourse et al., 2008), in particular involving membership into essentially adult organized crime organizations or gangs. Unlike the risk factors identified in the classic gang theories and research, in certain countries such as Canada and the United States, not infrequently, youth join these multi-ethnic gangs even though they are from relatively stable middle-income families and neighbourhoods. The primary hypothesized risk factor is the desire for the immediate and exciting gangster lifestyle made popular in multi-media depictions usually of the American gangster ideal type. Central to this lifestyle, however, are strain theory risk factors based on immediate lifestyle benefits without the prosocial and non-criminal means of attaining them. Nonetheless, traditional risk factors for gang membership remain by far the most prevalent, that is, adolescents and young adults from socio-economically marginalized ethnic/racial groups and neighbourhoods with high concentrations of economic disadvantage and social discrimination (Corrado and Cohen, 2011a; Klein et al., 2001). The use of the CI for case management for a youth either at-risk for, or already involved in, an informal gang or a formal youth/adult gang, therefore, is to identify the specific set of risk/protective factors including onset of gang involvement so that the treatment strategy reflects the distinctive pathways associative with late adolescent or young adult onset.

Old risks better understood

The CI was based conclusively on restricting research about certain risk factors from the earliest developmental stage, such as avoiding excessive use of alcohol during pregnancy. Consumption of originally unknown levels of alcohol caused fetal alcohol disorder and, in turn, early onset aggression and violence and an increased risk for serious and violent offending in adolescence and adulthood. Similar causal connections were asserted about maternal smoking, mother/fetal exposure to environmental lead, and maternal use of marijuana or cocaine. There was also, in the criminological literature, the idea that "low self-control" (LSC) was a key predictive variable for serious delinquency and criminality. More recent research has confirmed and expanded on the understanding and explanation of LSC in terms of executive functions (EF) or specified cognitive processes defined as "planning, organized searching, inhibition, working memory, set shifting, flexible thinking, strategy employment, and linguistic fluency" (Agin, 2010, p. 137). The complex behaviours associated with EF are mediated by the frontal lobes. Executive function based disorders include attention-deficit/hyperactivity disorder (ADHD), FASD, autism, learning disabilities (LD), and traumatic brain injury (Watson and Wesby, 2003). These developmental psychopathologies linked to LSC are associated with serious criminality. For example, in one study of young adult criminals, approximately half (51%) of males and females (44%) had histories of childhood psychopathology (Copeland et al., 2007). More specifically, in another study, 60% of FASD full spectrum individuals were involved in the criminal justice system (CJS) with approximately half sent to jail/prison (Savage et al., 2007). Regarding FASD, during the last decade, there has been a more detailed specification both conceptually and diagnostically concerning the range: the least morphological changes and impairments being Alcohol Related Neurodevelopment Disorder (ARND) and the most severe identified as Fetal Alcohol Syndrome (FAS).[1]

Part of the FASD risk factor involves its association with low IQ. In one study, children at 7 years of age exposed to maternal binge drinking were twice as likely to have IQ scores in the mental retardation range and have a 2 1/2 times greater likelihood of clinically significant levels of delinquent behaviour (Baily et al., 2004). In terms of general long-term criminal trajectories, prenatal exposure to alcohol was a predictor of alcohol abuse as adults (Molina et al., 2007). While there has been ongoing research concerning minimum amounts of alcohol that can be safely consumed, Agin (2010) asserted that "there is no threshold below which alcohol use during pregnancy is safe: Its use even at low levels has harmful effects on later child behaviour. The effects are observed at average levels of alcohol exposure as low as one drink per week" (p. 133). This controversy is critical given the estimations of alcohol consumed during pregnancy. For example, one US estimate was that 10–26% of pregnant women drank during pregnancy resulting in 40,000 children with varying levels of brain insults (Chambers et al., 2005). Nearly half (43%) drank in the first three months as they did not know they were pregnant. Also, there were substantial variations by low income women and ethnicity; nearly 1/3 of non-Hispanic, Black non-Hispanic and English-speaking Hispanic drinking past conception compared to only 1/20 (16%) of Spanish-speaking Hispanics. These ethnic differences likely reflected differing rates of acculturation to the broader US cultural norms regarding drinking (Chambers et al., 2005). The highest rate of binge drinking was in the 18 to 24 age group, while young pregnant moms were most likely to both smoke and drink during pregnancy and most frequently addicted to both of these toxicities during pregnancy (Ebrahim, Diekman, Floyd, and Decoufle, 1999; Rochman, 2012). In the US, Blacks and Indians have the highest prevalence of FAS (Wilford et al., 2006).

Like FASD, autism spectrum disorder (ASD) has been associated with early onset aggression and violence as well as longer-term trajectory of serious and violent offending. ASD comprises five diagnostic categories: autism; Rett syndrome; Asperger syndrome; childhood disintegrative disorder; and pervasive developmental disorder otherwise not specified (PDD: NOS). However, it is very likely that the range of spectral disorders will be reduced along with fewer traits or indicators in the proposed revisions for the Diagnostic and Statistical Manual of Mental Disorders Five (DSM V). Asperger syndrome and PDD: NOS would no longer be part of ASD. Under DSM IV, a person can qualify for the ASD diagnosis by exhibiting six or more of 12 behaviours, whereas under the proposed definitional change the person more narrowly would have to exhibit three deficits in social interaction and communication and at least two repetitive behaviours (Carey, 2012).

These changes will likely result in fewer clinically recorded cases of ASD. Currently, this spectral disorder is four times more likely for boys (Park, 2009). Although there has been an intense media debate concerning the cause of ASD, mainly associated with the assertion that infant and childhood disease inoculations are the culprit, there is no simple genetic explanation of the majority of autisms.

Instead, there is support for the far more complex processes involving epigenetic risk factors, especially during pregnancy. The long list of risk factors include impact of maternal psychosocial stress; maternal fever; maternal genetics; hormonal status; use of certain medications; fetal hypoxia; advanced maternal/paternal ages; history of miscarriage; childhood cancer; autoimmune disorders; schizophrenia; elevated blood levels of mercury; PCBs; immune toxicities; maternal iodine deficiencies from pesticides; and maternal Lyme disease-related chronic infection (Agin, 2010).

According to Agin (2010), the prevalence of psychosis in the US is between 2% to 3% of a population of approximately 312 million. In contrast to this small percentage, the prevalence of at least less severe mental disorders in a lifetime is much higher, with closer to one-quarter of the US population with either anxiety disorders (by far the most pervasive), mood disorders (including major depressive disorders), impulsive control disorders (such as ADHD), or substance disorders (including alcohol and hard drugs such as cocaine and heroin). An important theoretical theme directly related to the use of the Cracow Instrument is the causal pattern or genesis of both of these traditionally general or broad categories of mental illness. Agin (2010) argued that more recent neurological and genetic/epigenetic research has blurred the distinction within the general categories as well as between the categories. Within the psychosis category, this is most obvious with mixed psychosis such as schizoaffective disorder, which combines schizophrenic traits and bipolar traits. The blurring between the more general categories is evident in the umbrella construct, schizophrenia spectrum disorders that encompass the schizotypal and schizoid personality disorders at the less severe end of this continuum. While these severe disorders typically have young adult full onset, certain disorders such as schizoaffective disorder more frequently have an older adult full onset. This blurring or overlap is hypothesized to reflect the overlap in both genes and gene expression (linked to fetal development affected by many of the above mediating factors such as stress, toxins, infections, season of birth, and nutritional deficiencies) for the categories of psychoses. For example, maternal stress is related to low birth weight for healthy full-term newborns which, in turn, is related to adolescent and adult depression disproportionality for girls and women (Patton et al., 2004; Rice et al., 2006). Another key example is smoking during pregnancy and its correlation with offspring impulsivity and aggression, especially important since teenage mothers have the highest prevalence (46%) of smoking in the first trimester when the fetal brain is most susceptible to the toxicities in tobacco smoke (Correia and Linhares, 2007). Agin (2010) also asserted that "low socio-economic status increases the prevalence of infection, exposure to toxins, poor nutrition, and many other prenatal impacts that maybe involved in fetal brain damage and in the aetiology of later mental illness" (p. 222).

It has been found that high concentrations of caffeine in fetal blood negatively affect fetal brain development including higher risk for fetal death (Bech, Nohr, Vaeth, Henriksen, and Olsen, 2005; Cornelius, Goldschmidt, DeGenna, and Day, 2007). The "culture of poverty" creates maternal stress and related higher uses of tobacco, alcohol, and the highest prevalence of obesity, especially in high density urban neighbourhoods with high concentrations of economic disadvantage, high crime rates, single parent young families, inadequate housing, low community social/political cohesion and which have the highest levels of serious violent crime and intergenerational adult/youth gangs (Wilkinson and Marmot, 2003). Agin (2010) explained how acute psychosocial maternal stress during pregnancy is related to an increased probability of offspring with ADHD, schizophrenia, depression, and adult criminality.

There also is greater understanding of the impact of fetal lead exposure to the development of aggression and violence in children and older youth. Historically, this particularly has been endemic to industrial-urban environments and impoverished neighbourhoods with older housing structures for over a century and is related to child violence, adult criminality and violent crime rates. Lead poisoning, for example, is one of the strongest predictors of criminal behaviour for African Americans from birth to young adulthood and, more generally, for long-term murder rates, that is, since 1900 (Denno, 1990; Nevin, 2007; Stretesky and Lynch, 2001, 2004). Similarly, there is recent research that has updated the importance of premature babies and low infant birth weights, especially prevalent and among teenage mothers. In the United States, there was a moderate to strong correlation (0.58) between low birth weight and violent crime (McDaniel, 2006). Differences between and within states concerning low birth weight and its relationship to crime is hypothesized to reflect differences between urban profiles and cities with high industrial air and water pollution (Centers for Disease Control and Prevention, 2002; Singh and Kposowa, 1994).

All of the above risk factors have been associated with neuropsychological developmental disorders. It has been estimated that 1 in 6 or 17% of US children have at least one neuropsychological developmental disability (ADHD, learning disability, chronic emotional/behavioural problems, speech defects, delay in growth or development, and deafness) or 11 million children under 17 (Agin, 2010). Again, nearly all of the research in the first decade of this century has confirmed the relationships between neuropsychological disorders and exposure during pregnancy to a wide range of risk factors. In addition, several new risk factors have been identified as well. Learning disorders and ADHD alone have been linked to DDT (dichlorodiphenyltrichloroethane); maternal smoking; low level of lead exposure; plus post-natal infections such as childhood viral infections, meningitis; head injury; encephalitis; epilepsy; and prescription drugs (Millichap, 2008). A disproportionate number of serious and violent young offenders in custody have these developmental disorders, especially LD (Cesaroni and Peterson-Badali, 2005; Corrado and Cohen, 2002; Teplin, Abram, McClelland, Dulcan, and Mericle, 2002).

It is not possible to review the extensive updating of all the risk and protective factors that have been identified, based largely on technological advances in measuring toxicities, their impact on neurological development, and then the related impact on aggression and violence. Even more complex is the understanding of these relationships with aggression and violence based on the revolutionary knowledge that has emerged from genome studies and, most recently, epigenetic research. However, another theme in reviewing some of the more recent traditional risk factors included in the CI is that it lends support to the need to develop case management strategies for distinctive pathways of risk/protective factors.

Specific pathways to serious young offending and related specific risk management strategy themes

Despite the consensus about the key LSC risk factor being serious and violent offending (SVO), there has been a longstanding debate about whether there is a single or multiple pathways of risk/protective factors to SVO (Loeber and Farrington, 2000). The proponents of a single pathway assert that inappropriate parental socialization of children, with a focus on discipline styles in responding to children, causes or reinforces their LSC; therefore, the risk management strategy obviously needs to concentrate on parenting styles and related family risk/protective factors such as parental education, involvement, and child health. In other words, despite the single pathway, the risk management strategy is not necessarily simplistic. It is beyond the scope of this chapter to describe the multiple pathway models; however, the general theme of multiple pathways is important in the utilization of the CI for case management, essentially because of the more recent research strongly suggesting that there are distinctive initial risk factors that likely need to be considered in developing the most effective strategies for treatment. In other words, once the full range of CI risk/protective factors for serious and violent young offenders has been identified, the next case planning step is to discern the potential key initiating risk factor such as FASD, ASD, or trauma and then to identify the subsequent pattern of risk/protective factors in order to devise the specific set of treatment programming, assuming that appropriate programs are available. In effect, pathways can assist or guide case planning strategies.

In a recent article, Corrado and Freedman (2011) presented five pathways of risk factors for involvement in the criminal justice system and linked or corresponding intervention programming, again, with the focus on the initial and distinctive key risk factor. In order to utilize this approach for CI case planning use by practitioners for targeted interventions for serious and young violent offenders, the Corrado and Freedman (2011) five pathways were slightly modified for SVOs.

The first pathway is based on in utero risk factors or *prenatal risk factors* (see Figure 2.1). Many of these risk factors were identified in the original CI and were discussed above including a wide range of toxins and diseases (Corrado and Freedman, 2011). As discussed above, the most recent research has led to Agin's (2010) assertion that "more than 200 industrial environmental agents [e.g., high exposure to polychlorinated biphenyls (PCBs), dioxins, pesticides, and ionizing radiation] have been demonstrated to have neurotoxic effects in humans – with probable critical windows of vulnerability for the fetus – and the neurodevelopmental disorders caused by these industrial chemicals may constitute a 'silent pandemic' in modern society" (p. 40). He explained further that many of these toxins, including PCBs, act as endocrine disrupters and function as hormones, which can result in obvious adverse effects on development; other toxins such as polycyclic aromatic hydrocarbons actually affect the structure of the DNA, thereby effecting gene expression and creating irreversible damage.

Another critical risk factor discussed above is FASD because, in the absence of early focused intervention, it is strongly related to early and persistent expressions of aggression. This aggression and violence pattern then is exacerbated if additional CI identified risk factors are present in subsequent developmental stages especially in late childhood and/or adolescent onset SVO. It is therefore critical for intervention programs such as the Home Nurse Visiting support healthy pregnancies through proper maternal diet and a cessation, if relevant, in substance use.

The *childhood personality disorder* pathway (see Figure 2.2 pathway) is distinguished by the presence of an early personality disorder, for example, conduct disorder or oppositional defiant disorder (Corrado and Freedman, 2011). Children presenting with one or more of these disorders (comorbidity) are likely to have a more difficult time developing strong positive attachment to their parent(s) or caregiver(s). The symptomology of these disorders further often lead to early bullying behaviours, difficulties in developing stable relationships, and other major behavioural problems that are often displayed at school and in the classroom (DeLisi and Vaughn, 2011). These social and academic strains are related to the resistance to authority and low discipline, rather than definitively organic-based cognitive

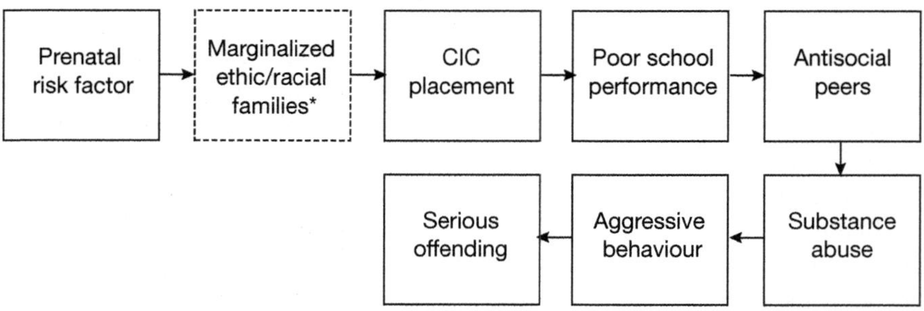

Figure 2.1 Prenatal risk factors pathway

Note: *Risk factors in dotted lines have likely always been present, but take on new meaning as others accumulate.

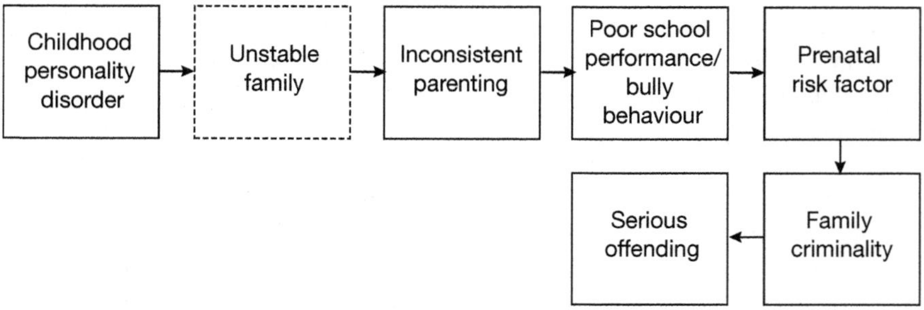

Figure 2.2 Childhood personality disorder pathway

dysfunctions. A risk management strategy for this pathway needs to consider educating the family and school on the specific personality disorder – as well as any comorbid conditions – and how to respond both verbally and behaviourally to the symptom-related behaviours. Also, specific forms of discipline and positive and non-stigmatizing rewards are important for these young people. Without such interventions, including additional counselling from a child psychologist and, in some cases, medication, these behaviours can ultimately result in serious offending due to the symptoms of the personality disorder and the young person's frustration with the condition.

Childhood temperament model (see Figure 2.3 pathway) is distinguished by two potential initiators – high reactive temperament involving extreme irritability and aggressivity in response to novel social situations, authority and strong discipline and low reactive temperament involving equanimity and passivity in response to the above contexts. Unlike the previous pathways, there is a strong genetic base for these extreme temperaments, which can be recognized as early as when the child is only four months old (Kagan, 1994, 2010). The related risk factor is when parent(s) fail to adjust their bonding and parenting styles according to the two temperaments (i.e., less structure and more sensitive discipline for high reactive infants and toddlers and more structure and non-physical discipline to low reactive children), negative attachment styles toward parent/caregiver are more likely for these children. The negative attachment relationships increase the likelihood of either internalizing or externalizing behaviours later in the child's development (DeLisi and Vaughn, 2011).

The essential case management strategy involves identifying the extreme temperament types and then providing access to education programming to expose the parent(s) to the appropriate parenting style. Similarly, other authority figures such as older siblings, teachers and coaches also need to be informed. Early intervention for families of children with this trajectory profile can reduce the possible fracturing of the family and subsequent placement in care, both major risk factors for later developmental stages' serious and violent offending.

The childhood maltreatment pathway (see Figure 2.4) is focused primarily on the period from birth to five years of age, during which time experiences of child maltreatment can result not only in possible permanent brain damage, but also in

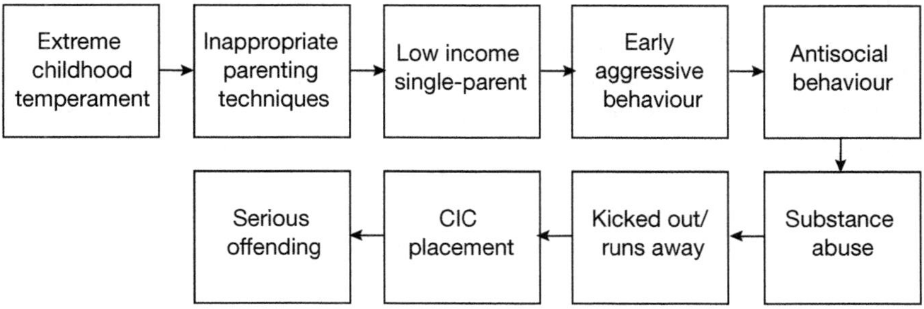

Figure 2.3 Childhood temperament pathway

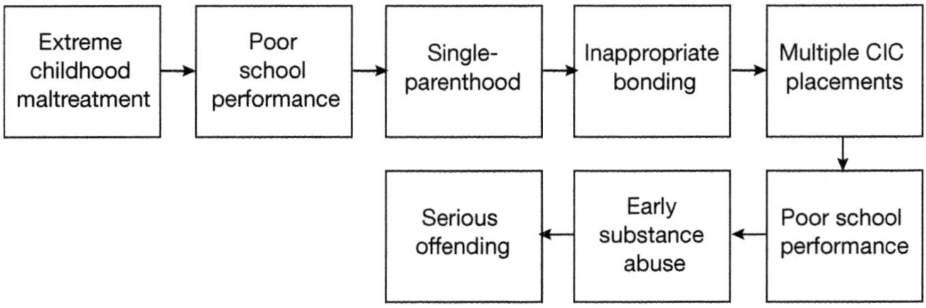

Figure 2.4 Childhood maltreatment pathway

severe trauma and PTSD. As mentioned above, whereas extreme physical and sexual forms of abuse are more likely detected, emotional and neglect forms of abuse are inherently more difficult to detect until much later developmental stages and, even then, without memories of such events, effective cognitive emotion-based therapies are more problematic. In the interim developmental stages, undetected trauma can then be exhibited in hostile and aggressive antisocial behaviours that are misunderstood and result in further damage resulting from disciplinary reactions from authority figures plus stronger interactive effects from additional risk factors presented in this pathway. Early detection is enhanced when comprehensive instruments such as the CI suggest that an infant, toddler or young child is at risk because of traditional and previous evidence of either actual abuse histories to siblings or other abuse risk profiles such as domestic spousal abuse. In other words, part of the immediate initial and necessarily tentative strategy for children in this pathway is to identify families that present a high risk for child abuse and, where confirmed and entrenched, out-of-home placement and childcare are immediate and long-term options. Whether the child remains in the home or is placed in care, proper diagnosis of the extent of the trauma can result in several therapeutic strategies including traditional cognitive and emotional approaches along with standard programs for PTSD for older children and youth. As with all the pathways, beyond responding to the initial key risk factor, specific additional programming is necessary depending on the remaining sets of risk factors such as drug dependency and poor school performance.

The final pathway builds from Moffitt's (1993) model regarding *adolescent onset* offending (see Figure 2.5). More recently, however, Moffitt et al. (2002) have asserted that adolescent onset offending typically is less serious than the Life Course Persistent type (i.e., child onset serious delinquency and subsequent serious and violent offending into adolescence and adulthood) and that offending desistence occurs at the end of adolescence. Moffitt et al. (2002; Moffitt and Caspi, 2005) have also modified the original models to include another types where adolescent onset offending continues into adulthood. As discussed above, more recent trajectory research has identified even more types including adult onset offending (Eggleston and Laub, 2002; Gomez-Smith and Piquero, 2005).

Our final pathway is concerned only with adolescent onset serious and violent offenders. In this pathway, peer group relationships are a particularly important

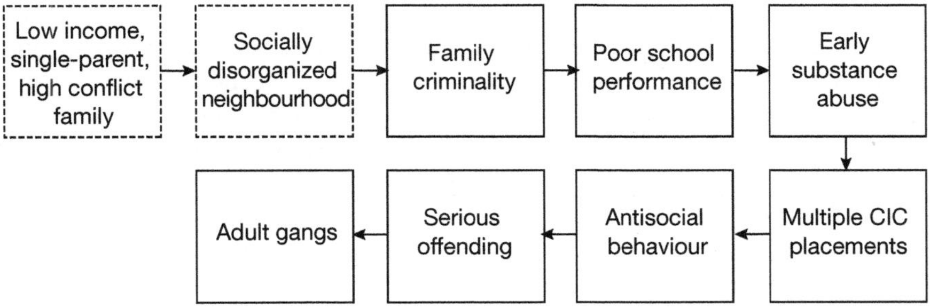

Figure 2.5 Adolescent onset offending pathway

risk factor, especially either informal "gang" types (i.e., no formal gang structure other than a leader and a small number of core followers), formal youth gangs, or adult formal gangs with youth members. As discussed above, either traditional risk factors for gangs or "more immediate thrill seeking" lifestyle risk factors in the absence of traditional ones need to be considered regarding intervention case management programming. For the latter type, the focus of programming is not on socio-economically and marginalized family and community social disorganization risk factors but, instead, on school-based education programs delivered by school and/or police gang officers concerning the high likelihood of being killed in gang violence or being sentenced to long-term imprisonment. These programs are directed at reducing the impact of initial gang recruitment efforts on vulnerable youth as they transition into young adulthood. Traditional gang interventions are concerned further with withdrawal from committed gang involvement and involve extensive community and family programs, including educational programs, trade skills training, cognitive-based therapies, substance abuse treatment, and independent living experiences (Corrado and Cohen, 2011b; Klein et al., 2001). It is also critical to address the young person's thought patterns and short- and long-term goals, as youth at this stage are making the choice to follow a criminal lifestyle comprising serious and violent offending. The CI can be utilized to identify risk factors for case management for traditional gang involvement but not the new type. Depending on the country, city, and neighbourhood, gang involvement typically varies substantially; however, recent trends indicate that gang involvement has increased in countries with a limited history of youth/young adult gangs such as Canada and several European countries such the Netherlands (Corrado and Cohen, 2011b; Klein et al., 2001).

Again, these pathway models are necessarily tentative and are designed as preliminary efforts to assist in utilizing the numerous and long list of often complex risk factors and the developmental stage sequencing. The central theme, though, is the importance of identifying the initial key risk factor in order to enhance the case planning effect on reducing serious and violent future offending. Many challenges remain in utilizing the CI for this purpose, and even more so for the development of pathway models for case management. Most importantly, there are obvious differences in the magnitude and expression of each risk factor. For example, one child may be low on the FASD spectrum, while another child may be extremely high. Despite the encouraging advancements made to neuroimaging and extensive new research in the areas of biology and genetics, there is still a lack of understanding of the specific effects that different exposure, for example, to certain toxins, can have on a developing child in the womb. It has been established that there are varying degrees of vulnerability based on the stage of development of the fetus. Certain noxious exposure will have a different impact at the ovum stage (when a single female reproductive cell is matured and ready to be fertilized) as compared with levels of exposure at the following stages: blastocyst (around five days after fertilization), morula (when there is an embryo composed of cells in a solid ball, at an early stage of embryonic development), embryo (when cell division and fetal development begin), and fetus (a more advanced development stage following the embryonic one) (Agin, 2010). Still, the precise microbiology and chemistry behind the toxins and their impact at the varying levels is yet unknown.

Beyond this, there are also two types of damage that can occur – one is *endophenotype*, or the internal traits that may cause some change, but cannot be seen; the other is known as *exophenotype*, the external traits that can be seen. Subsequently, there are many different types of threats to an individual's development which can occur at multiple stages, thus resulting in potentially major differences in impact and which may be visibly expressed or not. This evidently can make it extremely difficult to recognize and establish existing risk traits. "[W]e have no idea about the possible damage by a single molecule or of a few molecules or of a thousand molecules of a specific toxin that gets to an ovum or blastocyst or morula or embryo or fetus" (Agin, 2010, p. 106). Despite the multitude of risk factors that have been identified in the CI and other comprehensive risk management instruments such as the MASPAQ – Measures of Adolescent Social and Personal Adaptation, Quebec/Mesures de l'adaptation sociale et personnelle pour les adolescents québécois (Le Blanc, 1996), it is not possible to predict their impact on a specific youth. Similarly, regarding little understood risk factors, such as children in care, there can also be major differences in children and adolescents' experiences prior to, during, and post being in care (Corrado and Freedman, 2009; Corrado et al., 2011).

Conclusion

Given the impressive recent research that has amplified our understanding of traditional risk and protective factors largely related to the revolutionary advances in genetic and now epigenetic research, it will be necessary to continually update instruments such as the CI regarding both old and new risk factors. The related necessity is to develop case management pathway models that simplify the developmental sequencing of the array of risk factors so that practitioners can better identify and sequence the multiple programming needs of serious and violently offending children and young adults.

Note

1 Brain scans for FAS show changes in brain morphology regarding certain critical brain EF structures (e.g., thickening of corpus callosum, caudate nucleus re. learning) controlling behaviour. Brain scanning technology likely will be more common diagnostically especially since clinical assessment techniques require extensive resources to identify the less severe FASD types in the absence of changes in facial morphology. Facial dysmorphology include, for newborn, short eyelid fissures, thin upper lip and absent philtrum or groove between middle of upper lip and nose. Children also can show ptosis (dropped eyelids), upturned nose and flat nasal bridge, underdeveloped ears and cardiac defects.

References

Agin, D. (2010). More than genes: What science can tell us about toxic chemicals, development, and the risk to our children. New York, NY: Oxford University Press.

Bailey, B., Delaney-Black, V., Covington, C., Ager, J., Janisse, J., Hannigan, J., and Sokol, R. (2004). Prenatal exposure to binge drinking and cognitive and behavioural outcomes at age 7 years. *American Journal of Obstetrics and Gynecology,* 191(3), 1037–43.

Bech, B. H., Nohr, E.A., Vaeth, M., Henriksen, T.B., and Olsen, J. (2005). Coffee and fetal death: A cohort study with prospective data. *American Journal of Epidemiology,* 162(10), 983–90.

Broidy, L. M., Tremblay, R. E., Brame, B., Fergusson, D., Horwood, J. L., Nagin, D. S., Vitaro, F. (2003). Developmental trajectories of childhood disruptive behaviors and adolescent delinquency: A six-site, cross-national study. *Developmental Psychology,* 39(2), 222–45.

Carey, B. (2012, January 19). New definition of autism will exclude many, study suggests. *New York Times*. Retrieved from http://www.nytimes.com/2012/01/20/health/research/new-autism-definition-would-exclude-many-study-suggests.html.

Caspi, A., McClay, J., Moffitt, T. E., Mill, J., Martin, J., Craig, I. W., Taylor, A., and Poulton, R. (2002). Role of genotype in the cycle of violence in maltreated children. *Science*, 297(5582), 851–54.

Centers for Disease Control and Prevention (2002). Racial and ethnic disparities in infant mortality rates – 60 largest U.S. cities, 1995–1998. *Morbidity and Mortality Weekly Report*, 51(15), 329–32.

Cesaroni, C. and Peterson-Badali, M. (2005). Young offenders in custody: Risk and adjustment. *Criminal Justice and Behavior*, 32(3), 251–77.

Chambers, C. D., Hughes, S., Meltzer, S. B., Wahlgren, D., Kassem, N., Larson, S., Riley, E. P., and Hovell, M. F. (2005). Alcohol consumption among low-income pregnant Latinas. *Alcoholism: Clinical and Experimental Research*, 29(11), 2022–8.

Cooke, D. J., Hart, S. D., and Logan, C. (2005). Comprehensive Assessment of Psychopathic Personality Disorder: Institutional Rating Scale, Version 1.1. Unpublished manual.

Copeland, W. E., Miller-Johnson, S., Keeler, G., Angold, A., and Costello, E. J. (2007). Childhood psychiatric disorders and young adult crime: A prospective, population-based study. *American Journal of Psychiatry*, 164(11), 1668–75.

Cornelius, M. D., Goldschmidt, L., DeGenna, N., and Day, N. L. (2007). Smoking during teenage pregnancies: Effects on behavioral problems in offspring. *Nicotine & Tobacco Research*, 9(7), 739–50.

Corrado, R. R. (2011). Comprehensive risk management instruments for serious and violent young offenders: Challenges and advantage. In T. Bliesener, A. Beelmann, and

M. Stemmler (eds), *Antisocial behaviour and crime: Contributions of developmental and evaluation research to prevention and intervention*. Göttingen, Germany: Hogrefe.

Corrado, R. R. and Cohen, I. M. (2002). A needs profile of serious and/or violent Aboriginal youth in prison. *FORUM on Corrections Research*, 14(3), 20–4.

Corrado, R. R. and Cohen, I.M. (2011a). Aboriginal youth at risk: The role of education, mobility, housing, employment, and language as protective factors for problem and criminal behaviours. In P. Dinsdale, J. White, and C. Hanselmann (eds), *Urban Aboriginal communities in Canada: Complexities, challenges, opportunities*. Toronto, ON: Thompson Educational Publishing (pp. 153–72)

Corrado, R. R. and Cohen, I. M. (2011b). Review of school-based intervention and prevention programs for gang involved Aboriginal youth. Report submitted to Ministry of Indian and Northern Affairs, Canada.

Corrado, R. R. and Freedman, L. (2009). Children in care and the criminal justice system: A review of the research literature. Report prepared for the Office of the Representative of Children and Youth, BC.

Corrado, R. R., and Freedman, L. (2011). Risk profiles, trajectories and intervention points for serious and chronic young offenders. *International Journal of Child, Youth and Family Studies*, 2(2.1), 197–232.

Corrado, R. R., Freedman, L., and Blattier, C. (2011). The over-representation of children in care in the youth criminal justice system in British Columbia: Policy and theory issues. *International Journal of Child, Youth and Family Studies*, 2(1/2), 99–118.

Corrado, R. R., Watkinson, A., and Cohen, I. M. (2005). Theoretical and empirical developments in the utilization of psychopathy as a predictor of serious and violent young offending. In A. Czeredercka, T. Jaskiewicz-Obydzinska, R. Roesch, and J. Wojcikiewicz (eds), *Forensic psychology and law: Facing the challenges of a changing world*. Krakow: Institute of Forensic Research Publishers (pp. 409–23)

Correia, L. L. and Linhares, M. B. M. (2007). Maternal anxiety in the pre- and postnatal period: A literature review. *Latin American Journal of Nursing*, 15(4), 677–83.

Côté, S., Vaillancourt, T., LeBlanc, J. C., Nagin, D., and Tremblay, R. E. (2006). The development of physical aggression from toddlerhood to pre-adolescence: A nationwide longitudinal study. *Journal of Abnormal Child Psychology*, 34(1), 71–85.

Cullen, F. T., Wright, J. P., Brown, S., Moon, M. M., Blankenship, M. B., and Applegate, B. K. (1998). Public support for early intervention programs: Implications for a progressive policy agenda. *Crime and Delinquency*, 44(2), 187–204.

Dawson, S. E., McCuish, E. C., Hart, S. D., and Corrado, R. R. (2012). Assessing psychopathy with the CAPP and PCL:YV: Utilizing a case study to understand the manifestation of psychopathic traits in youth. *International Journal of Forensic Mental Health*, in press.

DeLisi, M. and Vaughn, M.G. (2011). The importance of neuropsychological deficits relating to self-control and temperament to the presentation of serious antisocial behaviour. *International Journal of Child, Youth and Family Studies*, 1 and 2, 12–35.

Denno, D. W. (2007). *Biology and violence: From birth to adulthood*. New York, NY: Cambridge University Press.

Ebrahim, S. H., Diekman, S. T., Floyd, L., and Decoufle, P. (1999). Comparison of binge drinking among pregnant and nonpregnant women, United States, 1991–1995. *American Journal of Obstetrics and Gynecology*, 180(1), 1–7.

Eggleston, E. P. and Laub, J. H. (2002). The onset of adult offending: A neglected dimension of the criminal career. *Journal of Criminal Justice*, 30(6), 603–22.

Farrington, D. P. (2005). Childhood origins of antisocial behavior. *Clinical Psychology and Psychotherapy*, 12(3), 177–90.

Gomez-Smith, Z. and Piquero, A. R. (2005). An examination of adult onset offending. *Journal of Criminal Justice*, 33(6), 515–25.

Haberstick, B. C., Lessem, J. M., Hopfer, C. J., Smolen, A., Ehringer, M. A., Timberlake, D., and Hewitt J. K. (2005). Monoamine oxidase A (MAOA) and antisocial behaviours in the presence of childhood and adolescent maltreatment. *American Journal of Medical Genetics,* 135B(1), 59–64.

Hosking, G. and Walsh, I. (2010). *International experience of early intervention for children, young people and their families*. Surrey, England: Wave Trust.

Kagan, J. (1994). *Galen's prophecy: Temperament in human nature*. New York: Basic Books.

Kagan, J. (2010). *The temperamental thread: How genes, culture, time, and luck make us who we are*. New York: Dana Press.

Kazemian, L. and Le Blanc, M. (2004). Exploring patterns of perpetration of crime across the life course offense and offender-based viewpoints. *Journal of Contemporary Criminal Justice,* 20(4), 393–415.

Kim-Cohen, J., Caspi, A., Taylor, A., Williams, B., Newcombe, R., Craig, I. W., and Moffitt, T. E. (2006). MAOA, maltreatment, and gene-environment interaction predicting children's mental health: New evidence and a meta-analysis. *Molecular Psychiatry*, 11(10), 903–13.

Klein, M. W., Kerner, H.-J., Maxson, C. L., and Weitekamp, E. G. M. (eds) (2001). *The Eurogang paradox: Street gangs and youth groups in the U.S. and Europe*. New York, NY: Kluwer-Plenum.

Lacourse, E., Dupéré, V., and Loeber, R. (2008). Developmental trajectories of violence and theft. In R. Loeber, D. P. Farrington, M. Stouthamer-Loeber, and H. R. White (eds), *Serious theft and violence: Risk and promotive factors from childhood to early adulthood*. Mahwah, NJ: Lawrence Erlbaum Associates Publishers (pp. 231–68)

Le Blanc, M. (1996). *MASPAQ: Mesures de l'adaptation sociale et personnelle pour les adolescents québécois. Manuel et guide d'utilisation* (3rd edition). Montréal, École depsychoéducation, Groupe de recherche sur les adolescents en difficulté, Université de Montréal. Logiciel MASPAQ (Windows et MacIntosh).

Loeber, R. and Farrington, D.P. (2000). Young children who commit crime: Epidemiology,developmental origins, risk factors, early interventions, and policy implications. *Development and Psychopathology,* 12(4), 737–67.

Loeber, R. and Hay, D. (1997). Key issues in the development of aggression and violence from childhood to early adulthood. *Annual Review of Psychology,* 48(1), 371–410.

Loeber, R., Farrington, D. P., Stouthamer-Loeber, M., and White, H. R. (2008). *Violence and serious theft: Development and prediction from childhood to adulthood.* Mahwah,NJ: Erlbaum.

Loeber, R., Stouthamer-Loeber, M., Farrington, D. P., and White, H. R. (eds) (2008). *Violence and serious theft: Development and prediction from childhood to adulthood.* New York, NY: Routledge.

Loeber, R. N., Slot, N. W., and Stouthamer-Loeber, M. (2008). A cumulative developmental model of risk and promotive factors. In R.N. Loeber, N. W. Slot, P. H. van der Laan, and M. Hoeve (eds), *Tomorrow's criminals: The development of child delinquency and effective interventions*. Farnham, UK: Ashgate (pp. 133–61).

Lösel, F. and Bender, D. (2006). Risk factors for serious and violent antisocial behaviour in children and youth. In A. Hagell and J. R. Dent (eds), *Children who commit acts of serious interpersonal violence: Message for best practice*. London, England: Jessica Kingsley Publishers (pp. 42–72).

Lussier, P., Corrado, R., Healey, J., Tzoumakis, S., and Deslauriers-Varin, N. (2011). The CRACOW Instrument for multi-problem violent youth: Examining the postdictive validity with a sample of preschoolers. *International Journal of Child, Youth and Family Studies,* 2(2.1), 294–329.

McDaniel, M. A. (2006). Estimating state IQ: Measurement challenges and preliminary correlates. *Intelligence,* 34(6), 607–19.

Millichap, J. G. (2008). Etiologic classification of attention-deficit/hyperactivity disorder. *Pediatrics,* 121(2), 358–65.

Moffitt, T. E. (1993). Adolescence-limited and life course-persistent antisocial behavior: A developmental taxonomy. *Psychological Review,* 100(4), 674–701.

Moffitt, T. E. and Caspi, A. (2005). Life-course persistent and adolescence-limited antisocial males: Longitudinal follow-up to adulthood. In D. M. Stoff and E. J. Susman (eds), *Developmental Psychobiology of Aggression.* Cambridge, UK: Cambridge University Press (pp. 161–86).

Moffitt, T. E., Caspi, A., Harrington, H., and Milne, B. J. (2002). Males on the life-course persistent and adolescence-limited antisocial pathways: Follow-up at age 26 years. *Development and Psychopathology,* 14(1), 179–207.

Molina, B. S., Pelham, W. E., Gnagy, E. M., Thompson, A. L., and Marchal, M. P. (2007). Attention-deficit/hyperactivity disorder risk for heavy drinking and alcohol use disorder is age specific. *Alcoholism: Clinical and Experimental Research,* 31(4), 643-54.

Nevin, R. (2007). Understanding international crime trends: The legacy of preschool lead exposure. *Environmental Research,* 104(3), 315–36.

Odgers, C., Vincent, G. M., and Corrado, R. R. (2002). A preliminary conceptual framework for the prevention and management of multi-problem youth at risk for violence. In R. R. Corrado, R. Roesch, S. D. Hart, and J. K. Gierowski (eds), *Multi-problem violent youth: A foundation for comparative research on needs, interventions, and outcomes.* Amsterdam: IOS Press (pp. 302–30).

Park, A. (2009, May). A genetic clue to why autism affects boys more. *Time Magazine.* Retrieved from http://www.time.com/time/health/article/0,8599,1899756,00.html.

Patton, G. C., Coffey, C., Carlin, J. B., and Olsson, C. A. (2004). Prematurity at birth and adolescent depressive disorder. *British Journal of Psychiatry,* 184(5), 446–7.

Rice, F., Harold, G. T., Shelton, K. H., and Thapar, A. (2006). Family conflict interacts with genetic liability in predicting childhood and adolescent depression. *Journal of the American Academy of Child & Adolescent Psychiatry,* 45(7), 841–8.

Rochman, B. (2012, January). Half of teen moms don't use birth control: Why that's no surprise. *Time Magazine.* Retrieved from http://healthland.time.com/2012/01/20/why-its-not-surprising-that-half-of-teen girls-who-give-birth-shun-birth-control/.

Salekin, R. T. and Lynam, D. R. (eds) (2010). *Handbook of child and adolescent psychopathy.* New York, NY: Guilford Press.

Savage, C. L., Anthony, J., Lee, R., Kappesser, M. L., and Rose, B. (2007). The culture of pregnancy and infant care in African American women: An ethnographic study. *Journal of Transcultural Nursing,* 18(3), 215–23.

Singh, G. K. and Kposowa, A. J. (1994). A comparative analysis of infant mortality in major Ohio cities: Significance of socio-biological factors. *Applied Behavioral Science Review,* 2(1), 77–94.

Stretesky, P. B. and Lynch, M. (2001). The relationship between lead exposure and homicide. *Archives of Pediatrics and Adolescent Medicine,* 155(5), 579–82.

Stretesky, P. B. and Lynch, M. J. (2004). The relationship between lead and crime. *Journal of Health and Social Behavior,* 45(2), 214–29.

Teplin, L. A., Abram, K. M., McClelland, G. M., Dulcan, M. K., and Mericle, A. A. (2002). Psychiatric disorders in youth in juvenile detention. *Archives of General Psychiatry,* 59(12), 1133–43.

Thornberry, T. P. (2005). Explaining multiple patterns of offending across the life course and across generations. *Annals of the American Academy of Political and Social Science,* 602(1), 156–95.

Thornberry, T. P. and Krohn, M. D. (2005). Applying interactional theory to the explanation of continuity and change in antisocial behavior. In D. P. Farrington (ed.), *Integrated developmental and life-course theories of offending.* New Brunswick, NJ: Transaction Publishers (pp. 183–209).

Tremblay, R. E. and Japel, C. (2003). Prevention during pregnancy, infancy and the preschool years. In D. P. Farrington and J. W. Coid (eds), *Early prevention of adult antisocial behaviour.* Cambridge, UK: Cambridge University Press (pp. 205–42).

Tremblay, R. E., and Nagin, D.S. (2005). The developmental origins of physical aggression in humans. In R. Tremblay, W. Hartup, and J. Archer (eds), *The developmental origins of aggression.* New York, NY: Guilford Press.

Tremblay, R. E., Japel, C., Pérusse, D., McDuff, P., Boivin, M., Zoccolillo, M., and Montplaisir, J. (1999). The search for the age of 'onset' of physical aggression: Rousseau and Bandura revisited. *Criminal Behaviour and Mental Health,* 9(1), 8–23.

Tremblay, R. E., Nagin, D. S., Séguin, J.R., Zoccolillo, M., Zelazo, P.D., Boivin, M., Pérusse, M., and Japel, C. (2004). Physical aggression during early childhood: Trajectories and predictors. *Pediatrics,* 114(1), 43–50.

Vincent, G. M., Vitacco, M. J., Grisso, T., and Corrado, R. R. (2003). Subtypes of adolescent offenders: Affective traits and antisocial behaviour patterns. *Behavioural Sciences and the Law,* 21(6), 695–712.

Watson, S. M. R. and Westby, C. E. (2003). Strategies for addressing the executive function impairments of students prenatally exposed to alcohol and other drugs. *Communication Disorders Quarterly,* 24(4), 194–204.

Wilford, J. A., Leech, S. L., and Day, N. L. (2006). Moderate prenatal alcohol exposure and cognitive status of children at age 10. *Alcoholism: Clinical and Experimental Research,* 30(6), 1051–9.

Wilkinson, R. and Marmot, M. (eds) (2003). *Social determinants of health: The solid facts* (2nd ed.). Copenhagen, Denmark: World Health Organization.

3 Juvenile delinquency and justice and policing in Italy

A. C. Baldry, C. Giacomantonio, S. Maccioni and G. Scardaccione

A child, by definition, is a person not yet completely matured (either physically or, especially, mentally). It is because of this lack of maturity that the Italian legal system provides a special protocol for juvenile trial proceedings, designed and built for and around the person who commits a crime and is under age. This is done to guarantee his or her sound development and possible rehabilitation. In the Italian juvenile justice system, Art. 2 of Presidential Decree 448/88 identifies the institutions and agencies involved, at various stages and as legally defined, in the proceedings in the administration of juvenile justice: the public prosecutor at the juvenile court, the judge for preliminary investigations at the juvenile court, the juvenile court, the attorney general at the court of appeal, the circuit court of appeals for minors and the surveillance judge for minors.

The juvenile court

Since 1934, the Italian juvenile justice system has been administered by an ad hoc body created to deal with all matters relating to minors, the so-called Juvenile Court:[1] just because he has not completed the process of development, the child has a complex personality, sometimes problematic, and has not yet reached an equilibrium. The purpose of the special courts is to best understand the wrongdoings, the risk factors but also the needs of the juvenile for a proper rehabilitation. For this reason a specific court is established and it consists of usual judges plus lay judges (specializing in biology, criminal anthropology, psychology, social sciences, pedagogy and psychiatry, or medicine). These courts provide for those technical legal competences also needed to better and fully understand the juvenile.

Jurisdiction

The juvenile court in Italy is in charge of all crimes committed in the area in which the court of appeal is established. This allows for an especially large local jurisdiction, guaranteeing, on the one hand, a sufficient number of court proceedings and, therefore, more experience for the components of the court; and, on the other hand (from a forensic/penal standpoint), a more comprehensive monitoring of young deviants. The jurisdiction's responsibilities are divided into three sectors:

civil (the court handles all civil cases that relate to children who are in foster care or are declared in such condition for adoption), criminal (the court has jurisdiction for all crimes committed by juveniles under 18), and administrative (the court hears applications for re-education measures).

Composition for juvenile criminal trials

In criminal trials for juveniles, the court has a different composition for each of the procedural phases of the trial: the court for preliminary investigation (GIP) is the only case of a (stipendiary) single judge; the court for the preliminary hearing (GUP) is a panel consisting of a single stipendiary judge and two lay members (a man and a woman); and, finally, the court in the trial is composed of two judges and two lay people (this is also the composition of the surveillance court, whose powers are established in Art. 70 of the penitentiary law).

The surveillance court

As described above, Art. 2 of Presidential Decree 448 appoints, among jurisdictional bodies, a surveillance judge for minors. This single magistrate, along with the surveillance court (with which he shares the tasks), is responsible for all the penal measures issued for persons who have committed a crime before the age of 18. The peculiarity of this jurisdiction, however, is that it extends until the juvenile has completed his or her twenty-fifth year. The reason for this provision is found in the non-specification of the term of the security measures: owing to the extension of its jurisdiction, in fact, "the court continues to exercise jurisdiction long after the offender [ceases] being under age, meaning that there are different ways of looking at even dangerous crimes when committed by a juvenile as compared with an adult" (Ricciotti, 2007, p. 251) .

Appeals

Given the general reference to the rules of the Code of Criminal Procedure made by Art.1, Presidential Decree 448/88, the regulations issued by the juvenile court may be challenged for the same reasons and in the same manner as in ordinary proceedings. The body that has jurisdiction in cases of appeal is a special department set up in each court of appeal, which is composed of three stipendiary judges and two lay members, selected according to the same criteria as previously described. With regard to the trial's proceedings, the provisions of Book IX of the Code of Criminal Procedure are followed.

Obviously, also for appeals to the Supreme Court of Cassation and for reviews, the other two possible courses of action, the regulatory provisions are contained in the Code of Criminal Procedure.

Public prosecutor

Under Art. 4 of the Royal Decree-Law 1404/34, the public prosecutor in the juvenile court "must promote and conduct the prosecution for all crimes committed by children under 18 . . . therefore all the reports, exhibits, denunciations, complaints, actions, petitions and requests related to crimes committed by children under 18 are sent to him". In addition to these powers related to criminal matters before the juvenile court, the public prosecutor also has all the powers that the law gives public prosecutors in the ordinary courts (in particular, in civil matters, the public prosecutor has the task of promoting the legal recognition and the practical implementation of the rights of the child).

Judicial police

As is the case of the ordinary courts, in the juvenile court, too, there is a section of the judicial police. This section, however, is "specialized": these are staff with specific skills and training assigned to the juvenile section (Art. 5 of Presidential Decree 448/88).

Extra-judicial organization

Social services for minors

Social services refers to "all activities relating to the preparation and provision of services or benefits intended to remove and overcome situations of need, except those provided in the administration of justice" (Art. 128, paragraph 2, law no. 112/98, cited definition by law no. 328/00). This definition has sanctioned the distinction (previously made only by interpretation) between the general social welfare and judicial social welfare systems.

On the one hand, the social welfare system for minors was created to ensure that children are provided with everything they need materially, from goods to services, including education, to ensure their proper development and growth (i.e., to prevent deprivation of any kind). Generally,[2] local health services take care of these requirements.

Social services for minors within the judicial context, on the other hand, ensure that the judicial authorities acquire all the information they need to take proper decisions. Moreover, no less important, this service is meant to implement orders issued by the judicial authorities for the children. The justice system's social service function is implemented by the centers for juvenile justice. Collaboration between these centers and the judicial authorities is, of course, most frequently related to criminal matters, as provided by the DPR 448/88.

The two services (local-welfare and national-judicial) coordinate their own activities, and, in the case of minors under protective measures, they collaborate with each other as provided by Art. 19 of the Presidential Decree 448/88.

Department of Juvenile Justice

The Department of Juvenile Justice (DJJ), created in 1984 (DM 08/06/1984), is one of the four departments of the Ministry of Justice and has jurisdiction in matters of protection, legal protection of minors and implementation of criminal orders issued by the juvenile courts. Its work is carried out through decentralized structures called *centers for juvenile justice*, which are located throughout the state's territory. In addition, the DJJ has its own central committee that coordinates the activities of all the welfare services for minors of the country.

First Reception Center

The First Reception Centers host minors under arrest, in custody or escorted until they are heard by a judge (within 96 hours of the arrest) ensuring that minors are kept in custody but not actually in prison or jail. A team from the center issues the first information report on a child's social and psychological situation and on the resources locally available for a specific case. This is done to provide the relevant judicial authority with the information needed to define, if necessary, the protective order most appropriate to the detained juvenile.

Community

The communities are private or public structures that ensure the implementation of any of the judicial authority's orders against young offenders, as provided by Art. 18, 18-bis, 22, 36 and 37 of Presidential Decree 448/88. With the aim of letting the juvenile gain responsibility, an individualized education program is prepared (for each incoming child), which, of course, directly involves the child and which also takes into account the child's and family's resources, as well as the opportunities offered by the area where he lives. These communities, as mentioned above, are of two types: *public*, which means organized directly by the centers for juvenile justice, in cooperation with local authorities, and *authorized* (private), which means authorized and subject to agreement between centers for juvenile justice and external structures locally recognized.[3]

Court cases

Before examining the institutions typical of Italian juvenile criminal justice, it is necessary to briefly describe some interesting and general aspects of the system.

- As previously noted, Art. 1 of the Presidential Decree 448/88 expressly provides that the provisions of the Code of Criminal Procedure can be applied *mutatis mutandis* to the process for minors. This does not mean that the juvenile court is required to apply only those provisions of the Code "as they can be applied to a minor", but rather that the court must follow the same rules created for the process for "adult persons", but always having regard to the particularities of the subject before it.

- The assistance provided to the child during the process is tripartite: (1) affective (parents or eligible person indicated by the minor himself and admitted by the judge); (2) psychological – social (the representatives of social welfare, always present); and (3) legal (attorney). A minor's criminal process takes place behind closed doors in order to protect the child and his or her privacy. Art. 684 of the Criminal Code provides penalties for anyone disclosing information or documents related to juvenile proceedings that are protected by confidentiality laws.
- A special feature: a juvenile older than 16 years of age has the opportunity to request a public hearing.
- In the minors' justice system, a victim is not allowed to start a civil action.
- The juvenile trial does not allow any of the ordinary special procedures used for adults: the application of the penalties by agreement of the parties (so-called settlement) and the decree proceeding are excluded.

Preliminary investigation

Already at the preliminary investigation stage, from a purely procedural perspective, the will of the legislature, which is to turn the judicial process into a tool for the rehabilitation of a juvenile who has committed a crime, can be clearly seen: the prosecutor (assisted by the police), in carrying out the investigation, is concerned with collecting all relevant information to assess the minor, the context of his or her origin, the available resources in the area and possible expectations for the future (Pennisi, 2004, p. 258).

Personality evaluation

An assessment of a juvenile's personality is needed in order to assist the judge to determine best measures to be applied in each case.[4] In other words, the function of an assessment is to discover the most appropriate response to an offender's deviant behaviour, through the evaluation of the offender and his or her origins, and to apply every useful measure possible to assist the offender to overcome the conditions that resulted in the criminal episode (Pennisi, 2004 p. 562).

The findings from the personality assessment, which are considered mandatory, are different from any "judicial examination" that is carried out by the expert witness as early as the pre-trial stage. This assessment helps decide eventual specific disposition provisions in juvenile cases, namely, acquittal for immaturity, not prosecuting for irrelevance of the fact and, eventually, probation.

Pre-protective measures

Arrest in flagrante delicto

To arrest a minor, it is necessary that the offense that was committed is a crime punishable by life imprisonment, imprisonment of not less than nine years, sexual violence or, finally, an offense provided by Art. 380 c.p.p. (crimes for which you can have preventive custody). The reasoning underlying these restrictions is that the psychological impact of an arrest on a child may be greater than the application of other measures at a later stage (temporarily distant from the fact). In addition, the law also provides options to the arrest of a child; that is to say that, contrary to what usually happens, the officers and agents of the judicial police are never obliged to proceed with an application of this kind of measure (the arrest), but they must carefully assess all options (taking into account the type of crime committed and, as mentioned, the personality of the juvenile).

Custody

The arrangements for custody are governed by Art. 17, Presidential Decree 448/88. An arrest may occur (by the prosecutor and justice police agents) when a juvenile is strongly suspected of a crime and when there is a concrete risk of escape. The arrest can be specified in those cases of arrest *in flagrante delicto*, with a further restriction: the related offenses should not have a minimum prescribed sentence of under two years imprisonment.

Escorting

Escorting can be provided in cases where it is not possible to arrest *in flagrante delicto* or arrest. This consists of accompanying juveniles to the offices of the justice police and holding them until they can be delivered to the parents, foster parents, or even to persons authorized by the parents or other legal guardians.[5] Children may not, however, be held beyond 12 hours. Of course, once a child is entrusted to an authorized caretaker, the officials/justice police officers should make sure that the person to whom the child has been entrusted will make the child available to the public prosecutor and will, as well, monitor the child's behaviour.

Precautionary measures

In the Italian juvenile system there is a principle that states that provisions should be taken according to the crime committed and by always taking into account the resources and the needs of the juvenile, as expressed in Art. 19, Presidential Decree no. 448/88. In particular, these are applicable precautionary measures such as prescription (see below), restriction to home, placement in the community, or preventive custody.

In the event of a breach of these imposed measures (and never in the case of aggravation of the "precautionary needs", as is the case for adults), the court may replace the violated measure with one immediately more severe. This possibility, known as *the waterfall method*, is typical of the Italian juvenile justice system.[6] As for removal or replacement with a *less* afflictive measure, however, it is not allowed to deviate from what is contained in the discipline provided by Art. 299 c.p.p.

The choice of which measure to apply to a specific case depends on the criteria prescribed by the Code (danger of suppression of evidence, a recurrence of criminal acts, escape), as well as on the court's application of the further specific requirements indicated by the second paragraph of Art. 19, Presidential Decree 448/88: the need not to disrupt the educational processes in place. This means, simply, that the court should prefer a measure that does not limit a juvenile in his or her developmental process.

The judge for preliminary investigations (JPI) at the juvenile court has jurisdiction to order the application of precautionary measures (at the request of the prosecutor or *de plano*). The criteria on which the judge will consider applying a measure are those provided by the findings indicated in Art. 9 of the Presidential Decree 448/88 and the reports of social services (which, as noted already, the judicial authority (JA) may use at every stage and level of the proceedings).

The "special" regime planned for minors is followed even in respect of those who reach 18 years during the execution of an order (up to the age of 21) or before the execution of the measure.

Prescriptions: requirements of a positive character

The young people are required to comply with certain provisions related to study, work or other activities to help them in their development. These are designed thus to stimulate the process of maturation and responsible behaviour of the child.

Restriction to home

Under this measure, the youth is obliged to stay in the family home or in another place of private residence. The judge, in order not to limit educational opportunities, may allow the juvenile to move away from the residence to carry out those activities considered constructive for its growth.

Placement in community

This measure entails the admission of a minor to a public structure or a structure authorized by the magistrate. The function of this measure is to continuously monitor the child and prevent its free movement. As in the case of home detention and for the same reasons already described, the juvenile may be allowed to leave the placement facility to carry out certain activities that are judged constructive and useful to growth.

Precautionary custody

This measure involves the custody of the juvenile at a penal institution for minors. It is applicable only in the case of crimes punishable with life imprisonment or a sentence of not less than nine years imprisonment (unless, of course, the juvenile has violated the placement in community, as according to the mechanism mentioned above).

Conclusion of the preliminary investigations

At the end of the investigations, the public prosecutor decides whether to acquit the case (either because there is not enough evidence or for other procedural aspects) or to prosecute.

Irrelevance of the actions committed

Another option granted to the prosecutor (and exclusive to the juvenile justice system) is to ask the JPI to issue a pronouncement of acquittal on the basis of irrelevance of the fact. In fact, Art. 27 of the Presidential Decree 448/88 provides:

> During the preliminary investigation if it appears the fact is tenuous and the behaviour is occasional, the prosecutor may ask the judge ruling not to prosecute for irrelevance of the fact when the further course of the proceedings might affect the educational needs of the child.

It is evident, from this paragraph, what the three conditions of applicability of the option in question are.

From a procedural point of view, the process is simple: the court, at the request of the public prosecutor, immediately sets a hearing to decide the issue. On this occasion, the child, the legal guardian and, if any, the injured party must be heard. After this hearing, the judge pronounces acquittal to grant the request or vice versa with the order of restitution of the acts to the public prosecutor. The same minor (who, because with this measure guilt is acknowledged, may have an interest in an acquittal on the merits) and the attorney general at the court of appeal that has jurisdiction may bring an appeal against the decision not to prosecute.

Preliminary hearing and special tools

The preliminary hearing takes place in the same manner as the procedure for "adults". The judge, after verifying the appearance of the parties before the court[7] (we should remember that the notice of the preliminary hearing in this type of procedure must be sent not only to the accused, but also to those with the authority of parents and to juvenile services), admits the parties themselves to the discussion.

Possible outcomes for the preliminary hearing are:

- decree ordering a trial.
- not to proceed on the basis of irrelevance of the fact (see above).
- not pursued for legal pardon (referred to also as "forgiveness").
- not pursued for extinguishment of the offense in case of successful probation.
- dismissed for lack of criminal responsibility.
- sentence or alternative sanction penalty (see below).

Legal pardon

Legal pardon, as provided by the Criminal Code (Art. 169), implies the recognition of the culpability of the minor, but, in fact, extinguishes the offense; *pardon* could be better understood by the term *forgiveness*. Granting the pardon, the judge decides to waive punishment of the guilty, opting for a mere "warning", believed to be more fruitful in terms of re-education (i.e., it is believed that the juvenile can benefit more from the process itself, rather than the execution of a sentence). The legal pardon may be granted either during the preliminary hearing (where it is often granted) or during the trial, but never during the preliminary investigation, because the precondition of the recognition of the guilt of the juvenile requires the exercise of prosecution. In order to grant a "pardon", the court must consider a number of requirements provided by legislation, such as the following:

a) The punishment that would be fine if convicted (with specific reference to the fact) must not be longer than two years' imprisonment or €1,500 in the event of a financial penalty (taking account of the reduction provided for in Art. 97 c.p.).
b) The juvenile offender must have no other sentences.
c) There must be a positive prognosis regarding the future conduct of the juvenile.

The "forgiviness" is recorded in the criminal database (known as "criminal record"), but it is canceled at 21 years of age. It is noteworthy that an older age has been provided for the removal of records related to pardon than the one provided for the removal of entries relating to other "indulgent decisions", such as irrelevance of the fact, non-attribution and the extinguishment of the offense for successful probation (the elimination of the latter from the criminal record can take place at 18 years of age). The reason is that in this way the court demonstrates that the responsibility of the juvenile has been reached; moreover, that it has been established not necessarily for a minor or occasional offense and that the extinction of the offense was taking place with the granting of the benefit, and not subsequent to probation.

Probation

The institution of probation was introduced into the Italian legal system in 1988 with Art. 22 and 29 Presidential Decree 448. Although from the beginning it was similar to the probation[8] of other jurisdictional systems, it is actually more similar to "diversion" (Mantovani, 1984, p. 503), an arrangement under which the accused is given the opportunity to "divert" legal proceedings by voluntarily completing various requirements in terms of education and rehabilitation programs.

Probation for a juvenile involves the possibility of suspending the trial for a certain period of time (never more than three years for offenses with a maximum penalty of not less than 12 years, or one year for the others) and entrusting the child to juvenile services who then monitor activities of both the juvenile and of support and treatment.[9] After the expiry of the defined period, in an ad hoc hearing, assisted by the reports of social services, the judge evaluates the outcome of the activities undertaken during the suspended period of time and, if deemed all is completed successfully, issues a decision not to prosecute for expunging of the offense, allowing the youth to be diverted from the criminal circuit (without conviction). This ruling may be appealed in the ordinary ways.

Despite having foreseen the possibility of applying probation for any type of offense (there are no objective limitations), the legislature provides that the judge, to enable diversion, is required to evaluate the personality of the child and the motivations that led him or her to commit crimes (subjective limit).[10] This means, in other words, that the judge will have the responsibility of evaluating the possibility of getting judicial elements from the probation period, depending on the subject's ability to achieve positive lifestyle changes (Ricciotti, 2007, p. 70).

There are several essential characteristics of the Italian system of probation. First, as is evident, juvenile services play a fundamental role, in particular due to the distinction referred to above, in providing the required services for the administration of justice. However, Art. 27 of disp. Att. Min. (*juvenile implementing dispositions*) provides for collaboration between the relevant state juvenile services and local social services in order to prepare a specific plan of action for the minor. This plan insures that the juvenile and the family all work together for the well-being of the juvenile. This plan must include a program making sure that the juvenile undertakes activities that increase his or her sense of responsibility. This can also be done with reparation of the consequences of the crime and promotion of reconciliation with the victim. It is possible for the JA to provide the simultaneous application of a precautionary measure, such as community placement. Services should regularly keep the judge informed. More precisely, they must inform the president of the college who ordered the measure about the progress of the plan, suggesting possible variations depending on new needs arising. In the case of repeated and serious breaches of the imposed requirements, the order for suspension of the trial can be revoked.

Hearing

In the event that the judge for the preliminary hearing orders a trial, a proper trial proceeds, following the rules of the 1989 Code. Obviously, given that these are juvenile proceedings, there are some differences compared with ordinary trial procedures, such as the following:

- Hearings are held "in camera", closed to the public.
- It is forbidden to disclose and publish information or images that would allow the identification of the child involved in the proceedings (Art. 13 DPR 448/88).
- Examination of the accused is held not by the parties, as provided by Art. 503 CCP, but by the presiding judge (Art. 33 DPR 448/88), who filters out any questions or objections presented by prosecutors and lawyers.
- Once the ruling is issued, the president of the judging college explains to the juvenile the reasons for the decision, and, of course, the consequences that this decision will have for him.

Conclusions

Criminal procedures against juvenile offenders in Italy are characterized by the fact that the principle of the "recovery of the young offender" is an additional component of the objective of ascertaining the truth, the typical function of an "ordinary" trial. The Constitutional Court has held that this should be the aim because it represents a "special interest and duty of the State to recover the child", the punitive claim being subordinate to the recovery of the child.[11] We can therefore conclude the following:

- The trial is an educational opportunity: the rules must be applied to the juvenile process in relation to the educational needs; the duty of the judge to explain the meaning of procedural activities and decisions depends on the need to educate the child; the opportunity to arrange for his or her escorting is provided to favor the explanation of the meaning of proceedings and decisions; and, finally, the determination of probation with the consent of the juvenile helps the educational process.
- The trial must not disrupt the educational processes the juvenile is involved in. This is the explicit purpose of the precautionary measures and of the finding not to proceed based on irrelevance of the fact, as well as the reason for the prohibition of publication and dissemination of information about juvenile proceedings.
- The trial is an opportunity to make sure that the educational processes takes place. To achieve this objective, investigations are conducted to assess the personality of the accused juvenile, and the diversion project is designed to involve the resources of the child's living environment (Adduci, 2005).

Executive phase

The Italian juvenile justice system involves a series of specific measures to prevent the juvenile's remand to prison. A prison sentence is applied only in extreme cases, as a last measure.

Supervised release

In general, this measure prevents the prisoner from going to prison, if the punishment (imprisonment) is less than two years (for the adults), two years and six months (for those who are aged 18 years, but under 21), and finally three years for minors. The general conditions of applicability are established in Art. c.p. 164. The benefit may be granted only once and can be revoked if, within five years for crimes or two years for simple violations, the juvenile gets a sentence for another crime of the same nature. It is quite possible that the judicial authority, in granting probation, will require the fulfilment of specific conditions. In this regard, it is frequently required in the juvenile system that the offender takes steps to ameliorate harmful or dangerous consequences resulting from the offense. Finally, probation is entered in the criminal records of minors, and once they become adults it is transmitted to the ordinary criminal record, as provided by Art. 15 Presidential Decree 448/88.

Alternative sanctions

Art. 30 of the Presidential Decree 448/88 provides that the court applies alternative sanctions to a minor who has been sentenced to imprisonment for not more than two years. Nonetheless, although this provision allows the application of such sanctions in the abstract to the vast majority of cases, the judge cannot rely on it in practice if there has not previously been an assessment of the personality and attitudes of the child.

A final interesting feature of alternative sanctions in juvenile protocols is found in Art. 32 Presidential Decree 448/88, which provides for the possibility of the public prosecutor's requesting the application in the preliminary hearing. If this is granted the penalty to be imposed is reduced by half (almost as if with this legislation there is a need to compensate for the lack of the application of the penalty at the request of the parties, which is not provided for in this type of procedure).

Alternative sanctions include the following:

- *Half-imprisonment* (which is applied for adults in the case of a penalty of less than one year) is the obligation to spend at least ten hours a day in prison. The exact period of stay is determined on case-by-case basis by the competent supervisory judicial authority, depending on the demands of work and study of the child.
- *Controlled freedom* (penalty of less than six months) is a prohibition from leaving the municipality of residence and the obligation to regularly report to the police and not travel.
- *Alternative sum to pay* (custody shorter than three months): Art. 660 c.p.p. and 181 d. att. c.p.p. provides for the conversion of the period of imprisonment ruled in the sentence into a sum to be paid to the state in order to pay off the debt to justice system.
- *Parole*: allows the execution of the sentence well in advance. Parole has an extinguishment nature. For children, it may be granted at any time, regardless of the punishment and whatever the residual term to be served.

Alternative measures to detention include the following:

- *Diversion* by juvenile social services which has the same length of penalty provided in the sentence, and social services regularly report on the progress of the program to the juvenile's monitoring judge.
- *House detention* means that the penalty is served in the home or in another private residence of the convicted. At 21 years of age, this provision ends.
- *Probation* allows the child to spend part of the day outside the prison to carry out educational activities, work or any activity for the child's reintegration.

Art. 11 provides special probation institutions that work in conjunction with the outside community. Art. 12, however, establishes the so-called multi-functional daytime services.

Custodial sentence

It is clear, then, that in the Italian juvenile justice system, only in extreme cases do juveniles serve their sentences in prisons. The IPMs (Istituto Penale Minorile, penal institutes for minors) are structures created to house youngsters aged between 14 and 21 years, who have committed crimes while under age, and are subject to the precautionary measures of custody in prison or in expiation of a final sentence to imprisonment. If the sentence issued lasts beyond the point when they will turn 18, they still have the right to stay in juvenile detention centers. Once they turn 21 they will spend the remaining sentence in an adult prison. Within the IPM, professional educators and psychologists not only provide individualized plans for re-education, but they are also in direct and constant contact with the prisoners, which is crucial to the young subjects' serious critical re-examination stage of their lives. The work done by the treatment team, in collaboration with juvenile social services, allows for an extensive risk assessment and risk management procedures to try to understand the needs and risks of minors and provide responses best suited to reducing the risk of revictimization. Risk assessment would assist in determining whether there are grounds for alternative sanctions such as diversion, home detention, and probation.

The role of the lawyer in the juvenile criminal trial

The lawyer (namely, the defender) has, in the field of juvenile law, unique and atypical features, compared with those of other areas. This statement is understood in the context of the dual nature of the juvenile justice process which is not, and cannot be, reduced to a mere process of fact-finding (as happens in the ordinary courts); rather it should be understood secondarily, and perhaps more importantly, as a trial of the child's personality, where the best interests are done in name of the juvenile, even if this contrasts with the classical approach toward most defendants, that of finding the offender guilty.

Therefore, the defender has a double role: on the one hand, he or she is the guarantor of technical assistance, always needed to ascertain the liability of the juvenile according to the principles of law; on the other hand, that of a guarantor of the psychological growth of the juvenile experiencing the proceedings. This means, in other words, that the defender of the juvenile will be faced with the difficulty of matching two requirements (a technical and a moral one), creating a peculiar defense aimed at ascertaining the offense as well as the psycho-legal insights related to the personality of the young offender and to his or her educational needs. So it is easy to interpret the combined provisions of Art. 11 of Presidential Decree 448/88 and 15 of the implementing rules, which provide for the public defender a duty of specific training in the juvenile field.

Given the social purpose that the Presidential Decree 448/88 imprints on the juvenile justice process, it is imperative that the defender first and foremost has the ability to build and manage the processes of communication and interaction, "identifying the forms, strategies, timing adjusted in accordance with relevant stakeholders". He or she must not only technically defend the minor from the accusation, but also solicit responses that are appropriate and assist the juvenile to share in working through the process rather than being a mere spectator at his own trial. On the other hand, if this does not take place, then the rehabilitative goal of the juvenile process is not met. The lawyer must be able to use his own communicative competence, building a proper relationship with the child, "capturing and decoding the messages and signals that the juvenile suggests". Also of utmost importance is the ability to work with other people who are involved, such as the parents and social services, with whom the lawyer must maintain an ongoing relationship in order to stimulate the involvement of each in their own field of expertise.

As for the parents, although it is useful to collaborate with them (who, presumably, know their child well), it is important that the youngster does not come to perceive the relationship with the parents as a complicity to obscure the child's own centrality in the case. In other words, the lawyer should not be perceived as "defender of the parents", which would significantly undermine the fiduciary relationship with the young offender, and, therefore, the entire path of accountability.

Essential to the success of the process is also the dialogue between the defender and social services. With this dialogue, the lawyer has the opportunity to acquire basic information about the youngster and, above all, thorough knowledge, at a time prior to trial, of the psycho-social report the social services themselves write that is destined to go to the judge. Moreover, to the defender is guaranteed the function to "drive" the social services; that is to say, that he can seek further observation of the personality of the juvenile if needed and propose additional or alternative diversion projects. Finally, of considerable importance, in cases where this is relevant, the relationship of the defender with the person harmed by the crime also needs to be taken into account in some degree so that possible avenues of reconciliation and restitution can be explored. In conclusion, in the juvenile justice field, the purpose of the lawyer is to use communication modalities related to the educational function of the process, preparing a comprehensive defense of the case, without losing the so-called historical sense of the advocacy.

Notes

1 This is one of the specialized departments referred to in Article 102 of the Constitution so, unlike the other courts, it is not subdivided into more departments.
2 It is not unnecessary to specify "generally", because from 1977, with DPR 616 and then with the Presidential Decree 448/88, functions of a judicial nature were also assigned to these services.
3 The community, both public and authorized, has certain requirements established by law: (a) family-like community-dwelling, with the presence of minors who are not

subject to criminal prosecution and with no more than ten children; (b) the presence of qualified staff for all the different disciplines; and (c) the collaboration of the institutions concerned and of the resources of the territory.

4 Article 9 of the Presidential Decree no. 448/88 provides as follows: "1. The prosecutor and the judge gather elements of the conditions and personal resources, family, social and environment of the child in order to assess their eligibility and level of responsibility, assess the social significance of the fact and place the appropriate measures and take any other measures. 2. Similarly, the judge and the prosecutor can always take information from people who know the minor and hear the opinion of experts, without any formality."

5 Article 18-bis of Presidential Decree no. 448/88, introduced by legal Decree no. 12/92.

6 As known, in fact, under the Code of Criminal Procedure, in the prosecution of adults, the court may, at its sole discretion, replace the measure violated by any of the other which would be considered more appropriate in the specific case.

7 Immediately after this, the judge, if the defendant has appeared, asks the child if he or she plans to give consent to the procedure settlement in the current phase. This consent is necessary to arrive at a result that will be discussed shortly. Otherwise the indictment will be mandatory, unless the preliminary hearing judge deems the guilt of the child.

8 A probation order means the release of the convicted person under certain conditions, which are administered under the supervision of the prison service for the duration of the period. At the end of the period the person is considered free and the sentence served.

9 With the decision to suspend the trial, the judge may issue regulations aimed at repairing the consequences of the crime or to promoting reconciliation with the offended person, if possible.

10 It is essential that it appears that the child has committed the crime not because of a predisposition to crime, but rather from a state of temporary discomfort.

11 Decision no. 49/1973.

References

Adduci, V. (2005). *Il principio della minima offensività e le modalità di definizione del processo penale minorile* (The notion of "minimal offensiveness" and the forms of settlement in the juvenile trial) www.altrodiritto.unifi.it/adduci/index.

Mantovani, F. (1984). *Il problema della crimalità* (The problem of criminality), CEDAM, Padova.

Pennisi, A. (2004). *La Giustizia Penale Minorile: formazione, devianza, diritto e processo* (The juvenile criminal justice: training, crimes, rights, and trials) Giuffrè, Milano.

Ricciotti R. (2007). *La giustizia penale minorile* (The juvenile criminal justice), CEDAM, Padova.

4 Juvenile delinquency and justice in Cyprus

A. Kapardis

> Treatment of children, who are victims of the conditions in which they are living and children who have violated the law, is a reflection of a society's culture and value system.
>
> (Junger-Tas, 2006: 505)

Cyprus gained its independence from Britain in 1960, has been a member of the European Union since 2004 and has a common law legal system. It has a population of approximately 760,000, 13% of whom are non-Cypriots. Its main cities are Nicosia (300,600), Limassol (219,900), Larnaca (128,100) and Paphos (73,600), and, in January 2005, 28% of the population was under the age of 20. People may purchase and consume alcohol at the age of 18, and males 18 years of age have to do military service. One-fifth of pupils in secondary schools are foreign-born, with half of those being second generation. Population density is approximately 140 per square kilometre. The 2009 Human Development Index for Cyprus is 0.914, ranking the Republic of Cyprus 32nd of 182 countries.[1] On the basis of official criminal statistics, the average involvement of non-Cypriots in crime in general is 19%. Without ignoring their limitations, regarding comparative crime rates, drawing on Aebi et al.'s (2006) *European Sourcebook of Crime and Criminal Statistics – 2006*, in Cyprus there were 944 offences per 100,000 of the population compared with 697 in Malta, 10,343 in Finland and 3,490 in the Czech Republic. In addition, Cyprus had 20 offenders per 100,000 of the population in 2002 compared with 178 for Malta, 484 for Finland and 60 in the Czech Republic. Despite such comparatively low crime rates, crime in Cyprus is a major cause for concern (*Cyprus Barometer*, 2006: 73). Finally, it is well established in criminology that there is a correlation between juvenile delinquency and belonging to a large-size, low socio-economic status family (West and Farrington, 1973, 1977). A study of poverty in Cyprus by the Economic Research Center of the University of Cyprus, adopting the EU definition of *households in poverty* as those that are 60% below the median income, found that the following were in poverty: 21.4% of households generally; 13% of couples with three or more children; and 37% of single-parent families.

Excluding some changes over the last half century, the criminal justice system (i.e., criminal law, police and policing, corrections and the Department of Social

Services tasked with administering non-custodial penalties) in the Republic of Cyprus is the same as in 1960. With three notable exceptions, this fact is reflected in the existing system of juvenile justice. The three exceptions are (a) the closing down in 1986 of the Lambousa Reform School (the only one available), (b) the introduction of Community Service Orders in 1996 and (c) the change of the age of criminal responsibility from 10 to 14 years in 2007. In considering crime in Cyprus in general, and delinquency in particular, the reader needs to remember that the local society has undergone a number of social influences due to rapid urbanization, the Turkish military invasion of Cyprus in 1974[2] that resulted in the occupation of 40% of its territory, forcing a de facto partition of the island and a third of its population (Greek-Cypriots) to flee their ancestral homes and to become refugees; significant improvement in educational and economic standards; the presence since the early 1990s of a significant minority of non-Cypriots among the local community; and, finally, mass tourism since the 1980s – sociological factors which, as in other southern European countries, have impacted on the family and reduced the significance of such agents of social control and socialization as teachers, parents and the clergy.

Research into juvenile delinquency in Cyprus is a relatively recent phenomenon. For the purposes of the present book, juvenile delinquency and justice is discussed with reference to the Republic of Cyprus and to the free areas of the Republic because the government is unable to exercise control in the northern part of Cyprus that is occupied by Turkey which, since its unilateral declaration of independence in 1983, is only recognized by Turkey.

In writing about juvenile delinquency and juvenile justice the present author uses the definitions of the Council of Europe Committee of Ministers, Recommendation 20 of 2000, namely, that *delinquency* is treated as acts dealt with under criminal law, although, as Junger-Tas (2006) reminds us, "Some countries include antisocial or deviant behaviour in their juvenile penal law" (p. 505). As far as the *juvenile justice system* is concerned, it is "a formal system that is part of a wide approach to delinquency, including the police, the prosecutor system, the probation system, and youth institutions, but also agencies such as health, education, and social welfare" (p. 506).

Delinquency: the official picture

As criminologists do not tire of reminding their readers, for a number of reasons, official statistics on delinquency are not a reliable index of the real volume of delinquent acts committed due to the existence of the "dark" figure of crime – the amount of crime not reported to the police and/or not recorded in official criminal statistics (see Maguire, 2007). Self-report and victimization surveys can be used to obtain a more accurate picture of the volume, types and trends in delinquency. This chapter first examines the picture of delinquency in Cyprus that is constructed using official data and then examines self-report surveys. Utilizing police criminal statistics for juveniles, during the three-year period 2009 to 2011, a total of 529 juvenile cases were reported to the Cyprus police, of which 31% were serious and

69% non-serious. In order to obtain a good idea of juvenile cases reported to the police diachronically, Table 4.1 shows the number of juveniles involved in the commission of serious criminal offences during the 12-year period 2000 to 2011.

Table 4.1 shows fluctuations in the number of juveniles reported to and investigated by the police for serious offences. As will be seen below, although self-report surveys indicate that delinquency has been increasing over the last two decades, this is not reflected in police statistics. Drawing on the present author's experience as a criminologist in Cyprus, four plausible explanations for this discrepancy are (a) in response to "newsworthy" deviant behaviour by young people (e.g., youth violence during a football match – see Kapardis et al. (2006) – or a teacher getting attacked by a pupil in a secondary school or clashes between groups of pupils from different schools), the media over-report such events in a stereotypical way, characterizing them as if they happen all the time, thus creating moral panics; (b) the public and schools become more likely to report what they have come to consider as antisocial behaviour to the police; (c) the police come under pressure and publicly announce "a tougher approach" to such antisocial behaviour; and, finally, (d) parents of young people arrested by the police contact "significant, powerful individuals"[3] in politics and/or in the police to ensure the case against their children is dropped. Thus, the fluctuations reflect a dynamic interplay of the aforementioned factors. Interpreting official juvenile delinquency statistics becomes even more difficult when we remember that there has been no research, along the lines of the British Crime Survey (see Kershaw et al., 2008), into crime victimization or crime reporting by the public at large in Cyprus.

Table 4.2 shows that in the two-year period in question, whether we look at the situation in terms of number of cases or of individuals, in Cyprus, as in other countries, the great majority of juveniles commit property offences (predominantly burglary, followed by theft). Although the incidence and prevalence of drug offences and the use of firearms and explosives is low, it is nevertheless a cause of concern because of the fact that this is most likely to be the tip of the iceberg.

Table 4.1 Serious offences reported to the police involving juveniles, 2000–11

Year	*No. of serious offences*	*No. of juveniles*	*Males*	*Females*
2000	268	461	453 (98%)	8 (2%)
2001	235	379	376 (99%)	3 (1%)
2002	252	382	377 (98.6%)	5 (1.4%)
2003	199	351	325 (92.5%)	26 (7.5%)
2004	128	209	194 (92.8%)	15 (7.2%)
2005	168	257	246 (95.7%)	11 (4.3%)
2006	261	478	474 (99%)	4 (1%)
2007	145	267	259 (97%)	8 (3%)
2008	270	390	358 (91.8%)	32 (8.2)
2009	171	242	231 (95.4%)	11 (4.5%)
2010	239	397	381 (95.9%)	16 (4.1%)
2011	119	170	166 (97.7%)	4 (2.3%)

Table 4.2 Types of main serious offences reported to the police involving juveniles, 2010 and 2011

Offence	*2010*		*2011*	
	Cases	*Persons*	*Cases*	*Persons*
Illegal gathering and affray	5	15	4	14
Causing grievous bodily harm	3	3	3	3
Theft[a]	15 (6%)			
	21 (5%)	10 (9%)	19 (11%)	
Robbery and extortion	1	2	0	0
Burglary and related offences	182 (78%)	301 (77%)	71 (62%)	90 (51%)
Arson and attempts	0	0	1	1
Criminal damage[b]	5 (2%)	20 (5%)	5 (4%)	10 (6%)
Forgery	5 (2%)	20 (5%)	5 (4%)	10 (6%)
Attempted burglary	5	5	3	3
Explosives	6	9	4	10
Firearms	3	3	1	1
Drugs	3	3	5	15
Sexual	2	4	3	5
Other serious offences	4	4	3	3
Total	239	410	118	184

a Theft of property of value less than 794 euros is a minor offence (Arts 255 and 262 of the Criminal Code.

b If the property damaged is less than 794 euros it is a minor offence (Art. 324(1) of the Criminal Code).

Delinquency: self-report studies

Excluding criminological research into delinquency in Cyprus in the 1980s by Kapardis (1985, 1986), self-reported delinquency studies did not appear until the 1990s due to a lack of criminologists. In 2008 the present author was appointed chairman of the School Violence Committee with a brief to examine existing scientific knowledge about delinquency in general and school violence in particular, to review the intervention programmes in place dealing with delinquency and to recommend concrete measures to be adopted to tackle the phenomenon more effectively and efficiently. Drawing on the committee's report (see Kapardis et al., 2008), Peristianis et al. (1995) reported a deviance survey of 450 youth aged 14 to 21 years that found fights in public places to be the most common form of violence and that 5.2% and 0.4% of the respondents had used soft and hard drugs, respectively. Using a national stratified sample of grades 8 and 9 of junior secondary school (n = 1327), Papadopoulos et al. (2000) reported that 59% broke the law by drinking alcohol when out in the evenings, and 1% took hard drugs (e.g., cocaine, heroin, ecstasy), and, finally, that the degree of delinquency was inversely related to their scholastic achievement. Kokkinos and Panayiotou (2002) used psychological tests and a questionnaire to examine correlates of aggressive and violent behaviour among 202 secondary school pupils aged 11 to 15 years in one urban and one rural school in Nicosia. It was found that pupils who were both the perpetrators and the victims of violence showed the severest form of psychopathology; the *disturbed behaviour* and *self-esteem* scores predicted bullying behaviour while *oppositional defiance* predicted being a victim of bullying; and 82% of bullies and 81% of bullying victims had parents with low educational levels.

Concerning the use of drugs, this was found to be 5% among senior secondary school pupils in a sample of 915 by Papadopoulos and Konstantinopoulos (2005). Another survey of 960 secondary school pupils aged 14 to 18 and a sample of 400 young people aged 18 to 21 by the Intercollege Research and Development Centre (2004) found that 44% had driven a motorcycle without a licence, 38% had consumed alcohol and got drunk, 37% had used violence against another pupil, 19% had caused criminal damage to property and 13% carried a knife, etc. to school but, interestingly enough, concluded that the problem of juvenile delinquency was not serious! Papavasiliou et al. (2006) surveyed a sample of 593 primary grade school children and 1673 secondary school pupils in the district of Nicosia and found that in highland areas, 3.6% had committed theft and 2.7% had taken illegal drugs. Finally, Alabritis (2007) carried out an in-depth study of school teachers as victims of aggression and violence at work and reported that 12.4% in secondary schools had been threatened with physical harm, 50% had been the subject of verbal attacks, 9.6% had been pushed intentionally by pupils and, not, surprisingly, only 40% would intervene to break up a fight in the school yard.

In the context of the second International Self-reported Delinquency Study (ISRD-2), six countries that joined the European Union in 2004 (Cyprus, Czech Republic, Estonia, Lithuania, Poland and Slovenia) carried out their own surveys of crime, risky behaviour and victimization in their respective capitals (see Steketee et al., 2008). Using a stratified national sample of 2385 pupils from 16 junior secondary schools and the self-report ISRD-2 questionnaire that focuses on delinquent behaviour, the survey had two goals: (a) to measure the prevalence and frequency of delinquent behaviour in order to supplement national criminal statistics; (b) to test a number of theoretical perspectives in criminology (i.e., Hirschi's 1969 social control theory, Gottfredson and Hirschi's notion of self-control in their 1990 *General Theory of Crime*, Cohen and Felson's 1979 routine activities approach and, finally, Sampson et al.'s 1999 emphasis on neighbourhood factors) by identifying a number of correlates of delinquency such as age, gender, ethnicity, social class, lifestyle and social bonds. The sample comprised 49% boys, 11% non-Cypriots and 12% individuals not living with both their parents.

Regarding risk factors in the family, serious domestic discord characterized 12% of the respondents' parents, 8% shared no activity whatsoever with their parents, 22% would not tell their parents they would return home from an evening out and 29% did not tell their children what time in the evening they were to come home, 36% did not know who their children's friends were, 53% did not insist on the time-limit they themselves had set for their children to return home in the evening and, finally, 4% of the parents had no idea where their adolescent children went when they went out. Risk factors at the level of the school included the fact that 44% of the students did not like going to school, 17% had played truant in the previous 12 months, and 7% had repeated a class. As far as serious forms of antisocial behaviour are concerned, the (under-aged) respondents had consumed alcohol (20%), got drunk on alcohol (11%), taken illicit drugs (7%), stolen from a shop (11%), committed a burglary (7%) and 4% had used or threatened to use force. Regarding the extent of substance abuse, in the last 12 months before the survey, 12% had been involved in a group fight, 7% had caused criminal damage to a bus and 10% had bullied someone. As social psychologists remind us, people's attitudes are related to their behaviour, and it was interesting to find that 10% of the respondents believed that using violence is a way of gaining their peers' respect, 15% considered violence a form of entertainment, 30% were of the view that life without violence is boring and, finally, 59% would retaliate if someone was violent towards them.

A comparison of the findings for Nicosia versus other capitals of the countries participating in the survey showed that the secondary school students in the capital of Cyprus had the highest incidence of group fights at 16% but the lowest incidence for having consumed alcohol (27%), for theft (3%), carrying an offensive weapon (3.2%) and using hard drugs (2.4%). In support of Hisrchi's control theory, the data analysis also found that a juvenile's likelihood of exhibiting delinquent behaviour was significantly lower if he or she enjoyed a stronger bond with their family, the school and the local community, whereas the likelihood was significantly higher if there were frequent fights in the family and, finally, a juvenile's risk of being the victim of school violence (including bullying) was significantly higher the weaker his or her bond with the family and the school. However, when the Nicosia respondents were compared with their counterparts in the other five capitals on the basis of a composite score for the strength of their bond with the family, the school and the local community, it emerged that the juveniles surveyed in Nicosia had the strongest such bonds.

The reader should note at this point that a Cyprus-wide *Youth Aspiration Survey* of over 1600 youth aged 15 to 24 between November 2007 and March 2008 carried out by the University of Nicosia and KEDEMA (2009) with funding from the United Nations Development Programme reported that 89% of Greek-Cypriots live with their parents, 79% of which are in two-parent families, and 10% in single-parent families. The survey used a proportionate stratified random sampling procedure and face-to-face interviews and concluded that "the family unit continues to play a strong role in modern Cypriot society and features heavily in the lives of Cypriot youth" (p. 16).

The ISRD-2 survey in Cyprus confirmed that an adolescent exhibiting serious antisocial behaviour (i.e., one or more of alcohol abuse, drug use, serious antisocial acts, playing truant and victimizing other adolescents) have characteristics from the following list:

- Often goes out in the evenings.
- Does not spend time with his or her parents but with friends in groups of four or more.*
- His or her friends consist of both genders and constitute a close-knit clique.*
- Commits delinquent and antisocial acts in his or her free time.*

- Is not interested in school and does not read books.
- Socializes with peers who have already exhibited serious delinquent behaviour.*

In addition to being significant correlates of continuing antisocial behaviour, the characteristics with an asterisk are good predictors that an adolescent will also abuse alcohol, take illegal drugs, or play truant at school. In support of Hirschi's control theory, the survey also found that juveniles with low self-control were significantly more likely to show the types of serious antisocial behaviour mentioned above.

Juvenile justice: legal aspects

Three definitions are relevant in considering juveniles and juvenile delinquency and justice in Cyprus. First of all, *a child* is defined in Article 1 of the Convention for the Rights of the Child as "every human being under the age of 18, unless considered an adult by existing legislation". The said Convention was incorporated by Law 243/1990. The Children's Act (Cap. 352) defines *a child* as a person under 18 years of age. Secondly, the Criminal Code of Cyprus (Juveniles Act, Cap. 157), distinguishes juveniles as *children* (persons under the age of 14 years) and *young persons* (persons aged 14 years and over but under 16 years of age). Finally, Article 14 of the Criminal Code, as amended by Art. 2 of Law 18(1)/2006, states that "a person aged under 14 years is not criminally responsible for any act or omission". Prior to 2006, the age of criminal responsibility was in fact ten years. This means one cannot meaningfully talk about long-term trends in official delinquency and juvenile justice.

The procedure for dealing with a juvenile under the age of 16 years is as follows: when an offence committed by a juvenile is reported to the police, it is investigated by the local criminal investigation department who also inform the local social welfare services officer who prepares for the Committee for the Handling of Juvenile Offenders ("Juvenile Committee") a standard socio-economic report on the juvenile and his family circumstances. The police file on juveniles aged 14 to16 years is then reviewed by the juvenile committee which consists of a district welfare officer (Department of Social Services) and the deputy district police officer and makes a recommendation to the attorney general (AG) as to how the case will be disposed of. If the case involves a traffic offence or a drug offence, the case is not dealt with by the juvenile committee. A juvenile drug offender, for example, is processed by social workers in the police drug squad who divert the juvenile to a drug treatment programme. If the juvenile undertakes the treatment programme, he or she is issued with a "certificate of programme completion" and the drug squad recommends to the AG that the case be disposed of as *nolle prosecui.* In fact, the drug-treatment diversion option is available to young offenders aged 14 to 24 years. There is a juvenile committee in each of the five districts of Cyprus. In making a recommendation to the AG, the juvenile committee takes into account the social enquiry report and the recommendation/comments of the Police Juvenile Bureau[4] contained in the police crime file.

The Juvenile Delinquents' Act, Cap. 157 provides for a juvenile court consisting of a district court judge. The juvenile court sits either in a different building or on different days and times from when the judge normally sits. In practice, the same district judge sits as a juvenile court judge in the same courtroom as he normally does but at different times. The juvenile court procedure is provided in Art.10 of the Juvenile Delinquents' Act. When hearing juvenile cases, only those who are parties to or are directly involved in a case are allowed to be in the courtroom. Unless they have permission from a juvenile court judge, journalists are not allowed to publicize identification details of a juvenile. When a juvenile enters or departs the courtroom, care must be taken to ensure he does not come across any adult offenders. In addition, if a juvenile needs to be detained, he should not be held in the prison but in police cells and care must be taken to ensure the only persons he encounters are relatives. Generally speaking, the approach of the juvenile court is relatively informal and, in considering disposition, the judge has the benefit of a social worker's report on the personal circumstances of a juvenile. Article 12 provides the judge with a number of measures in dealing with a juvenile offender: to dismiss the case, to impose a probation order, a probation order with a requirement for unpaid community service, a supervision order, to place the juvenile in the care of a relative or other suitable person, or to order that he be sent to a juvenile correctional institution for a period of time,[5] or to impose a compensation order or, finally, to impose a term of imprisonment if the defendant is a "young person" (see above). Existing case law provides that a juvenile should not be incarcerated if he can be adequately dealt with by means of the other disposals mentioned. If imprisoned, a young person is not allowed to associate with adult prisoners.

In dealing with a juvenile or young person under the age of 25 years who has no previous convictions and who only uses illegal drugs, the maximum sentence a judge can impose is one year's imprisonment.[6] However, on the basis of Law 5(1)1994, harsher sentences can be imposed on juveniles and young persons convicted of violent offences in the context of sport events such as football matches. In 1987 Cyprus ratified the 1985 European Convention for Violence and Inappropriate Behaviour in Sport Events and football matches in particular. As far as juveniles in need of care and protection are concerned, in those cases where they are victims of cruelty or neglect or are exposed to moral and physical danger, a court may order (Art, 63, Children's Law, Cap. 352) that a juvenile[7] be sent to a reform school, be placed in the care of a suitable person who is willing to undertake his care, be bound over to his parents or guardian to exercise the appropriate care and guardianship or, even, that a supervision order be imposed providing that the juvenile be supervised by a social worker for a period not exceeding three years. Article 66 of the Children's Law provides for a parent or guardian who is unable to exercise control over a juvenile to apply to the court for a supervision order.

The most commonly used court order is the probation order. The Probation Law, Law 46(1)96, gives the judiciary a great deal of discretion in dealing with a juvenile in order to enable a judge to respond to an offender's needs by focusing both on the offence as well as on the circumstances of the juvenile and his character, to individualize the sentence, thus aiming for rehabilitation rather than punishment. A probation order is one such non-custodial measure. A probation order places a juvenile under the supervision of a social worker for up to three years, may contain conditions the juvenile must comply with (such as to do a certain number of hours' voluntary unpaid community work[8] or to attend school classes for certain period of time[9]) and may be imposed in addition to an order to pay compensation for the harm caused or for costs. A juvenile must consent before a condition for community service or school attendance is included in a probation order. A probation officer is responsible for the implementation of such an order and if a juvenile breaches conditions of the order, the probation officer may report him to the court which may impose a fine without any effect on the probation order or may cancel the order and impose a penalty on the juvenile for the original conviction. Article 10 of the Probation Law empowers the court, if it deems appropriate, to discharge the defendant with or without conditions. If the juvenile commits another offence during the period of his discharge with conditions set by the court, he is sentenced for the original conviction.

The reader should note, however, that, as Judge Antonis Liatsos (2009) has pointed out, the Juvenile Delinquents' Act, Cap. 157, has not been reformed for over 50 years[10] despite the fact that both delinquency, as will be shown below, has taken on new and alarming dimensions and juvenile justice internationally (see Junger-Tas, 2006) has come a long way in terms of the prevailing philosophy and broad range of non-custodial measures available to respond to the phenomenon. Additionally, the present juvenile justice system in Cyprus can be criticized for the following:[11]

- Judges trying juvenile cases do so on a part-time basis in addition to trying adult offenders and without any specialized knowledge or training to deal with the plethora of difficulties posed by juveniles.
- When a district court sits as a juvenile court, it does not enjoy the support of specialist professionals.
- The social workers who oversee the implementation of probation orders are few in number, not trained, and in no position to supervise their clients effectively and efficiently or to work with their families. To make things worse, being public servants, they finish work at 2.30 p.m. every day in the summer months and at 3 p.m. in the winter months and do not work for the rest of the day.
- There is no coordination between the courts and probation officers as far as rehabilitation is concerned.
- Even though Art. 3 of the Probation Law provides that the government should appoint probation officers, it was only very recently that a small number were appointed.
- There are no comprehensive rehabilitation programmes for juveniles, including education-based ones, and there are also very few community service schemes.
- Finally, there has been no real debate in Cyprus on such crucial issues as the type of philosophy that should underpin the police and the courts' treatment

of juvenile offenders and whether there should be a separate juvenile system or the rights of the victim.

Sentencing by the courts

According to Walker (1999: 135), a defendant's young age must be the oldest characteristic used by the courts to justify a lenient sentence. The rationale here is that a juvenile can be considered as less responsible for his behaviour and, consequently, less culpable for the offence because, compared with an adult offender, he is more likely to be influenced by others and to be led astray as his ability to control his actions is, generally speaking, less developed (Ashworth, 2000, pp. 139–40). In fact, such thinking underlies the practice whereby in Cyprus, as in many other countries, it is unusual for juveniles to be prosecuted for offending, and every effort is made to divert them from the system of criminal justice by making use of alternative responses such as giving the juvenile a formal warning. The powers of the AG to decide how to dispose of a juvenile case by means of a prosecution or *nolle prosecui* or by means of a formal warning by the police is given by Art. 113 of the Constitution. Interestingly enough, however, an archival study by Kapardis (1986) documented the fact that, in deciding whether to prosecute a juvenile before the courts or to dispose of the case in other ways, the Juvenile Delinquents' Committee[12] discriminated against juveniles of low socio-economic status and/or those whose parents had separated or divorced and in favour of those delinquents who came from high socio-economic status 'powerful' families that had the right connections in one or more of the agencies making up the Juvenile Delinquents' Committee and were thus in a position to influence its decision making.

As far as sentencing principles are concerned when dealing with a juvenile, Judge Efi Papadopoulou (1991) stated that the basic question why the defendant should be punished "becomes the more difficult to answer when confronted by juveniles and young persons. . . . When considering what sentence to impose, a juvenile, more than with any other defendant, must be treated as a person with the right to a better future. The aim of the sentence must be his rehabilitation and not so much his punishment." This view has been repeatedly stated in judgments of the Supreme Court: "Juvenile delinquents are usually victims of their social environment and their cases must be treated with special attention and care by the courts"; "There is no doubt that when having to sentence a juvenile, a judge must use imprisonment as a last resort in the defence of law and order" (Papadopoulou, 1991: 5147). One way the courts can avoid a sentence of imprisonment is by suspending the sentence for a period of time and setting conditions. The suspended sentence was introduced by the Law[13] Concerning the Suspension of a Sentence with Conditions in Particular Cases (N95/72). As the law stands today, a court can suspend a sentence of imprisonment if it is justified by the totality of the circumstances of the case and the personal situation of the defendant, especially when a juvenile is a first offender. A judge wishing to avoid as much as possible the unwanted side-effects of imprisonment for a juvenile but also to satisfy the need for a deterrent sentence can make use of the *Law Concerning the Sentencing and Serving of a Sentence of Periodic Imprisonment* (N94(1)/06). Art. 3 of that law provides that when a court decides, on the basis of any law, to imprison any person, whether juvenile or adult, for up to three years, it can (once it is satisfied that the defendant is a person suitable[14] for such a disposition, as provided in Art. 6(1) of the Law) order that the sentence be served in sequences of weekly periods. Paragraph 2 of Art. 3 defines *weekly period* as commencing at 20.00 hours on Friday and ending at 05.00 hours on Monday morning.

Even in those cases that call for deterrence, the weight of the guidance provided in relevant Supreme Court judgments is expressed in the case of *Ioannou and another* (1986) 2 *Cyprus Law Reports* at 149. Their justices made it clear that even where a deterrent sentence seems appropriate in theft and burglary cases, this cannot detract from the need to individualize the sentence in light of a defendant's young age and lack of previous convictions. In that case, the Supreme Court of Cyprus concluded that "the emphasis laid on deterrence by the judge of first instance was misplaced, for in the case of young offenders it must be balanced by the strong interest of society in the reform of the accused". However, the need for the court to individualize the sentence ceases to exist and the justification for an exemplary sentence prevails when dealing with juveniles convicted of such serious offences as carrying a firearm or being in possession of explosives or who have a criminal record and have failed to utilize previous opportunities to reform afforded them by the courts. It must be remembered, of course, that (a) the cases that are decided by the Supreme Court are not necessarily representative of the general population of juvenile cases decided by the district courts and (b) it is by no means certain that the district courts uniformly comply with the sentencing principles enunciated in a number of relevant Supreme Court decisions. Let us, therefore, next take a close look at the disposition of juvenile defendants by the criminal courts in Cyprus.

Prosecuting juveniles

Drawing on an analysis (unpublished) by the present author of data pertaining to a total of 341 juveniles who were involved in criminal offences reported to and investigated by the police in 2008, the following was found: 11% were foreigners, 50% were prosecuted, six juveniles were tried by a juvenile court (all convicted) and 96.5% by a district court (96% convicted). The decision to prosecute was made by the district welfare officer in 45% of the cases and by the AG in 55% of the cases. The decision not to prosecute 158 juveniles was made by the district welfare officer in 32% of the cases and by the AG in 68%. The decision not to prosecute 99 juveniles was made in 57% and 43% of the cases by the district welfare officer and the attorney general, respectively. Boys comprised 96% of those prosecuted; 96% were aged 14 to 15 years.

But what became of those not prosecuted? Bearing in mind that 92% of them had committed non-serious criminal offences and 62% were charged with property offences, the method of disposition was as follows: committed to the care of the director of welfare services (2.3%), before the court as a child in need of care and protection (1.1%), preventive supervision (13.4%) and official reprimand (83%). Unfortunately, there has been no study of the impact, if any, of the official reprimand by a senior police officer, the official warning given those juveniles not prosecuted. Regarding those proceeded against: 96% were boys; 96% were aged 14 to 15 years[15] and 65% were charged with non-serious criminal offences.

Turning our attention next to juveniles vis-à-vis the courts, of the 170 proceeded against, 91% were convicted (4% by a juvenile court, 96% by a district court and only four juveniles were females), 5% were disposed of as *nolle prosecui*, in 2.3% the case was dismissed and in one case the charge was withdrawn. Of those convicted, 40% were given a probation order, 25.3% a community service order, 18% a fine, 5% a suspended term of imprisonment, and 2% were fined and bound over to keep the peace, one juvenile was given absolute discharge and, finally, 1.2% were imprisoned. Interestingly enough, all convicted juveniles were first offenders and all four female juveniles proceeded against were given a probation order. The sentences imposed show that the courts do their utmost not to incarcerate juvenile offenders.

It is known that a number of defendant characteristics are relevant in considering the severity of the sentence (Ashworth, 2000; Kapardis, 2010b: pp. 195–227; Kapardis et al., 2003). Interestingly enough, even though pleading guilty is considered a mitigating factor and all those convicted had, in fact, pleaded guilty, it did not stop juvenile judges incarcerating three and imposing a suspended prison sentence on six juveniles. Having a criminal record and especially previous convictions for the same offence is an aggravating factor in sentencing in Cyprus as elsewhere (Kapardis et al., 2003: 75–6). Of the 154 juveniles convicted, there were only four females and they all received a probation order, all juveniles convicted were first offenders whereas 8% had other offences taken into consideration, with 1 (1–3), 4 (4–6) and 3 (7+). It would seem that juvenile judges in Cyprus imprison juveniles convicted of property offences, without a criminal record but who plead guilty and 'assist' the police to clear up more crime and in most such cases they suspend the sentence. One possible explanation for such an approach in sentencing criminal defendants is that judges wish to emphasize retribution and deterrence, both individual and general (see Walker, 1999). Regarding the use of Community Service Orders (CSOs) by the courts, the evaluation study of the use of CSOs in Cyprus by Kapardis (2006) found that only 6% were breached.[16] Finally, it is generally believed that "justice delayed is justice denied". The average time that elapsed between commission of an offence and completion of the proceedings or the disposal of the case in 2008 was 16.1 months (*Criminal Statistics*, 2008: 150).

Conclusions

With very few exceptions, the criminal justice system of Cyprus, in general, and its juvenile justice in particular, have been the same since 1960 when Cyprus became an independent country after 82 years of British rule. This is a major cause of concern in view of the various and important reforms in juvenile justice internationally the last few decades. As a number of researchers have found, official criminal statistics in Cyprus, as indeed in other countries, grossly underestimate the volume of juvenile delinquency in the Republic of Cyprus. It may be a comforting thought that Cypriot researchers have found that junior secondary pupils' bond with the family, the school and their local community remains rather strong compared with other European countries such as the Czech Republic, Estonia, Lithuania, Poland and Slovenia.

Examination of relevant legislation and the approach of the authorities (police, courts and social services) in Cyprus in dealing with juvenile offenders shows the following:

(i) Despite their good intentions, the police lack an adequately staffed and trained specialist juvenile bureau and their handling of officially processed juveniles appears to be influenced by outside interference.
(ii) Regarding the treatment of juveniles by the courts in the absence of a juvenile court per se, a significant proportion (50%) of cases are not prosecuted and most (83%) of those not prosecuted are given a formal warning/reprimand by the police. Unfortunately, there has been no research into the impact of such treatment on juveniles' subsequent behaviour. The most common form of disposition for those convicted is probation (40%), followed by community service order (25%) and fine (18%). Only 1% were imprisoned whereas 5% were given suspended terms of imprisonment. Existing Supreme Court case law emphasizes rehabilitation in dealing with juvenile offenders.
(iii) The lack of a national strategy for juvenile delinquency and justice means the juvenile justice system is failing juvenile offenders in Cyprus for it does not offer them the benefit of rehabilitation programmes in any real sense. Those of low socio-economic status appear to be the worst off at all stages of the criminal justice system. It is not an exaggeration to say that, in contravention of Art. 3 of the 1989 UN Convention on the Rights of the Child, the juvenile justice system in the Republic of Cyprus has for decades been failing to serve the best interests of juveniles.

There is no doubt an overhaul of the ways in which the police handle suspected juvenile offenders, the courts sentence juvenile defendants and, finally, the social services implement such court orders as probation and community service is long overdue.

Notes

1 Human Development Report 2007/2008, Country Fact Sheets: Cyprus, available at: http://hdrstats.undp.org/2008/countries/country_fact_sheets/cty_fs_CYP.html
2 Turkish armed forces still occupy the northern part of Cyprus in violation of international law and successive UN resolutions, and the island remains divided.
3 In the sense of being able to influence decisions by the police.
4 Established in 2007.

5 Unfortunately, Lambousa Reform School, the only one available that reopened in Limassol after the Turkish invasion of 1974, was closed down in 1986 and, consequently, there is no secure correctional juvenile institution per se in the Republic of Cyprus.
6 See *Narcotic Drugs and Psychotropic Substances Law* 29/77 as amended by Law 20(1)/92.
7 In this case a person under the age of 16 years.
8 In which case we have a "Probation Order with Community Service Requirements".
9 In which case we have a "Probation Order with Education Requirements".
10 In April 2012, a bill is still pending in Parliament that will reform juvenile legislation in Cyprus.
11 For some of the criticisms of the juvenile justice system, I have drawn on Liatsos (2009).
12 The committee consists of a representative of (a) the Department of Social Services, and (b) the district police officer, who formulate a joint recommendation (prosecution, no prosecution but official warning) to be considered by the AG.
13 It was subsequently amended by Laws 41(1)/97 and 186(1)/03.
14 In deciding a defendant's suitability for a term of periodic imprisonment, a court should take into account the nature of the offence (e.g., violent behaviour at sports events), the character of the defendant and the Special Enquiry report provided by the Department of Social Services.
15 In 2007, the age of criminal responsibility was raised from 10 to 14 years. Consequently, subsequent criminal justice statistics on juveniles in Cyprus differ.
16 See Kapardis (2009) regarding the use of non-custodial sanctions by the courts in Cyprus.

References

Aebi, M. F. et al. (2006). *European sourcebook of crime and criminal justice statistics*. The Hague: WODC.

Alabritis, M. (2007). School violence and aggression: Teachers as victims of violence in state schools in Cyprus. Doctoral Thesis, Department of Social and Political Sciences, University of Cyprus [in Greek].

Ashworth, A. (2010). *Sentencing and criminal justice* (5th edition). Cambridge: Cambridge University Press.

Cohen, L. E. and Felson, M. (1979). Social change and crime rate trends: A routine activities approach. *American Sociological Review*, 44, 588–608.

Council of Europe Committee of Ministers Recommendation 20 (2000) to Member States on the role of early psychosocial intervention in the prevention of criminality (adopted by the Committee of Ministers on 6.10.2000 at the 724th meeting of the Ministers' Deputies).

Criminal Statistics (2008). Statistical Service (Report No. 35), Ministry of Finance, Republic of Cyprus, Nicosia, Cyprus.

Cyprus Barometer (2006). Marfin Laiki Bank, Nicosia, Cyprus. Accessed 3 August 2007. http://www.laiki.com

Gottfredson, M. R. and Hirschi, T. (1990). *A general theory of crime*. Stanford CA: Stanford University Press.

Hirschi, T. (1969). *Causes of delinquency*. Berkeley CA: Berkeley University of California Press.

Intercollege Research and Development Centre (2004). *A survey of juvenile delinquency* [in Greek]. Nicosia.

Junger-Tas, J. (2006). Trends in international juvenile justice: What conclusions? In J. Junger-Tas and S. H. Decker (eds), *International handbook of juvenile justice*. New York: Springer (pp. 503–32).

Kapardis, A. (1985). Lambousa Reform School, Cyprus: A study of its population (1979–1983) and its effectiveness. *Cyprus Law Review* 4, 1821–32.

Kapardis, A. (1986). Juvenile delinquency and delinquents in Cyprus. *Cyprus Law Review* 4, 2371–9.

Kapardis, A. (2006). The Community Service Order in Cyprus. Unpublished consultancy report to the Ministry of Justice and Public Order [in Greek]. Ministry of Justice and Public Order, Republic of Cyprus, Nicosia.

Kapardis, A. (2009). Non-custodial measures in Cyprus/_. In Yiotopoulos-Marangopoulos (ed.), *A Volume on Penal Sciences in Honour of Aglaia Tsitsoura* [in Greek]. Athens: A. N. Sakkoulas (pp. 283–302).

Kapardis, A. (2010a). Cyprus. In J. Junger-Tas (ed.), *Juvenile delinquency in Europe and beyond*. New York: Springer (pp. 245–51).

Kapardis, A. (2010b). *Psychology and law* (3rd edition). Cambridge: Cambridge University Press.

Kapardis, A., Alambritis, M., Antoniou, S., Panayi-Karayianni, M., Papadopoulos, M., Sismani-Papacosta, E. and Varelis, T. (2008). Report of the School Violence Committee [in Greek, 145 pages, unpublished]. Nicosia: Ministry of Education and Culture: Republic of Cyprus.

Kapardis, A., Loizou, C. and Peristianis, N. (2006). Hooliganism in Cyprus. *Monatsschrift für Kriminologie und Strafrechtsreorm*, 3, 206–17.

Kapardis, A., Solomonides, H. and Stefanou, E. (2003). *Sentencing in Cyprus: Penological aspects, principles and case law* [in Greek]. Athens: A. N. Sakkoulas.

Kershaw, C., Nicholas, S. and Walker, A. (2008). *Crime in England and Wales, 2007/2008. Findings from the British Crime Survey and Police Recorded Crime*. London: Home Office.

Kokkinos, M. K. and Panayiotou, G. (2002). Disturbed behaviour, bullying experience and victimization among juveniles. In M. K. Kokkinos (ed.), *Aggression: Proceedings of the 4th Cyprus Psychology Conference* [in Greek]. Nicosia, Cyprus: Cyprus Psychologists Association.

Liatsos, A. (2009). The legal framework in Cyprus: Juvenile delinquents and sentencing-practices, weaknesses and suggestions [in Greek]. Paper presented at Seminar on Juveniles, Crime and Criminal Justice, organized by the Department of Law, University of Cyprus and the Cyprus Police Academy, Nicosia, Cyprus. Unpublished.

Maguire, M. (2007). Crime data and statistics. In M. Maguire, R. Morgan, and R. Reiner (eds), *The Oxford handbook of criminology*. Oxford: Oxford University Press (pp. 241–301).

Papadopoulou, E. (1991). Juvenile delinquents: Terms of imprisonment and effectiveness. *Cyprus Law Review*, 33, 5143–58.

Papadopoulos, M., Yiallourides, G., Theodorou, M., Georgiou, M., Konstantinou, M. and Stavrou, A. (2000). A Cyprus-wide self-reported juvenile delinquency survey among junior- and senior-secondary school pupils [in Greek, unpublished]. Cyprus, Nicosia: Ministry of Education and Culture.

Papadopoulos, M. and Konstantinopoulos, K. (2005). *Use of legal and illicit addictive substances by senior secondary school students* [in Greek]. Nicosia: Ministry of Education and Culture.

Papavasiliou, X. V. , Andreou-Filimi, A., Dimitriou, D., Mavrikiou, P. and Konstantopoulos, A. (2006). Juvenile delinquency trends in early and middle adolescence by school pupils in Cyprus [in Greek]. Paper presented at the 18th Panhellenic Conference, *Child, Health and Culture*, Greek Association of Social Pediatrics and Health Promotion, Crete, Greece.

Peristianis, N., Michaelidou, S. and Makrides, G. (1995). A juvenile delinquency survey in Cyprus [In Greek]. Nicosia: Intercollege Research and Development Centre.

Sampson, R. J., Morenoff, J. D., and Felton, E. (1999). Beyond social capital: Special dynamics of collective efficacy of children. *American Sociological Review*, 64, 633–60.

Steketee, M., Moll, M. and Kapardis, A. (2008). *Delinquency in six EU Member States*. Utrecht, Netherlands: Verwey-Jonker Instituut.

University of Nicosia and KEDEMA (2009). Cyprus Human Development Report 2009. *Youth in Cyprus: Aspirations, lifestyles and empowerment.* Nicosia, Cyprus: United Nations Development Programme.

Walker, N. D. (1999). *Aggravation, mitigation and mercy in English criminal justice*. London: Butterworths.

West, D. J. and Farrington, D. P. (1973). *Who becomes delinquent?*. London: Heinemann.

West, D. J. and Farrington, D. P. (1977). *The delinquent way of Life*. London: Heinemann.

5 Community-based intervention programs for released incarcerated serious and violent young offenders

Challenges and opportunities

R. Corrado and A. M. F. Peters

The late childhood and adolescent dynamic and static factors associated with increased risk for delinquency, general criminal offending, and serious/violent offending have been well established (Howell, 2009; Loeber and Farrington, 1998b; Mulder et al., 2011; Myner et al., 1998). Far more recent research, as discussed in Chapter 1, has identified similar risk factors for the earliest developmental age stages. In contrast, there is more limited research concerning the effectiveness of treatment programs addressed to reduce risk, and protective factors, especially those associated with serious and violent offending (Farrington and Welsh, 2007; Greenwood et al., 2001). One general theme that has emerged from the complex and sophisticated meta-analytic studies of the few appropriately designed evaluation studies is that few treatment programs demonstrated large effect sizes; again, especially for the serious and violent young offenders. In other words, the understanding of how to reduce the likelihood for either the onset of such offending or its persistence with effective treatment programs has not progressed at the same rate as the identification of the risk and protective factors. This is not surprising given that the development of treatment programs with high effect sizes is inherently considerably more challenging than both the development of theories and the identification of risk/protective factors for a complex phenomenon such as serious and violent young offenders. For example, the Cracow risk management instrument illustrates the enormous number and complexity of risk and protective factors that have been asserted to be necessary to consider for developing case plans for individual young offenders, yet, to date, specific treatment programs to address various combinations of such factors at the successive developmental stages have not been identified and integrated into this instrument or any other similar comprehensive instrument. One reason for this omission is simply that such programs do not exist or still need to be validated. Another program challenge, though far narrower in scope and complexity than the above challenges, involves the identification of effective program interventions for incarcerated serious and violent offenders released into their communities at the end of their custodial sentences. This chapter will review, first, the key risk assessment instruments utilized in custodial institutions to assist in creating case management plans while in custody; second, rehabilitative programs for serious/violent high-risk young offenders in the community; and, third, an experimental community program currently employed in Vancouver, British Columbia.

A long-standing debate, especially in certain countries such as Canada, the United Kingdom and the United States, has been whether custodial institutions by their very nature preclude or, at least, seriously inhibit the effectiveness of treatment programs for serious and violent offenders. The essence of this debate is, on the one hand, the assertion that custody for such offenders is necessary to protect society from further violent victimizations through incapacitation; and, additionally, that custody serves as a form of general and specific (i.e., society-directed as opposed to individually aimed) deterrence and provides direct access to treatment programs. On the other hand, there is the assertion that custody simply aggravates the risk factors for incarcerated offenders while reducing their protective factors because the prison experience is invariably an authoritarian, aggressive and violent environment that precludes any lasting treatment programming impacts. The predominance of one assertion or the other likely explains the substantial variation in the use of custody discussed in the next section.

Incarcerating young offenders

The custody political debate

The United Nation's Convention on the Rights of the Child states that custody is to be employed only as a "last resort" and for the "shortest possible time" (United Nations, 1989; Natale, 2010). Yet even in European Union countries, there is considerable variation in the use of custody. In England and Wales, for example, custody continues to be a common option utilized by the courts (Barry, 2011; Council of Europe, 2004; Muncie, 2001; Natale, 2010). The Netherlands also experienced a surge in the use of custody from the mid-1990s until recently, and, furthermore, nearly half (46%) of the youth in custody did not have a serious offending history (Junger-Tas and Dünkel, 2009). In contrast, Belgium, Denmark, Finland, Germany, Holland, Italy, Norway and Scotland had lower youth incarceration rates (Arthur, 2010; Muncie, 2001). For example, in Italy, in addition to youth only being sentenced to custody in the most serious cases, judges often employ a pardon, in combination with specialized police monitoring in the community (Muncie, 2001).

In terms of the above debate concerning custody and its impact on deterrence and the protection of the public, the drop in custody use and its limited use were not associated with any increases in youth delinquency and problems (Council of Europe, 2000; Goldson, 2005; Muncie, 2001; Junger-Tas and Dünkel, 2009; Natale, 2010).[1] Not surprising, England (Paperny, 2011) and Ireland (Arthur, 2010) have introduced policies and reforms to reduce the use of custody. Even the conservative American states of Texas and Utah have substantially reduced the use of custody (Paperny, 2011). However, even though after the introduction of the Youth Criminal Justice Act in Canada in 2003 the numbers of youth in custody were drastically reduced (Calverley, 2006; Calverley et al., 2010; Kong, 2009), Canada's conservative government passed an Omnibus Crime Bill (Bill C-10), the Safe Streets and Communities Act, in 2012 that will impose an increased use of pre-trial detention for repeat young offenders and serious property offences, as well as the possibility of custodial sentences for young offenders who have had a number of extrajudicial sanctions (Department of Justice Canada, 2011; Parliament of Canada, 2012).

For proponents of the highly restrictive use of custody for even serious and violent offenders, a critical assertion is that youths import an array of high-risk factors and few protective factors into authoritarian institutions that make effective treatment interventions very difficult.

A profile of risk factors of youth in custody

The most common risk factors typical of incarcerated young offenders include unstable (e.g., mobility, family breakdown) and unhealthy living conditions (e.g., abuse, poverty, family criminality); frequent contact with the child welfare system including removal from family and placements in care; low self-esteem; persistent academic problems including high drop-out rates; antisocial/criminal adult role models; substance use and abuse; poor social skills; a history of traumatic experiences (e.g., multiple forms of abuse, neglect, abandonment) and mental illness, most frequently, depression and anxiety (Cesaroni and Peterson-Badali, 2010; Sedlak, 2009; World Health Organization, 2003); poor coping mechanisms (Sorensen et al., 1998); history of self-harm or suicidal ideation (Natale, 2010; Sedlak, 2009); and low self-control (DeLisi et al., 2003). In addition, youth incarcerated geographically far from home experience isolation and, often, severe stress (Natale, 2010). A recent study of a sample of incarcerated young offenders further confirmed several of the above characteristics being imported into custody, such as multiple out-of-home placements, unstable home life, poverty, experiences of physical abuse, sexual abuse, emotional abuse, substance abuse, gang involvement, and prior offending and detention (DeLisi et al., 2011).

Particularly vulnerable to the negative impact of custody are those young offenders with comorbid psychiatric disorders (Washburn et al., 2008). A mental health study in one of the largest custodial facilities in Chicago, Illinois, found that approximately 57% (56.5%) of females and approximately 46% (45.9%) of males met the criteria for two or more of the disorders mentioned above (Abram et al., 2003). Moreover, one-fifth of females (17.3%) and 20% of males had one at least one major mental disorder. An earlier study by the same researchers revealed that approximately two-thirds of males and three-quarters of females could be diagnosed with one or more psychiatric disorders (Teplin, Abram, McClelland, Dulcan, and Mericle, 2002).

A related concern is the availability of diagnostic and treatment resources/programs for youth in custody. Studies revealed that many incarcerated youth did not receive the necessary services regarding their diagnosed mental health conditions (Shelton, 2005). Even where such services were provided, the vast majority of mental health professionals in the youth custody institutions did not have accredited mental health training and qualifications (Sedlak and McPherson, 2010). A comparative research review involving Britain, Canada, the United States, Australia and the Netherlands confirmed the continued discrepancy between the mental health needs of detained young offenders and the provision of mental health services (Penner, Roesch, and Viljoen, 2011).

Incarcerated youth are exposed to additional risk factors that aggravate future offending likelihoods (DeLisi et al., 2011; Barry, 2011; Steinberg, Chung, and Little, 2004). Equally disconcerting is the threat of self-directed harm related to overwhelming custody-aggravated stress and anxiousness, especially for younger youth and those who have already been exposed to familial aggression (Cesaroni and Peterson-Badali, 2010; Gover et al., 2000). The additional risk factors were the exposure to or witnessing of aggression and violence in custody (Lahm, 2008), the use of segregation to punish non-compliance with rules, and the potential loss of program access for similar rule infractions. Yet, there are protective custodial structural factors as well, such as programming and treatment, including medication, and isolation for protection from aggressive, problematic youth (Prevost, 2011). Again, the youth most vulnerable to the negative structural risk factors were identified as having had the highest degree of adjustment problems because of numerous pre-existing or imported and multiple developmental and mental health risks (Cesaroni and Peterson-Badali, 2005).

The provision of health and mental health services along with providing, more generally, a less antagonistic and violent physical and program environment were strongly associated with their enormous cost (Goldson, 2005; Welsh and Farrington, 2011). Not surprising, this cost included the provision of diagnostic services at in-take and for later case management planning.

Risk assessment and programming challenges in custody

Typically, incarcerated young offenders do not spend extended periods of time in custodial settings with the exception of certain US states and non-liberal democratic countries (Winterdyk and Reichel, 2010). In Canada, for example, for the infrequent lengthier custody sentences served only in youth correction facilities (typically youth under 18 years of age), the maximum period was three years. Far more predominant, for example, in 2008/2009, 43% of youth were in custody for less than one month, whereas 47% were in custody for between one and six months (Milligan, 2010). Regarding youth remanded to custody, slightly more than half (54%) of youth were released in less than a week (Calverley et al., 2010). According to a recent self-report survey in the United Kingdom (where the range of time sentenced to custody can be four months to two years) that involved a sample of incarcerated male young offenders, 21% of the young offenders had been in custody for less than one month; 54% for between one and six months; and the remaining 26% more than six months (Summerfield, 2011).

Paradoxically, the above typical short custodial sentences constitute challenges to both case planning and participation in targeted program services. First, even for young offenders serving such short sentences, their risk profiles can be severe, as described above, and, therefore, expedient and full diagnoses or accessible prior case information are needed to develop a comprehensive case plan. Second, beyond accessing general education programs common in custody, more specialized treatment programs for learning disorders (e.g., various types of dyslexia), alcohol/drug dependency, anger/impulse management, trauma, and specified mental disorders such as conduct disorders, fetal alcohol spectrum disorder (FASD), autism spectrum disorder, and suicide vulnerability, require intense and often lengthy time involvement. Developing case plans is substantially more challenging when comorbidity needs (i.e., multiple mental health disorders within an individual) have to be considered. Finally, treatment motivation, responsivity, and readiness have been identified as essential to successful program participation and effectiveness (Ward, Day, Howells, and Birgden, 2004). Fortunately, case planning has been enhanced by decades of the development of risk assessment instruments.

Risk assessment instruments

For the in-take assessment stage, Andrews, Bonta et al. (1990) pioneered the Risk-Need-Responsivity (RNR) three-core principles/components model. First, there is the identification of an individual's risk of re-offending and the determination of appropriate services to correspond with this risk: this is *the risk principle*. The second component, the *need principle*, is the determination of the young person's recidivism risk and protective factors that have been empirically identified as being amenable to modifications through treatment programming. The final component, the *responsivity principle*, is the assessment of the responsivity to any treatment by examining the strengths and abilities of the individual offender in terms of learning and acquiring new skills. Andrews et al. (1990) emphasized the central role of cognitive-behavioural programs in conjunction with other specialized skills programming and the need to tailor these programs to the type of young offender (e.g., females, Aboriginals, sex offenders). Assessment indicators for criminality and recidivism consist of the traditional factors including antisocial personality, pro-criminal attitudes, social supports for crime, substance abuse, family relations, school and/or employment, and leisure activities. More recently, additional areas for assessment were further specified, for example, self-esteem and major mental illness, such as bipolar disorder and schizophrenia (Bonta and Andrews, 2007).

Validation research on the RNR model has emphasized the importance of establishing positive relationships, with both the offender and, also, the correctional employees because it is these individuals who facilitate a positive environment for all individuals involved, and, therefore, increase the likelihood of individual success and rehabilitation (Andrews and Bonta, 2006).[2] The concern with both the young offender and corrections staff is important for program effectiveness since historically it has been difficult to transfer the successful treatments from non-custodial contexts to custodial ones (Lipsey, 1999). Again, the emphasis on the comprehensive and systematic training of staff, careful implementation and rigour, and ongoing internal monitoring is essential to enhance treatment programming for serious and violent young offenders (Bernfeld, Farrington, and Leschied, 2001; McGuire, 2002; Ward et al., 2004).

As stated above several times, although risk assessment instruments utilized for case planning are not yet in standard use in correctional settings and community services (Howell, 2009), they are essential for incarcerated serious and violent young offenders. Again, the risk profiles for this type of offender typically are extensive and severe, though their custodial sentences often are short. Case planning, therefore, needs to consider interventions that begin in custody and then continue into community settings upon release (Catchpole and Gretton, 2003; LeBlanc, 1998; Penner, Roesch, and Viljoen, 2011; Wiebush, 2000). Hoge (2002) argued that risk assessment tools were sometimes avoided initially partly because of reliability concerns centered on the difficulties of training correctional staff to administer them as opposed to far fewer available specialists such as mental health workers, psychologists and psychiatrists. Another difficulty in the use of standardized risk and need assessment instruments is that they often are designed either for immediate and short-term case planning often focused on, for example, custody placement, suicide assessment, and aggression violence threats – for example, the Structured Assessment of Violence Risk in Youth (SAVRY) – or are not designed for the adolescent serious and young offender – for example, the Early Assessment Risk List for Boys (EARL20B) and the Early Assessment Risk List for Girls (EARL21G).

Comprehensive risk assessment tools that identify a wide range of risk and protective factors for serious and violent young offenders are now available. As discussed in Chapter 1, the Cracow Instrument (CI) is an example of a comprehensive age-risk management instrument. Developed by a research team of more than 30 scholars from around the world, the CI was designed to be used with populations of violent youth and cover all of the developmental stages of a young person, up to adulthood (Corrado, 2002). The majority of existing, widely validated, and descriptive assessment instruments focus on the adolescent stage, or late childhood and early adolescence – for example, the Youth Level of Service/Case Management Inventory (YLSCMI) and the Measure of Social and Personal Adaptation for Adolescents in Quebec (MASPAQ). Again, the CI requires information from various agencies responsible for the case management of violent young offenders and those at risk for violence to more effectively respond to the risk and protective factors of each young person. In effect, comprehensive information for case planning in custodial settings includes risk and protective factors as well as the history of prior treatment interventions from all the developmental stages leading up to the current age of the incarcerated young offender. A systematic review of as many risk and protective factors also is important in identifying the appropriate treatment strategy for complex and distinctive patterns of these factors that have been the focus of considerable theorizing and validation research in the last several decades in psychology and criminology. The serious and violent young offender trajectory of crime obviously has been central, but it is one among others.

Trajectories for serious young offending

The initial pathway identified with the serious and violent young offending trajectory, developed by several scholars, emphasized the early childhood onset of antisocial behaviours and related risk and protective factors (Loeber and Hay, 1997; Loeber et al., 1997; Loeber et al., 1999; Moffitt, 1993). Based on the traditional risk factors discussed above and the inclusion of more recently specified ones, Corrado and Freedman (2011) specified five pathways based on the initial "causal" risk factor and its sequential interactions with subsequent sets of risk factors through to adulthood: (1) exposure to prenatal risk factors such as substance use during pregnancy (e.g., frequent or binge consumption of alcohol) which can lead to fetal alcohol spectrum disorder; (2) childhood personality disorders, such as oppositional defiant disorder, conduct disorder, and attention-deficit/hyperactivity disorder; (3) extreme child temperaments, either high reactivity or low reactivity; (4) childhood maltreatment, such as early experiences of trauma, including physical and/or sexual abuse and neglect; and (5) adolescent onset criminal behaviour. Like the Cracow Instrument, the purpose of these pathway models is to assist case planners in developing a general treatment strategy dependent on the availability of specific programs associated with the distinctive set of risk factors that distinguishes incarcerated young offenders. The major assumption underlying this approach is that increasing the positive impact of any specific program targeting a particular risk requires an understanding of both the initial causal risk factor and its likely interaction with subsequent risk factors. For example, a young offender with FASD-related pathway versus a young offender with trauma-based pathway is more likely to benefit from a case plan that includes highly structured and lifelong assistance involving basic daily living rituals (e.g., housing, health, school, and employment) while the trauma pathway young offender likely can benefit from more short-term traditional emotional- and cognitive-based therapies. A second assumption is that there are validated treatment interventions for most of the risk factors identified with the five pathways (Corrado and Freedman, 2011; Leschied, 2011). The third assumption is that both comprehensive and specific risk-based instruments can provide the detailed historical information needed to identify the appropriate pathway for the individual incarcerated serious and violent young offender. The fourth assumption is that treatment strategies for these pathways for such offenders require community-based programs immediately extending and following from custodial programs. In other words, with the possible exception of the adolescent onset of serious criminal behaviour pathway, the array of risk factors, and absence of sufficient protective factors, along with the average short-term custodial sentences increase the likelihood that longer-term treatment programming extended into the community is imperative to enhance a prosocial, post-custody life-style and avoiding recidivism (Mears and Travis, 2004; Penner et al., 2011).

Another fundamental challenge to case planning in the community context is the continued presence of many, if not most, of the major risk factors that were associated with young offenders prior to their periods in custody. Even effective programs involving custodial education, anger management, and alcohol/drug dependency programs, can be offset by other individual risk factors such as major mental illness, as well as several family and community risk factors including no family or relatives or a socially isolated and impoverished single parent to return to; culturally and economically marginalized ethnic/racial family and neighbourhoods; and family criminality, especially father, and/or history of gang involvement (Snyder, 2004). Serious and violent young offender case planning often requires extensive community-based resources. Though very cost-effective compared with the enormous costs of youth justice processing through police and custody stays (Hawkins et al., 2010; Welsh and Farrington, 2000; Welsh and Farrington, 2011), these resources are often few in number in the community.

Serious young offender treatment and programming

Serious and/or violent offending is strongly associated with violent recidivism, and, accordingly, the most intensive approaches to rehabilitation and treatment are essential for young people who have committed a violent offence and who have a series of prior convictions (Corrado et al., 2003; Corrado et al., 2004). Serious young offenders have a high frequency of reoffending when they have multi-risk and low protective factor profiles (Corrado et al., 2003). As discussed above, five major challenges in reducing their recidivism are (1) insufficient diagnostic assessment of risk needs and protective factors at the initial in-take stage into youth criminal justice, particularly to custody institutions; (2) short-term custody stays and consequent limited-time exposure to complete programming and treatment; (3) insufficient community-based extension of custody programming; (4) poor young offender and family responsivity to community treatment; and (5) release to post-custody criminogenic community (i.e., socially disorganized, high concentration economic disadvantage, high-crime, youth-adult gangs, low-income housing, single parent, disadvantaged ethnic group families and neighbourhoods). Nonetheless, there is program evaluation research that indicates that some serious young offenders are amenable to community-based rehabilitation (Lipsey and Wilson, 1998). The essential advantages of community-based programs are access to longer-term or more complete interpersonal skills training, behavioural contracting, and individual counselling. These advantages are evident even for serious and/or violent young offenders (Henggeler and Schoenwald, 2011; Hoge, 2009; Lipsey, Wilson, and Cothern, 2000; Loeber and Farrington, 1998a; Loeber and Farrington, 1998b; Tate and Redding, 2005).

Model programs: criteria and characteristics

Several model programs have been validated utilizing experimental research designs (Trupin, 2007). One set of programs is The Blueprints for Violence Prevention Initiative initiated in the USin 1996 (Mihalic et al., 2001), including the addition of a youth and mental health component in 2000 (Skowyra and Cocozza, 2006). Currently, 11 programs are recognized as Blueprint model programs (Mihalic et al., 2001). These programs address youth with sets of multi-risk profiles for harmful behaviours including violence and aggression, substance abuse, and behavioural problems (Mihalic et al., 2001). More specifically, the primary focus of these Blueprint programs is on prenatal and early childhood strategies, home-visiting approaches, parent- and family-based approaches, social-cognitive approaches, and mentoring strategies.

Other innovative and validated programs consist of specialized probation caseloads, which sometimes include violent offender treatment programs (VOTP). Youth in these programs typically have been characterized by mental disorders, severe drug addiction or sex offending (Dünkel and Drenkhahn, 2003; Schoenwald et al., 2008).

The above programs focus on adolescent young offenders; another major effective treatment trend has been early intervention-based programs focusing on maternal/fetal health.

Home-visiting approaches

As discussed in several chapters, one of the fundamental bases of the CI is the link between perinatal risk factors and early onset and long-term aggression and violence behaviour trajectories (Lussier et al., 2011). Home-visiting programs involve specialized workers (e.g., nurses, psychiatrists and substance abuse counsellors) attending the homes of parents to inform them about essential maternal and fetal health needs (Thornton et al., 2002). Evaluations of the Blueprints Prenatal and Infancy Home Visitation by Nurses Program, which involves nurses attending the homes of expectant and new parents for routine visits until the child reaches the age of two, to assist them in stimulating the child's physical, cognitive, and social-emotional development, have been conducted. These studies demonstrated that participating in home visitations from nurses resulted in reduced maternal smoking, child abuse and neglect, as well as lower levels of depression and anger within families (Olds et al., 1997). Most importantly, the long-term impact indicated that these children were substantially less likely to be arrested and convicted of a crime (50% and 80%, respectively) than youth whose families had not had these visits (Olds et al., 1998).

Later developmental stage parent- and family-based approaches

Functional Family Therapy (FFT) is an exemplar treatment approach that effectively includes the entire nuclear family in the behaviour-modification process (Alexander and Sexton, 2000). FFT addresses the risk needs typically of youth between 10 and 18 years of age and families that have substance abuse issues and whose members have criminal lifestyles. Extensively trained FFT therapists design and implement individual/family strategies utilizing a multisystemic approach. FFT begins by establishing clear and obtainable objectives and encouraging the family's confidence in the process, while simultaneously decreasing any potential for resistance, that is, by presenting family and culturally specific aims, easing the ability to access services. The final stage involves teaching the family how to apply, more widely (e.g., at school, in the community), the skills they learned in the previous stage to other problems or difficult circumstances (Alexander and Sexton, 2000; Thornton et al., 2002).

Similar to FFT, Multisystemic Therapy (MST) is a multi-systems approach to managing aggression, emotional disturbances, problem behaviours and substance abuse in youth. This approach incorporates the entire family in an individualized treatment plan to address a variety of problems (e.g., drug use, aggression/violence, emotional problems) that may originate and/or be supported by the dynamics of the family and the relationships that have been established within it (Burns et al., 2000; Eddy and Chamberlain, 2000; Henggeler, 1982; Henggeler and Lee, 2003; Leve and Chamberlain, 2007; Lyons and Rawal, 2005).[3]

MST is one of the most empirically supported treatment strategies for reducing problems at home and with peers, decreasing the number of out-of-home placements, reducing the likelihood of youths' recidivating, and modifying drug use (Borduin et al., 1990; Borduin et al., 1995; Henggeler et al., 1992; Henggeler et al., 1999; Waldron and Turner, 2008). In addition, FFT and MST have been evaluated for cost-effectiveness, and figures demonstrate that they are much more economical than other interventions such as residential placement or custody (Alexander and Sexton, 2000; Barnoski, 2004; Burns et al., 2000; Greenwood and Turner, 2011; Mihalic et al., 2001). MST has been assessed as a "cost-efficient, community-based option to keep high-risk youth out of residential placements . . . without putting the community at risk" (Cunningham and Leschied, 1998, p. 558).

Individual-focused social-cognitive approaches

Validated social-cognitive approaches have focused on modifying antisocial thinking and behaviours (Howell, 2009; Vaske et al., 2011), as well as assisting youth in managing mental health needs, specifically anxiety, depression, suicidal ideation, and post-traumatic stress disorder (Schmied and Tully, 2009). This approach utilizes cognitive-behavioural therapy (CBT), which focuses on rectifying problematic cognition and situations and prosocial responses (Vaske et al., 2011). A recent meta-analysis examined the effects of CBT on violent behaviour specifically and revealed preliminary support for the therapy's usefulness for rehabilitating aggressive youth (Özabacı, 2011). Further research has also demonstrated transformations in antisocial thinking in youth as a result of CBT (Bogestad et al., 2010).

Mentoring strategies

One-on-one mentoring programs have been validated as effective in reducing recidivism, as well as general antisocial behaviours. A long-standing program is the Big Brothers/Big Sisters (BB/BS). This program is based on intimate exposure to healthy adult role models who provide certain generally limited-risk profile youth with prosocial experiences that young offenders can role-model in reacting to criminogenic environments which previously reinforced antisocial and criminal lifestyles. This approach has also demonstrated effectiveness for more serious, multi-risk profile youths (Grossman and Tierney, 1998; Henry, 2009; Mihalic et al., 2001).

Violent offender targeted treatment programs

Violent offender targeted treatment programs (VOTP) typically utilize cognitive-behavioural management therapies, including anger management for the most serious and violent offenders (Serin et al., 2009). Though validation studies have demonstrated mixed results regarding the effectiveness of VOTP, there is empirical support for certain programs (for example see Serin et al., 2009). Violent young offenders who completed a violent offender treatment program based in British Columbia had a lower incidence of violent and non-violent recidivism (Catchpole, 2002; Gretton et al., 2003).

Specialized caseloads for violent and mentally disordered young offenders

Specialized young offender probation caseloads have a long history, especially in the US, even though initial programs had mixed validity results. However, more recent versions of this approach have produced more promising findings (Council of State Governments, 2002; Skeem et al., 2006; Spriggs, 2008; The National Center for Mental Health and Juvenile Justice, 2009). Specialized young offender probation caseloads typically are reserved for young offenders with a high risk for violent and/or serious criminality profiles, such as gang membership, predatory sexual offending, drug use, and certain mental disorders associated with low self-control and aggressive impulsivity. Specialized probation caseloads frequently consist of between 10 to 15 probationers involving one to two probation officers with access to more intensive support and supervision within the community (Spriggs, 2008). A limitation to this approach is the inconsistency in maintaining appropriate levels of funding for intensive program resources for small caseloads, for instance, high cost for individual young offenders is politically problematic during periods of budget restrictions (Council of State Governments, 2002; Skeem et al., 2006).

Though there is limited research on specialized young offender caseloads, there is considerable validation support for adult caseloads, which has shown a significant increase in access to mental health services and a decrease in re-arrest rates for offenders referred to specialized caseloads (Manchak et al., 2008; Skeem and Louden, 2006). More recently, two experimental programs based on this approach were introduced in a major Canadian city.

Specialized young offender caseloads and related programs in Vancouver, BC, Canada

The Mentally Disordered Young Offender (MDYO) Caseload was created because of the challenges facing probation officers for young offenders with extensive mental health risk profiles. Referrals to the MDYO Caseload are made for youth who have been diagnosed with one or more DSM Axis I diagnosis including generalized anxiety, clinical depression, bipolar phobias, post-traumatic stress disorder, social or separation anxiety, psychosis, schizophrenia, and pervasive developmental disorders, such as autism spectrum disorder (American Psychiatric Association, 2000).

The Violent Offender/Gang Specialist (VO/GS) Caseload involves young offenders who have committed a violent offence, have known involvement with a criminal organization, or have been involved in a "high-profile" case involving a serious threat to public safety. At in-take into this program and subsequent six-month follow-up periods, youth in this program undergo a youth risk/needs assessment (YNRA). At any point where the YNRA is considered low, then the youth no longer remains in the program and is transferred to regular probation programming.

The MDYO and the VO/GS Caseloads involve intensive case programming regarding multi-risk profiles and therefore youth are given access to a wide range of treatment, programming, and monitoring. Regular integrated case management meetings are conducted by a specialized team, consisting of probation officers, psychiatrists, case managers, doctors, teachers, intensive support and supervision program (ISSP) workers. This team attempts to meet directly with the youth to review case planning for a variety of settings, such as in the living situation, at school, and in programming. These two specialized programs provide referrals to family and individual counselling, including parent–teen conflict resolution. An objective is to improve family relationships and prevent out-of-home placements by connecting the youth to therapists who are explicitly trained in family-systems theory and youth and family counselling approaches. The MDYO and VO/GS Specialized Probation Caseloads also employ mentoring and one-on-one services and alternative schools. The latter involve specialized teachers and low teacher-to-student ratios as well as education and related risk profile assessments that assist in the determination of individualized curricula. This includes, for certain youth, vocational/skills training programs to increase employment opportunities. These vocational programs combine trades and life-skills training (e.g., construction, fork-lifting, forestry, and woodwork). Substance-use programs are available in the community and in residential attendance programs, which are highly structured and include close monitoring of the youth. In addition, for those youth who have the sexual exploitation risk factor (i.e., have experienced traumatic sexual assault), there is the Onyx Voluntary Safe Care program, which offers case planning and support for young offenders who have had this often traumatic exposure.

The MDYO and VO/GS Caseloads are currently undergoing an evaluation review study; therefore, there is no current assessment of the validity of these programs. Though initial participant observation research has provided preliminary encouraging results (Peters et al., 2011), expectations for these innovative programs are necessarily limited because of the well-known validity threats established in the evaluation literature for such programs. These problems include the absence of culturally based programs for youth from highly marginalized ethnic and social groups, such as Aboriginal, African American, and Hispanic groups in North

America and Roma in Europe; bureaucratic/political/funding implementation and program continuation challenges; the presence of multiple and highly complex developmental pathways of risk/protective factors requiring specialized or distinctive treatment strategies, both short-term and long-term, as discussed in Corrado and Freedman (2011), and in Chapter 1; and finally, geographic barriers to accessing urban programs from non-urban locations, especially in countries with large, sparsely populated territories such as Canada, the US, Australia, Russia, and China.

Conclusion

The comprehensive risk management instruments, such as the Cracow Instrument, have provided, at least experimentally, the capacity to assess a wide and even exhaustive range of risk and protective factors that need to be considered in individual case management in youth justice and related disciplines and ministries. However, the ability to utilize instruments like the CI, as discussed in this text and elsewhere (Corrado, 2011), as well as the even larger challenges discussed in this chapter, should not discourage the experimentation with specialized programming for serious young offenders described above. There are overwhelmingly encouraging meta-analytic studies (Farrington and Welsh, 2003; see Farrington and Welsh, 2007; Koehler, Humphreys, and Lösel, 2011; Lipsey, Wilson, and Cothern, 2000; Tong and Farrington, 2006) that have demonstrated substantiated important reductions in such offending. In other words, developments in treatment strategies, while trailing advances in diagnostic instruments, nonetheless, have been very encouraging and therefore warrant continued innovative and comprehensive programming for the small numbers of seriously high-risk children and adolescents who, with few exceptions, are tragically evident in all advanced industrial societies.

Notes

1 Please refer to Cesaroni and Doob (2004) for more detailed international trends in youth offending.

2 Professionals involved in treatment and rehabilitation, however, should recognize that the targeting of low-risk offenders has actually been shown to increase their likelihood of becoming more criminal and reoffending (Andrews and Bonta, 2006; Andrews et al., 1990; Lowenkamp and Latessa, 2005).

3 Please see Schoenwald et al. (2000) for a more comprehensive overview of the principles and processes involved in MST, and Curtis et al. (2004) for the results of an MST meta-analysis.

References

Abram, K. M., Teplin, L. A., McClelland, G. M., and Dulcan, M. K. (2003). Comorbid psychiatric disorders in youth in juvenile detention. *Archives of General Psychiatry*, 60(11), 1097–108.

Alexander, J. F. and Sexton, T. L. (2000). *Functional family therapy*. Washington, DC: US Department of Justice, Office of Juvenile Justice and Delinquency Prevention.

American Psychiatric Association (2000). *Diagnostic and statistical manual of mental disorders* (4th ed., text revision). Washington, DC: Author.

Andrews, D. A. and Bonta, J. (2006). *The psychology of criminal conduct* (4th ed.). Newark, NJ: LexisNexis.

Andrews, D. A., Bonta, J., and Hoge, R. D. (1990). Classification for effective rehabilitation: Rediscovering psychology. *Criminal Justice and Behavior,* 17, 19–52.

Andrews, D. A., Zinger, I., Hoge, R. D., Bonta, J., Gendreau, P., and Cullen, F. T. (1990). Does correctional treatment work? A clinically relevant and psychologically informed meta-analysis. *Criminology,* 28(3), 369–404.

Arthur, R. (2010). Protecting the best interests of the child: A comparative analysis of the youth justice systems in Ireland, England and Scotland. *International Journal of Children's Rights* 18, 217–31.

Barnoski, R. (2004). *Outcome evaluation of Washington state's research-based programs for juvenile offenders.* Olympia, WA: Washington State Institute for Public Policy.

Barry, M. (2011). Explaining youth custody in Scotland: The new crisis of containment and convergence. *Howard Journal,* 50(2), 153–70.

Bernfeld, G. A., Farrington, D. P., and Leschied, A. W. (2001). *Offender rehabilitation in practice: Implementing and evaluating effective programs.* New York, NY: John Wiley.

Bogestad, A. J., Kettler, R. J., and Hagan, M. P. (2010). Evaluation of a cognitive intervention program for juvenile offenders. *International Journal of Offender Therapy and Comparative Criminology*, 54(4), 552–65.

Bonta, J., and Andrews, D. A. (2007). *Risk-Need-Responsivity Model for offender assessment and rehabilitation 2007–06.* Ottawa, Ont.: Public Safety Canada.

Borduin, C. M., Henggeler, S. W., Blaske, D. M., and Stein, T. (1990). Multisystemic treatment of adolescent sexual offenders. *International Journal of Offender Therapy and Comparative Criminology*, 34(2), 105–14.

Borduin, C. M., Mann, B. J., Cone, L. T., Henggeler, S. W., Fucci, B. R., Blaske, D. M., and Wilson, R. A. (1995). Multisystemic treatment of serious juvenile offenders: Long-term prevention of criminology and violence. *Journal of Consulting and Clinical Psychology*, 63(4), 569–78.

Burns, B. J., Schoenwald, S. K., Burchard, J. D., Faw, L., and Santos, A. B. (2000). Comprehensive community-based interventions for youth with severe emotional disorders: Multisystemic therapy and the wraparound process. *Journal of Child and Family Studies*, 9(3), 283–314.

Calverley, D. (2006). *Youth custody and community services in Canada, 2004/2005.* (850-02-X). Ottawa, Ont: Statistics Canada. Available: http://www.statcan.gc.ca/pub/85-002-x/85 002-x2007002-eng.pdf.

Calverley, D., Cotter, A., and Halla, E. (2010). *Youth custody and community services in Canada, 2008/2009.* Ottawa, Ont: Statistics Canada. Available: http://www.statcan.gc.ca/pub/85 002-x/2010001/article/11147-eng.htm#a3.

Catchpole, R. E. H. (2002, March). *Empirical findings from two provincial violent offender treatment programs: Risk assessment and treatment outcome.* Presented at the American Psychology and Law Society, Biennial Conference, Austin, Texas.

Catchpole, R. E. H., and Gretton, H. M. (2003). The predictive validity of risk assessment with violent young offenders: A 1-year examination of criminal outcome. *Criminal Justice and Behavior,* 30(6), 688–708.

Cesaroni, C. and Doob, A. N. (2004). Trends in youth crime: Has youth crime increased in the past few years? In C. Cesaroni, and A. N. Doob, *Responding to youth crime in Canada* (pp.117–41). Toronto, Ont: University of Toronto Press.

Cesaroni, C. and Peterson-Badali, M. (2005). Young offenders in custody: Risk and adjustment. *Criminal Justice and Behavior,* 32(3), 251–77.

Cesaroni, C. and Peterson-Badali, M. (2010). Understanding the adjustment of incarcerated young offenders: A Canadian example. *Youth Justice,* 10(2), 107–25.

Corrado, R. R. (2002). An introduction to the risk/needs case management instrument for children and youth at risk for violence: The Cracow instrument. In R. R. Corrado, R. Roesch, S. D. Hart, and J. K. Gierowski (eds), *Multi-problem violent youth: A foundation for comparative research on needs, interventions and outcomes.* Burke, VA: IOS Press (pp. 295–301).

Corrado, R. R. (2011). Comprehensive risk management instruments for serious and violent young offenders: Challenges and advantage. In T. Bliesener, A. Beelmann, and M. Stemmler (eds), *Antisocial behavior and crime: Contributions of developmental and evaluation research to prevention and intervention.* Göttingen, Germany: Hogrefe.

Corrado, R. R. and Freedman, L. (2011). Risk profiles, trajectories and intervention points for serious and chronic young offenders. *International Journal of Child, Youth and Family Studies*, 2(2.1), 197–232.

Corrado, R. R., Cohen, I. M., and Marino, F. (2003). Violent and non-violent young offenders: A comparison of demographics, multi-problem profiles, and psychopathic traits. In M. Vanderhallen, G. Vervaeke, P. Van Koppen, and J. Goethals (eds) *Much ado about crime: Chapters on psychology and law.* Belgium: Politeia.

Corrado, R. R., Vincent, G. M., Hart, S. D., and Cohen, I. M. (2004). Predictive validity of the Psychopathy Checklist: Youth Version: Psychopathic symptoms and recidivism. *Behavioral Science and the Law,* 22(1), 5–22.

Council of Europe (2000). *European sourcebook of crime and criminal justice statistics.* Strasbourg, France: Council of Europe.

Council of Europe (2004). *Council of Europe Annual Penal Statistics, Survey 2004.* Strasbourg, France: Council of Europe.

Council of State Governments (2002). *Criminal justice/mental health consensus report.* New York: Council of State Governments.

Cunningham, A. and Leschied, A. W. (1998). Alternatives to custody for high-risk young offenders: The multisystemic therapy approach. *European Journal on Criminal Policy and Research,* 6(4), 545–60.

Curtis, N. M., Ronan, K. R., and Borduin, C. M. (2004). Multisystemic treatment: A meta-analysis of outcome studies. *Journal of Family Psychology,* 18(3), 411–19.

DeLisi, M., Hochstetler, A., and Murphy, D. S. (2003). Self-control behind bars: A validation study of the Grasmick et al. scale. *Justice Quarterly,* 20, 241–64.

DeLisi, M., Trulson, C. R., Marquart, J. W., Drury, A. J., and Kosloski, A. E. (2011). Inside the prison black box: Toward a life course importation model of inmate behavior. *International Journal of Offender Therapy and Comparative Criminology,* 55(8) 1186–207.

Department of Justice Canada (2011). *Backgrounder: Safe Streets and Communities Act: Protecting society from violent and repeat young offenders.* Retrieved from http://www.justice.gc.ca/eng/news-nouv/nr-cp/2011/doc_32633.html.

Dünkel, F. and Drenkhahn, K. (2003). *Youth violence: New patterns and local responses: Experiences in East and West.* Mönchengladbach, Germany: Forum Verlag.

Eddy, J. M. and Chamberlain, P. (2000). Family management and deviant peer association as mediators of the impact of treatment condition on youth antisocial behavior. *Journal of Consulting and Clinical Psychology*, 68(5), 857–63.

Farrington, D. P. and Welsh, B. C. (2003). Family-based prevention of offending: A meta-analysis. *Australian and New Zealand Journal of Criminology,* 36(2), 127–51.

Farrington, D. P. and Welsh, B. C. (2007). *Saving children from a life of crime: Early risk factors and effective interventions.* New York, NY: Oxford University Press.

Goldson, B. (2005). Child imprisonment: A case for abolition. *Youth Justice,* 5(2), 77–90.

Gover, A. R., MacKenzie, D. L., and Armstrong, G. S. (2000). Importation and deprivation explanations of juveniles' adjustment to correctional facilities. *International Journal of Offender Therapy and Comparative Criminology,* 44(4), 450–67.

Greenwood, P. W. and Turner, S. (2011). Juvenile crime and juvenile justice. In J. Q. Wilson and J. Petersilia (eds), *Crime and Public Policy.* New York: Oxford University Press (pp. 88–129).

Greenwood, P. W., Caulkins, J. P., Wong, J. S., and Cicchetti, S. (2003). *The Deschutes County Community Youth Investment Program: An experiment in delinquency prevention* financing. Malibu, CA: Greenwood & Associates, Inc.

Gretton, H., Arabsky, S., Buchanan, T., and Rajlic, G. (2003, October). *Violent offender treatment program evaluation: Boulder Bay, Prince George and Kamloops executive summary.* Presented to the Executive of Youth Forensic Psychiatric Services, Burnaby, British Columbia.

Grossman, J.B. and Tierney, J. P. (1998). Does mentoring work? An impact study of the Big Brothers Big Sisters Program. *Evaluation Review,* 22(3), 403–26.

Hawkins, S. R., Lattimore, P. K., Dawes, D., and Visher, C. A. (2010). *Reentry experiences of confined juvenile offenders: Characteristics, service receipt, and outcomes of juvenile male participants in the SVORI Multi-site Evaluation.* Research Triangle Park, NC: RTI International.

Henggeler, S. W. (1982). Delinquency and adolescent psychopathology: A family-ecological systems approach. Boston, NJ: John Wright.

Henggeler, S. W. and Lee, T. (2003). Multisystemic treatment of serious clinical problems. In A. E. Kazdin and J. R. Weisz (eds), *Evidence-based psychotherapies for children and adolescents.* New York, NY: Guilford Press (pp. 301–22).

Henggeler, S. W. and Schoenwald, S. K. (2011). Social policy report: Evidence-based interventions for juvenile offenders and juvenile justice policies that support them. *Sharing Child and Youth Development Knowledge,* 25(1).

Henggeler, S. W., Melton, G. B., and Smith, L. A. (1992). Family preservation using multisystemic therapy: An effective alternative to incarcerating serious juvenile offenders. *Journal of Consulting and Clinical Psychology,* 60(6), 953–61.

Henggeler, S. W., Pickrel, S. G., and Brondino, M. J. (1999). Multisystemic treatment of substance-abusing and dependent delinquents: Outcomes, treatment fidelity, and transportability. *Mental Health Services Research,* 1(3), 171–84.

Henry, L. (2009). School-based mentoring: Big Brothers Big Sisters. *Educational Digest,* 74(5), 45–6.

Hoge, R. D. (2002). Standardized instruments for assessing risk and need in youthful offenders. *Criminal Justice and Behavior August,* 29(4), 380–96.

Hoge, R. D. (2009). *Serious and violent juvenile offenders: Assessment and treatment.* Paper presented at the 139th International Training Course: Visiting Experts' Papers.

Howell, J. C. (2009). *Preventing and reducing juvenile delinquency: A comprehensive framework* (2nd ed.). Thousand Oaks, CA: Sage Publications, Inc.

Junger-Tas, J. and Dünkel, F. (2009). Reforming juvenile justice: European perspectives. In J. Junger-Tas and F. Dünkel, *Reforming juvenile justice.* Dordrecht, Netherlands: Springer (pp. 215–33).

Koehler, J. A., Humphreys, D. K., and Lösel, F. (2011). *The effectiveness of treatment programmes to reduce juvenile reoffending in Europe: A systematic review and meta-analysis*. Paper presented at the American Society of Criminology Conference, Washington, DC, United States.

Kong, R. (2009). *Youth custody and community services in Canada, 2007/2008*. (85-002-X). Ottawa, Ont: Statistics Canada. Available: http://www.statcan.gc.ca/pub/85-002 x/2009002/article/10846-eng.htm#a4.

Lahm, K. F. (2008). Inmate-on-inmate assault: A multilevel examination of prison violence. *Criminal Justice and Behavior,* 35(1), 120–37.

LeBlanc, M. (1998). Screening of serious and violent juvenile offenders: Identification, classification, and prediction. In R. Loeber and D. P. Farrington, *Serious and violent juvenile offenders: Risk factors and successful interventions*. Thousand Oaks, CA: Sage Publications, Inc. (pp. 167–96).

Leschied, A. W. (2011). The correlates of youth violence: Evidence from the literature. *International Journal of Child, Youth and Family Studies*, 2(2.1), 233–62.

Leve, L. D. and Chamberlain, P. (2007). A randomized evaluation of Multidimensional Treatment Foster Care: Effects on school attendance and homework completion in juvenile justice girls. *Research on Social Work Practice*, 17(6), 657–63.

Lipsey, M. W. (1999). Can rehabilitative programs reduce the recidivism of juvenile offenders? An inquiry into the effectiveness of practical programs. *Virginia Journal of Social Policy and the Law,* 6, 611–41.

Lipsey, M. W. and Wilson, D. B. (1998). Effective intervention for serious juvenile offenders: A synthesis of research. In R. Loeber and D. P. Farrington (eds) *Serious and violent juvenile offenders: Risk factors and successful interventions* (pp. 313–45). Thousand Oaks, CA: Sage Publications, Inc.

Lipsey, M. W., Wilson, D. B., and Cothern, L. (2000). *Effective intervention for serious juvenile offenders*. Washington, DC: Department of Justice, Office of Justice Programs, Office of Juvenile Justice and Delinquency Prevention.

Loeber, R. and Farrington, D. P. (1998a). Never too early, never too late: Risk factors and successful interventions for serious and violent juvenile offenders. *Studies on Crime and Crime Prevention*, 7, 7–30.

Loeber, R. and Farrington, D. P. (eds) (1998b). *Serious and violent juvenile offenders: Risk factors and successful interventions*. Thousand Oaks, CA: Sage Publications, Inc.

Loeber, R. and Hay, D. (1997). Key issues in the development of aggression and violence from childhood to early adulthood. *Annual review of psychology,* 48(1), 371–410.

Loeber, R., Keenan, K., and Zhang, Q. (1997). Boys' experimentation and persistence in developmental pathways toward serious delinquency. *Journal of Child and Family Studies,* 6(3), 321–57.

Loeber, R., Wei, E., Stouthamer-Loeber, M., Huizinga, D., and Thomberry, T. (1999). Behavioral antecedents to serious and violent juvenile offending: Joint analyses from the Denver Youth Survey, Pittsburgh Youth Study and the Rochester Youth Development Study. *Studies on Crime and Crime Prevention,* 8(2), 245–63.

Lösel, F. (2001). Evaluating the effectiveness of correctional programs: Bridging the gap between research and practice. In G. Bernfeld, D. Farrington, and A. Leschied (eds), *Offender rehabilitation in practice: Implementing and evaluating effective programs* (pp. 67–90). Oxford, UK: John Wiley Press.

Lowenkamp, C. T. and Latessa, E. J. (2005). Increasing the effectiveness of correctional programming through the risk principle: Identifying offenders for residential placement. *Criminology and Public Policy,* 4(2), 263–90.

Lussier, P., Tzoumakis, S., Corrado, R., Reebye, P., and Healey, J. (2011). Pre/perinatal adversities and behavioural outcomes in early childhood: Preliminary findings from the Vancouver Longitudinal Study. *International Journal of Child, Youth and Family Studies*, 2(1/2), 36–64.

Lyons, J. S. and Rawal, P. H. (2005). Evidence-based treatments for children and adolescents. In C. E. Stout and R. A. Hayes (eds), *The evidence-based practice: Methods, models, and tools for mental health professionals*. Hoboken, NJ: John Wiley and Sons, Inc. (pp. 177–98).

Manchak, S., Skeem, J. L., and Johnson, T. (2008). *Specialty mental health vs. traditional probation*. Seattle: MacArthur Research. Retrieved https://webfiles.uci.edu/skeem/Downloads_files/twelvemonth_specialtyvtraditional.pdf.

McGuire, J. (2002). *Offender rehabilitation and treatment: Effective programmes and policies to reduce re-offending*. New York, NY: John Wiley.

Mears, D. P. and Travis, J. (2004). Youth development and reentry. *Youth Violence and Juvenile Justice*, 2(1), 3–20.

Mihalic, S., Irwin, K., Elliott, D., Fagan, A., and Hansen, D. (2001). *Juvenile justice bulletin: Blueprints for violence prevention*. Washington, DC: US Department of Justice, Office of Juvenile Justice and Delinquency Prevention.

Milligan, S. (2010). *Youth Court Statistics, 2008/2009*. (85-002-X). Statistics Canada. Available: http://www.statcan.gc.ca/pub/85-00-02-x/2010002/article/11294-eng.htm#a14.

Moffitt, T. E. (1993). Adolescence-limited and life course-persistent antisocial behavior: A developmental taxonomy. *Psychological Review*, 100, 674–701.

Mulder, E., Brand, E., Bullens, R., and van Marle, H. (2011). Risk factors for overall recidivism and severity of recidivism in serious juvenile offenders. *International Journal of Offender Therapy and Comparative Criminology*, 55(1), 118–35.

Muncie, J. (2001). Policy transfers and 'what works': Some reflections on comparative youth justice. *Youth Justice*, 1(2), 27–35.

Myner, J., Santman, J., Cappelletty, G. G., and Perlmutter, B. F. (1998). Variables related to recidivism among juvenile offenders. *International Journal of Offender Therapy and Comparative Criminology*, 42(1), 65–80.

Natale, L. (2010). *Factsheet: Youth crime in England and Wales*. London: CIVITAS Institute for the Study of Civil Society.

National Center for Mental Health and Juvenile Justice. (2009). *Advances and Innovations Emerging from the Mental Health / Juvenile Justice Action Network: 2009 Update* Retrieved http://www.modelsforchange.net/publications/247.

Olds, D. L., Eckenrode, J., Henderson, C. R., Kitzman, H, Powers, J., Cole, R., et al. (1997). Long-term effects of home visitation on maternal life course and child abuse and neglect. *Journal of the American Medical Association*, 278(8), 37–43.

Olds, D.L., Henderson, C. R., Cole, R., Eckenrode, J., Kitzman, H., Luckey, D., et al. (1998). Long-term effects of nurse home visitation on children's criminal and antisocial behavior: 15-Year follow-up of a randomized trial. *Journal of the American Medical Association*, 280(14), 1238–44.

Özabacı, N. (2011). Cognitive behavioural therapy for violent behaviour in children and adolescents: A meta-analysis. *Children and Youth Services Review*, 33(10), 1989–93.

Paperny, A. M. (2011, July 19). Canada's youth crime plans bewilder international observers. *The Globe and Mail*. Retrieved from http://www.theglobeandmail.com/news/national/time-to-lead/time-to-lead-archives/canadas-youth-crime-plans-bewilder-international-observers/article2102822/.

Parliament of Canada (2012). Legislative Summary of Bill C-10: 9 Amendments to the Youth Criminal Justice Act [Bill C-10, Part 4, Clauses 167–204 (Formerly Bill C-4)]. Publication No. 41-1-C10-E. Retrieved from http://www.parl.gc.ca/About/Parliament/LegislativeSummaries/bills_ls.asp?ls=c1009& arl=41&Ses=1&source=library_prb&Language=E#a16

Penner, E. K., Roesch, R., and Viljoen, J. L. (2011). Young offenders in custody: An international comparison of mental health services. *International Journal of Forensic Mental Health,* 10(3), 215–32.

Peters, A. M. F., Descormiers, K., Corrado, R. R., Manzardo, S., Freedman, L. L., Glackman, W. (2011). *Recidivism among serious and violent young offenders referred to specialized youth probation.* Paper presented at the American Society of Criminology Conference, Washington, DC.

Prevost, A. (2011). Empirical exploration of the importation, deprivation and integrated models concerning types of aggression in youth custody. (Doctoral dissertation). Retrieved from Simon Fraser University Theses, Dissertations, and other Required Graduate Degree Essays. (Electronic Theses and Dissertations No. etd6571).

Schmied, V. and Tully, L. (2009). *Effective strategies and interventions for adolescents in a child protection context.* Ashfield, New South Wales: Centre for Parenting & Research, NSW Department of Community Services.

Schoenwald, S. K., Brown, T. L., and Henggeler, S. W. (2000). Inside multisystemic therapy: Therapist, supervisory, and program practices. *Journal of Emotional and Behavioral Disorders*, 8(2), 113–27.

Schoenwald, S. K., Heiblum, N., Saldana, L., and Henggeler, S. W. (2008). The international implementation of multisystemic therapy. *Evaluation and the Health Professionals*, 31(2), 211–25.

Sedlak, A. J. (2009). Surveying youths in custody. *Corrections Today*, 71(6), 92–4.

Sedlak, A. J. and McPherson, K. S. (2010). *Youth's needs and services: Findings from the survey of youth in residential placement.* Juvenile Justice Bulletin.Washington, DC: Department of Justice, Office of Juvenile Justice and Delinquency Prevention.

Serin, R. C., Gobeil, R., and Preston, D. L. (2009). Evaluation of the persistently violent offender treatment program. *International Journal of Offender Therapy and Comparative Criminology*, 53(1), 57–73.

Shelton, D. (2005). Patterns of treatment services and costs for young offenders with mental disorders. *Journal of Child and Adolescent Psychiatric Nursing,* 18, 103–12.

Skeem, J. L., Emke-Francis, P., and Louden, J. E. (2006). Probation, mental health, and mandated treatment: A national survey. *Criminal Justice and Behavior*, 33(2), 158–84.

Skeem, J. L. and Louden, J. E. (2006). Toward evidence-based practice for probationers and parolees mandated to mental health treatment. *Psychiatric Services*, 57(3), 333–42.

Skowyra, K. and Cocozza, J. (2006). *A Blueprint for change: Improving the system response to youth with mental health needs involved with the juvenile justice system.* National Center for Mental Health and Juvenile Justice. Retrieved from http://www.ncmhjj.com/Blueprint/pdfs/ProgramBrief_06_06.pdf.

Snyder, H. N. (2004). An empirical portrait of the youth reentry population. *Youth Violence and Juvenile Justice,* 2(1), 39–55.

Sorensen, J., Wrinkle, R., and Gutierrez, A. (1998). Patterns of rule-violating behaviors and adjustment to incarceration among murderers. *Prison Journal,* 78, 222–31.

Spriggs, V. (2008). *Overview of the special needs diversionary program for mentally ill juvenile offenders, FY 2007.* Texas Juvenile Probation Commission.

Steinberg, L., Chung, H. L., and Little, M. (2004). Re-entry of young offenders from the justice system: A developmental perspective. *Youth Violence and Juvenile Justice* 2(1), 21–38.

Summerfield, A. (2011). *Children and young people in custody 2010–11: An analysis of the experiences of 15–18-year-olds in prison*. London: The Stationery Office Limited.

Tate, D. C. and Redding, R. E. (2005). Mental health and rehabilitative services in juvenile justice: System reforms and innovative approaches. In K. Heilbrun, N. E. S. Goldstein, and R. E. Redding, *Juvenile delinquency: Prevention, assessment, and intervention* (pp. 134–60). New York, NY: Oxford University Press Inc.

Teplin, L. A., Abram, K. M., McClelland, G. M., Dulcan, M. K., and Mericle, A. A. (2002). Psychiatric disorders in youth in juvenile detention. *Archives of General Psychiatry,* 59(12), 1133–43.

Thornton, T. N., Craft, C. A., Dahlberg, D. L., Lynch, B. S., and Baer, K. (2002). *Best practices of youth violence prevention. A sourcebook for community action.* Atlanta, Georgia: National Center for Injury Prevention and Control. Centers for Disease Control and Prevention.

Tong, L. S. J. and Farrington, D. P. (2006). How effective is the 'Reasoning and Rehabilitation' programme in reducing reoffending? A meta-analysis of evaluations in four countries. *Psychology, Crime and Law,* 12(1), 32–4.

Trupin, E. (2007). Evidence-based treatment for justice-involved youth. In C. L. Kessler and L. J. Kraus, *The mental health needs of young offenders: Forging paths toward reintegration and rehabilitation*. Cambridge, UK: Cambridge University Press.

United Nations (1989). *Convention on the Rights of the Child.* UN General Assembly Document, A/RES/44/25.

Vaske, J., Galyean, K., and Cullen, F. T. (2011). Toward a biosocial theory of offender rehabilitation: Why does cognitive-behavioral therapy work? *Journal of Criminal Justice*, 39(1), 90–102.

Waldron, H. B. and Turner, C. W. (2008). Evidence-based psychosocial treatments for adolescent substance abuse. *Journal of Clinical Child & Adolescent Psychology*, 37(1), 238–61.

Ward, T., Day, A., Howells, K., and Birgden, A. (2004). The multifactor offender readiness model. *Aggression and Violent Behavior,* 9(6), 645–73.

Washburn, J. J., Teplin, L. A., Voss, L. S., Simon, C. D., Abram, K. M., and McClelland, G. M. (2008). Psychiatric disorders among detained youths: A comparison of youths processed in juvenile court and adult criminal court. *Psychiatric Services*, 59(9), 965–73.

Welsh, B. C. and Farrington, D. P. (2000). Correctional intervention programs and cost–benefit analysis. *Criminal Justice and Behavior,* February, 27(1), 115–33.

Welsh, B. C. and Farrington, D. P. (2011). The benefits and costs of early prevention compared with imprisonment: Toward evidence-based policy. *Prison Journal Supplement,* 91(3), 120S–137S.

Wiebush, R. G. (2000). *Risk assessment and classification for serious, violent, and chronic young offenders*. Madison, WI: National Council on Crime and Criminology.

Winterdyk, J. and Reichel, P. (2010). Juvenile justice in the international arena. In P. L. Reichel, *The Handbook of Transnational Crime and Justice* (pp. 457–69). Thousand Oaks, CA: Sage Publications, Inc.

World Health Organization (2003). *Promoting the health of young people in custody.* Copenhagen, Denmark: WHO Regional Office for Europe.

6 Risk assessment and needs assessment

The EARN method

A. C. Baldry, A. Kapardis and C. Porcaro

The project

The European Assessment of Risk/Needs in Juvenile Violent Offenders (EARN in JVO) is a project that was funded by the European Union (Daphne program to combat violence against women and children) and co-financed by the Province of Caserta. The project was conducted under the auspices of the Department of Psychology of the Second University of Naples and coordinated by Professor Anna Costanza Baldry.

Aim of the project

The project lasted two years and included several phases and activities:

1) The implementation in Italy and Cyprus of a new method for the assessment of risks/needs of recurrence of violence for youths charged with violent crimes (Method EARN), based on the previous experiences from the United States (SAVRY: Borum et al., 2000) and from Canada (EARL B20: Augimeri et al., 2001; CRAKOW: Corrado, 2002).
2) Training on risk assessment for professionals (juvenile justice workers, law enforcement officials and lawyers) working with violent juvenile offenders.
3) Risk assessment by the professionals who provide interventions for the youth.
4) Development of intervention programs according to the assessment of risk /needs done with the EARN.
5) Evaluation of recidivism and review of the effectiveness of the interventions that had been implemented.
6) International conference in Rome; presentation of results.

Juvenile delinquency and risk assessment

Juvenile delinquency, in particular juvenile delinquency characterized by violent behaviors committed by pre-adolescents and adolescents, is an increasing problem in our society, damaging not only to the direct victims but also to the perpetrators who put at risk their entire futures. The violent crimes committed by minors (robbery, injury, beatings, attempted murder, murder, sexual violence, threats) are typically repeated over time; juveniles that perpetrate these types of crimes are likely to repeat them, regardless of whether or not they are stopped, arrested or convicted. The "timing" of the violence could be daily, weekly, monthly or yearly and could be characterized by not particularly severe crimes (e.g., beatings) or by a complex of behaviors, greater in severity and dangerousness (e.g., attempted murder, sexual violence). Preventing recurrences of these forms of violence should be one of the goals of all professionals who work in the juvenile justice services (law enforcement, social services, healthcare and schools). Combating all forms of juvenile violence with a focus, not just on repression, but on rehabilitation, and on restorative justice is the goal of more than 20 years of research on youth justice.

For decades, researchers in this field have tried to identify risk factors, characteristics and circumstances that increase the likelihood of youth perpetrating violent acts. As with all complex social phenomena, it is not possible to talk in terms of "cause": there are no causes of violent juvenile behaviors, but there are circumstances, characteristics related to the individual and his or her personality, social context, and family and past history – all of which are related to the perpetration of violence.

In addition to risk factors, it is useful to identify *protective factors*, those factors that protect against deviance, decreasing the probability that violent behaviors will occur or be repeated, offsetting the negative effect of risk factors. The protective factors also work as "buffers", mitigating the negative impact of some circumstances in the life of the youth or of his social and familial environment. In fact, finding appropriate and effective actions to reduce the risks of recurrence involves assessing not only the presence of risk factors but also the resources, or the protective factors, that are existence. The principle of risk assessment is that violence is a choice, a choice influenced by a number of social, biological, neurological and individual factors. This is not a deterministic approach to human behavior. It is possible to hypothesize, predict and assess which factors have led the child to decide to act violently and try to modify, reduce, or, even better, extinguish or neutralize them, thus reducing the risk of recurrence.

With a view to preventing and reducing recidivism, we must develop a risk management plan to minimize the circumstances, the risk factors that influenced the choice of violence, and maximize protective factors. When assessing risk, it is necessary to take into account the type of risk factors present and contextualize them; they could be static or dynamic, and their influence could be significant for some children but not for others. Assessment of risk aims ultimately to prevent the recurrence of violence itself because, by identifying the risk factors, professionals could design and implement interventions reducing the negative impact of those factors and thereby also reducing the possibility that the violent conduct recurs (Hart, 2001).

A structured approach such as the EARN is needed to better understand not only what the key problems of the child are but also to identify the needs of that child and provide the opportune rehabilitative answers, obviously in accordance with the provisions of law. Risk assessment involves risk management, the identification of the most appropriate intervention for that case, to avoid recurrence.

Social sciences and criminology cannot produce miracles; it cannot be expected that risk assessment will be equivalent to determining who will be violent again or when or what kind of violence will occur. Nonetheless, an approach based on risk assessment with a legal, psychosocial, clinical and criminological perspective can assist our understanding of possible circumstances and causes – risk factors (e.g., ineffective parenting, negative environment, personality disorders, substance abuse) – that have led the child to use violence in the past and to assess whether the presence of these factors could influence the probability of the use violence in the future.

Risk assessment is not a psychological diagnosis and does not require special clinical skills. It is an approach that can be useful to any professionals who work with juveniles who have committed violent crimes. It is not a static process, done only one time, but is dynamic and should be repeated each time new circumstances arise that may have affected the objective and subjective conditions relating to that child and, consequently, to the level of risk. Assessing risk does not mean simply discovering which factors are present but where and in what manner and time they can interact to increase the risk of recurrence of violence.

Planning for risk management should be implemented after an evaluation is conducted and can be based on four different phases: *monitoring*, *treatment*, *supervision* and, ideally, *programming for the safety of the victim* in the case of violent crimes committed against a victim (Hart, 2001; Kropp et al., 1999). Monitoring involves an ongoing assessment of risk and therefore constant attention and analysis to detect changes in the level of risk over time. When called for by changes that occur, strategies more suitable for the protection of the victim can be devised and implemented.

The tool

The EARN in JVO is a tool to assist juvenile justice system professionals in identifying risk and protective factors, assessing the risk of recurrence, and also identifying effective interventions, based on the needs and risks identified. This is not a psychometric test, which requires a score; the EARN is a checklist, a guide for professionals working in teams to identify the presence or absence of risk and protective factors.

Some risk and protective factors are static (do not change over time) and their influence (positive or negative) may also persist over time (e.g., had abusive parents or mother used alcohol during pregnancy). Other factors are dynamic; they can change over time. If a child who lived in a deprived environment, characterized by a high rate of delinquency, is placed in a home located in another area, in another neighborhood, the risk factor "deprived environment" will no longer have an effect.

The EARN was developed in Italy and in Cyprus in accordance with international experience, including the Canadian, American and English, and adapted to our social, cultural and regulatory environment. EARN is the result of a review of the national and international literature on juvenile delinquency, treatment, prevention, and antisocial behavior. The EARN is intended to be an easy-to-use toolkit that can be used at any time by practitioners in the juvenile justice system. The evaluation through the identification of risk and protective factors can be done at different times by different professionals. The checklist is composed of 32 factors divided into six domains (five risk factors: environmental, individual, familial, intervention, externalized behavior; one of protection).

Scoring

The coding of the 32 items is simple and consistent. For each of the risk factors, the compiler has to identify whether or not that factor is present and enter one of four codes: N = *not present*; P = *probably/partially present*; S = *present*; *and* – = *omitted /lack of information.*

Critical factors

The impact of risk factors depends on their frequency, severity and pervasiveness as well as the psychological characteristics of the children exposed to them. There are critical factors in an absolute sense, but each risk factor could be "critical" in interaction with individual, familial, and environmental contexts. Thus the EARN supports the codification of the critical factor in terms of presence/absence.

The compiler has to use the information about the child and his environment, as well as his own professional expertise, to assess which of 32 factors are more critical. This is important for two reasons: (1) for the intervention, those factors are, in fact, the critical dimensions on which the project should be focused and implemented depending on the resources available, and (2) for research purposes, evaluating which factors emerge as most critical is fundamental to increasing our ability to predict and prevent the occurrence of antisocial and deviant behaviors.

Final risk evaluation

Once the instrument has been completed and all the risk factors and any other factors deemed relevant to the understanding of the case are assessed, the compiler evaluates the overall risk on a three-level scale (*low*, *medium*, *high*) and proposes a plan of individualized intervention based on risk factors (especially the critical ones) and needs and resources of the child, considering the available resources.

I – Environmental domain

The environmental domain includes environmental factors of a medical, biological, physiological and social nature. Children who have had the misfortune to have deficits of both a physiological and social nature have a higher risk of perpetrating antisocial behaviors and violence (Brennan et al. 1997). The risk factors included in this section were selected on the basis of their correlation with antisocial behavior in adolescence and on their clinical impact on youth violence. The following are the risk factors related to environmental domain:

1. Maternal substance abuse during pregnancy.
2. Low socio-economic status.
3. Community disorganization.
4. School environment.

1. Maternal substance abuse during pregnancy

Research in this area has amply demonstrated that the neurological damage caused by the mother's exposure to substances such as alcohol and drugs (Conry and Fast, 2000) and their interactions increases the predisposition to criminal behavior. More recent research, instead, put the focus on the negative effects of exposure to cigarette smoke. Hodgins et al. (2001), for example, controlling a large number of spurious variables, found a high correlation between the mother's smoking and the juvenile's criminal behavior. Common sense leads us to believe that women who smoke during pregnancy are more likely to be influenced by other factors related to future antisocial behavior of their offspring (Hodgins et al., 2002). For example, these women have a higher probability, if they are young, of also using alcohol and drugs during pregnancy and of having an antisocial partner. Each risk factor that is present in addition to the use of cigarettes increases the risk that the child may be involved in violent types of deviant behavior (Corrado, 2002).

2. Low socio-economic status

The relationship between poverty and youth violence has been widely documented (Elliott et al., 1989; Farrington, 1989). The effect that poverty can have on violence, however, is linked to the presence of other variables (Reppucci et al., 2002). For example, the effect of low socio-economic status on the perpetration of violent behavior is linked, in the literature, on factors such as the disorganization of the environment where the child lives and grows (Sampson and Lauritsen, 1994).

Socio-economic conditions such as poverty and marginalization are certainly important, but they are not to be considered "causal" in a strict sense; what matters is the subjective meaning, combined with cultural conditions and the influence of group membership (De Leo, 1990). For the purposes of our work, it is still useful to consider this factor as a unique dimension when evaluating its effect on the genesis of certain "behaviors".

3. Community disorganization

The influence of a disruptive social and environmental context in which a youth grows up on the development of violent behavior varies significantly during the development of the child. The stronger and more direct relationship between the disorganization of the environment and violence has a stronger effect during adolescence (Maguin et al., 1995). In the early periods of development, the disorganization of the social and environmental context seems to operate indirectly through its influence on family variables (Surgeon General of the United States, 2001).

The indicators of disorganization of social and environmental context that have been shown to be linked to violence include the presence of violence in the neighborhood (Durant et al., 1994; Singer et al., 1995; Widom, 1989b), easy access to weapons, easy access to drugs (Maguin et al., 1995), the number of adults in the district involved in violent and antisocial behavior (Osgood and Chambers, 2000; Sampson and Lauritsen, 1994), the exposure to injury (McCord and Ensminger, 1995) and the lack of structured activities in the area (Bursik and Grasmick, 1993).

4. School environment

Research suggests that some schools encourage a culture of violence and students who attend these schools are at risk for both victimization and association with criminals. Farrington (1989) reported that children who attend schools with a high crime rate (at the age of 11) show more violent behavior in adolescence. The lack of structured and supervised activities within the school also contributes to the overall level of attachment that youth have to prosocial activities and institutions. Another important dimension of the school environment is the availability of resources and support from the community. The level of disorganization within the school cannot be inferred only from the characteristics of the community, even if schools situated in socially disorganized areas tend to have higher rates of violence (Laub and Lauristen, 1998).

II – Individual domain

The interaction of biological and psychological factors in children and adolescents may increase their vulnerability to the influence of a negative social environment. In many cases, this interaction is the main cause of antisocial behavior in adult subjects who have always lived in a social environment full of negative influences (Hare, 1993). We will consider, in this context, *biological factors*, such as the role of neurological damage in the implementation of violent behavior, and *psychological factors,* such as the ability to cope with stressful situations, the presence of empathy, or the ability to feel remorse, and we will consider the interaction between these two types of factors. The following are risk factors related to the individual domain:

5. Birth deficiency.
6. Poor school functioning.
7. Poor coping ability.
8. Impulsivity/risk taking.
9. Low empathy/lack of remorse.
10. ADHD symptoms.
11. Mental disease.

5. Birth deficits

In many studies, it was found that obstetric complications could lead to violent behavior because of damage to brain areas related to impulsivity (Litt, 1972). Prenatal and perinatal complications are factors that can have a significant impact on the subsequent development of the child. Obstetric complications/birth deficiencies include but are not limited to maternal health impairment (poor nutrition, infection), pregnancy with forceps, umbilical cord prolapse, pre-eclampsia (hypertension syndrome in pregnancy), premature birth, perinatal anoxia, abnormal weight, chronic diseases and disabilities already identified in the perinatal age.

6. Poor school functioning

Poor academic performance and academic failure are frequently cited as risk factors in the development of antisocial behavior of violent youths (Denno, 1990; Maguin and Loeber, 1996). Longitudinal studies indicate that young people who have missed many days of school are more likely to engage in violence both as teenagers and as adults (Farrington, 1989). Similarly, Maguin and associates (1995) reported an association between the number of transfers from one school to another and involvement in violent behavior. The encoding of this item includes measures of poor school performance and low commitment and interest and tenuous links with the school. For this item, the emphasis is on components of the cognitive and motivational functioning at school.

7. Poor coping ability

The process of *coping* is defined primarily as psychological dimensions involved in the process of adaptation to stressful situations (Holahan and Moos, 1986) and *low coping skills* as having no adaptive strategies to cope with stress at school, at home and in social and environmental contexts, in general. Augumeri et al. (2001) underlined the importance of coping skills as a measure of personal resilience (potential and internal resources) in relation to the antisocial behavior indicated.

External variables such as a parent/caregiver with a positive influence on the young, positive relationships with others, or even a high potential for learning can have a decisive effect on coping skills.

In an Italian study conducted on 1200 adolescents, there emerged a relationship between avoidance strategies (defined as *not effective*) and the presence of symptoms of discomfort (Menesini and Fonzi, 2005). Several authors (Endler and Parker, 1990; Seiffge-Krenke, 1993) have highlighted the protective role of some coping strategies; on the contrary, the prevalent use of avoidance strategies as well as difficulty monitoring and controlling emotions constitute a platform for maladjusted adolescents. Baldry and Farrington (2000, 2005) reached the same conclusion.

The encoding of this item requires an evaluation of the youth in such areas as self-esteem, adaptability and optimism.

8. Impulsiveness and risk taking

Impulsivity as a risk factor for violence is often characterized by behavioral and emotional instability, fluctuations in mood and behaviors (Hollander and Stein, 1995; Webster and Jackson, 1997; White et al., 1994). Impulsiveness may be seen in young people who act without thinking, who cannot wait for their turn in games, who ask meaningless questions in class or in conversations and who talk when they are asked to keep quiet. They often react with sudden and intense emotions without considering the consequences of their actions. The lifestyle of an impulsive young person is often characterized by dangerous and potentially harmful situations. Impulsivity is an important factor in predicting risk of violence in children (Augumeri et al., 2001), adolescents and adults (Rutter et al., 1998). A study by Giannotta et al. (2005) shows how high impulsivity plays a major role in substance abuse, especially if it is not moderated by protective factors such as parental relationships or positive friendships.

When evaluating this factor, it is important to consider factors such as emotional and behavioral instability, marked fluctuations in mood or behavior, tendency to act without thinking and difficulty staying alert and composed, especially when under pressure.

9. Low empathy/lack of remorse

A deficit in empathy and/or feeling remorse is one of the most powerful predictors of violence and deviant behaviors in adolescence. *Empathy* is defined as the identification, understanding and sharing of thoughts, feelings and intentions with another person (Eisenberg and Strayer, 1987). Empathy deficits were often found among violent youth (Cohen and Strayer, 1996; Ellis, 1982; Joliffe and Farrington, 2004). Gini et al. (2005) have examined how empathic responsiveness may be a protective factor for antisocial and deviant behavior or bullying.

We define *remorse* as the concern that comes from repentance for past behavior that has hurt others.

Although few studies have evaluated the link between the lack of remorse and violence, it appears to be a characteristic that could distinguish children and adolescents who exhibit serious and persistent patterns of antisocial and violent behavior (Christian et al., 1997; Frick, 1998; Frick and Ellis, 1999).

Encoding this item can be complicated because lack of empathy and remorse are constructs that are not directly observable but can be inferred from overt behaviors such as cruelty, bullying, insensitive behavior, pleasure in seeing others suffer and absent or inappropriate emotional reactions towards the suffering of others. Young people with low empathy do not understand what others think or feel; their expressions of emotions seem superficial, insincere and inconsistent with their actions and nonverbal behaviors. Young people with little capacity to feel remorse may look like they are "without conscience" and have little understanding of what is to blame. Factors that indicate little remorse are refusal to take responsibility for one's actions, a tendency to blame others, minimizing the detrimental effects of one's actions, and showing no aversion to repeatedly engage in damaging conduct (Borum et al., 2000).

10. ADHD symptoms

Inability to concentrate and attention deficit and hyperactivity disorder (ADHD) is an indicator that has good predictive power for violent behavior in childhood, adolescence and adulthood. Many studies (see *inter alia* Kumpulainen et al., 1998; Unnever and Cornell, 2003) found that attention deficit and hyperactivity disorder (ADHD) is a development problem that is frequently observed in bullying, whatever the role assumed by the child (bully, victim, bully-victim).

Children with ADHD are not always well accepted by their peers and having few friends makes them more vulnerable, display poor social skills and exhibit inappropriate behaviors that can lead to aggressive responses from their peers. Finally, ADHD children's learning problems and difficulties following the rules may encourage classmates to identify them as objects of scorn and derision (Pozzoli and Gini, 2006). Caravita and Fabio (2006) found that hyperactive children with ADHD and those diagnosed with mixed type of ADHD are more frequently reported by their classmates as bullies.

11. Mental diseases

The purpose of this item is the general assessment of the mental health of the child in relation to certain dimensions shown in the literature as those with the highest predictive power for violent delinquency. The evaluator will have to express an opinion on the basis of the clinical history of the child, his actual mental health and those elements that could represent the beginnings of a future disease. Neurocognitive deficits (including language, development, learning and mental deficits) contribute directly and indirectly to antisocial behavior; this effect was mainly revealed in deviant offenders (Moffitt, 1993).

Adolescents with a history of suicide attempts or self-harm show the highest levels of risk for future violence (Apter et al., 1995; Battle, Battle, and Tolley, 1993). All forms of suicidal behavior increase the likelihood of violence toward others (Garrison, 1993).

Serious mental health problems seem to have a moderate impact on violent behavior in adults (Hodgins, 1992), whereas the correlation between violent behavior and mental disorders seems to be more established in youth.

Disorders such as manifested anger, impulsivity and low empathy predispose individuals to violent and criminal behavior (Hare and Hart, 1992). This is particularly true for the personality disorders of cluster B of DSM IV (Antisocial, Histrionic, Borderline and Narcissistic) (Kropp et al., 1995). A study by Iani et al. (2002), conducted with 636 children with mental health problems who have committed deviant acts, found a prevalence of borderline personality disorder (15%), followed by other personality disorders (8.8%), conduct disorder (7.7%), depression (4.7%) and mild mental deficit (4.2%).

III – Familial domain

Family factors have received considerable attention in research on youth violence. It was demonstrated, and experience confirms, that the perpetrators of violent crimes often come from families that lived in a stressful and disorganized environment, with parents involved in antisocial activities and with a low level of education, and in situations where personal relationships are absent or greatly impaired. Included in this domain are particular aspects related to the ability of parents to care for their children, but we focus also on other characteristics of biological family members. The following are risk factors related to the family domain:

12. Parental history of mental diseases.
13. Maternal teenage pregnancy.
14. Early caregiver disruption.
15. Frequent changes of caregivers.
16. Family structure.
17. Ineffective parenting.
18. Family conflict–domestic violence.
19. Parental antisocial practices/attitudes.

12. Parental history of mental diseases

The heritability of antisocial behavior has been documented by epidemiological studies, but it is not entirely clear how large a role genetics and the socio-environmental context play (Carey and Goldman, 1997). Studies in twins and adopted children show that the genetic influence may explain about 40% of deviant behavior (Plomin et al., 1994), although these controversial results are the subject of continuing debate. The encoding of this item requires the examination of family psychiatric history. The compiler will include the list of mental disorders, personality disorders, and addictions.

13. Maternal teenage pregnancy

Many studies have shown that a child born from a teenage mother is more at risk of future offending (Morash and Rucker, 1989) and aggression (Baker and Mednick, 1984). Girls who become teenage mothers often have negative childhood experiences related to social disadvantages, which could put their own children at risk for poor education, general problems and crime (Fergusson and Woodward, 1999). Additional studies showed an association between the young age of the mothers and repeated acts of violent behavior by their children, as well as inadequate care to the newborn, the high risk of physically punishing their children and family instability. According to Fergusson and Woodward (1999), the risk of children with teenaged mothers becoming violent young children is considered; however, it is an effect mediated by variables such as family environment. There is an additive effect with other risk factors mentioned above.

14. Early caregiver disruption

During childhood and early adolescence, the lack of maternal care and the development of an insecure attachment to caregivers have been associated in several studies with violent behavior (Erickson et al., 1985). Early signs of detachment are useful predictors of future violent behavior (Farrington, 1991). There is also a body of research that suggests that the formation of a strong bond with parents who have antisocial and criminal behavior increases the risk that their children will engage in a series of violent and deviant behaviors.

15. Frequent changes of caregivers

This item measures the stability and consistency of the parents/caregivers in the life of the child. Multiple changes in a child's caregivers or in the living conditions of children with different caregivers are considered as critical risk factors for the future occurrence of violent offending, in particular if such changes occur before the child has reached the age of ten (Prentky and Righthand, 2003).

16. Family structure: single/multiparental

This item refers to the internal structure of the family and the distribution of resources among members. Lipman et al. (1998) showed that young people living in single-parent families are more likely to enact violent and deviant behavior than those from families where both parents are present. An even greater risk is present for those youths who live without parental figures or a caregiver.

17. Ineffective parenting

Several studies have shown a link between ineffective parenting and violent behavior. Children and young people who have a relationship with their parents based on a punitive style of discipline are more likely to consider such behaviors acceptable. The same is true for youth who do not receive good supervision and consistent rules of conduct.

A teenager who feels rejected and who feels the presence of a rejecting and unreliable parent develops a model of self as an unloved and unlovable person (Morris et al., 2003).

The quality of parent–adolescent relationships (comprising empathy and rejection) and parental practices (monitoring) on adolescent internalizing and externalizing disorders suggest that the link between parental monitoring and externalizing disorders is direct (Marta et al., 2004).

Parental monitoring is a factor of parental protection from a wide variety of symptoms connected to antisocial behavior, such as delinquency, drug use, early sexual relations, and promotes the development of prosocial skills (Caprara et al., 1998).

Other studies have also shown that there is an association between future violent behaviors and parenting style, characterized by low levels of control of their children, the absence of a daily family routine (Gorman-Smith et al., 1996; Patterson et al., 1992), lack of parental involvement, early experience of rejection and too permissive or coercive parenting styles.

18. Family conflict: domestic violence

The presence of violent behaviors in the family increases the risk of aggressive and violent behaviors in the offspring. There is evidence to support the idea that young people from violent homes, who have either experienced or observed violent behavior, have perpetrated significantly more violent acts than those who have not experienced violence in the home.

Not surprisingly, children who have experienced abuse and beatings have a significantly higher probability of being violent adolescents (Reiss and Roth, 1993). Also, family abuse and being neglected are closely related to serious psychological problems such as substance dependency (Dembo, Williams, Wothke, Schneidler, and Brown, 1992; Esbensen and Huizinga, 1991). An Italian study of factors in the mediation of traumatic child abuse underlined that, compared with their unabused peers, abused children have a prevalence of insecure and disorganized attachment styles, coping strategies of "distraction", below average intellectual level, internalized problems and borderline or clinical symptoms (Di Blasio et al., 2007).

19. Parental antisocial practices/attitudes

Many factors related to antisocial behaviors of parents are closely linked with violent behaviors in youth; in particular, a large number of studies suggest that having parents who commit crimes increases the risk that youth (children and adolescents) will commit violent crimes (Baker and Mednick, 1984; Farrington, 1989). It was found that young teens whose parents accept their children's violence at the age of ten are more violent than those whose parents did not tolerate certain types of behaviors (Maguin et al., 1995).

IV – Intervention domain

Intervention is an essential component of the prevention and management of juvenile delinquency.

The intent of this domain is to guide the decisions of the assessor to plan interventions appropriately for the youth and, where possible, for his family. The assessor is also asked to evaluate the response of the child and family to the proposed plan of intervention in terms of their acceptance and commitment. We refer to *intervention* as any program or strategy developed with the aim of prevention, treatment or management of future risk for violent antisocial behavior. The evaluation of individual responsivity to the intervention requires an understanding of the characteristics of the individual, the social context in which he lives and available resources in that particular area.

The domain of intervention requires the compiler to evaluate the success of interventions already undertaken, those currently required, the quality and availability of these interventions and the responsivity of the child and his family to the action plan proposed. The following are the risk factors related to the domain of intervention:

20. Failure of previous intervention.
21. Poor familial response to intervention.
22. Poor youth's response to intervention.
23. Inaccessibility to intervention.

20. Failure of previous intervention

The intent of this item is (1) to evaluate the support and skills that the child or the family has already acquired through past interventions, (2) to assist the evaluator in deciding the level of risk (many past interventions that have had success lowered the actual level of risk), and (3) to identify needs that are to be supported in the future work plan for risk management. This item requires listing the actions/programs not completed, partially completed or completed before the current assessment and is not limited to justice interventions but includes all past interventions that focused on the child and his family.

The categories of intervention are as follows:

- Medical intervention: includes support in hospital and medical care, psychiatric support, and so forth.
- Parental intervention: includes any action (of the local social services, counselors) with the family such as support with parenting skills, employment counseling, psychotherapy, family counseling and financial assistance.
- Interventions with the child: includes all programs centered on the child such as tutoring, educational plan, guidance work, psychotherapy and anger management.
- Educational interventions: structured activities in schools, monitoring activities designed to develop the involvement of parents.
- Intervention with peers: includes all those measures of horizontal management of conflicts and issues such as peer counseling, peer mediation, conflict mediation programs.
- Criminal justice interventions: includes all programs and activities ordered by the court for the child such as detention, probation, mediation and all other possible forms of 'diversion'.
- Civil justice intervention: includes all the interventions by the juvenile court.
- Community intervention: includes projects involving local communities.

21. Poor familial response to intervention

This item requires estimating how much the family will be responsive and receptive to the intervention plan being proposed. The support of parents and the inclusion of the family in the intervention are often essential components of the intervention with the child. Otherwise it is still relevant if the family maintains an active interest in treatment that deals exclusively with the child.

This assessment requires a review of past and present commitment. Indicators of receptivity may include the parents' encouraging the youth to participate in programs, involvement in the treatment plan, understanding and acceptance of the problems of the child.

22. Poor youth's response to intervention

This item requires estimating child responsivity and receptivity to the intervention plan being proposed. The assessment of responsiveness is not easy because, as professionals know well, it is necessary to consider the characteristics of the individual, of the proposed intervention and how the two interact. Personal characteristics that typically are associated with receptivity to intervention are good intelligence, verbal skills, insight, awareness of their own problems, interest in change, and external elements such as a solid relationship with the juvenile justice professionals.

23. Inaccessibility of intervention

This factor requires an assessment of local resources for the proposed plan. The level of integration among the existing network of social supports in the implementation of the program of intervention, should be carefully assessed.

V – Domain of externalized behavior

This domain includes all the child's acts of antisocial behavior even if such conduct did not result in a charge or an arrest. We define as *externalized* all those behaviors such as aggression and conduct problems that occur "outside" of the person (are aimed at others), and we define as *internalized* behaviors such as anxiety and depression (turned "inside").

These items were classified in one domain because (1) they are the target behaviors that the EARN approach aims to predict, prevent and manage and (2) because they are considered as the strongest predictors of serious delinquency and violence in adulthood. In children (8–12 years) these behaviors are the best predictors of possible future violent and deviant behavior; however, these behaviors could be normative in adolescence and many adolescents could exhibit antisocial behaviors without future deviant outcomes. For these reasons, the evaluator must carefully consider the age in which these behaviors have occurred for the first time. As the coding is based not only on conduct that has led to charges or arrests, it is useful to consider multiple sources of information (judicial files, self-statements, etc.) that allow us to assess general behavior and not just behaviors reported to the court. The following are risk factors related to the domain of externalized behavior:

24. History of violence and aggression.
25. General offending.
26. General behavioral problem.
27. Peer delinquency.
28. Use of substances.

24. History of violence and aggression

By the term *violence* we refer to any act of physical violence at a level sufficient to cause injury (e.g., cuts, broken bones, bruises) or death to the person or persons (regardless of whether the damage has actually occurred) and any act of abuse/sexual violence or threat of armed robbery. Typically, these acts should be of sufficient gravity as to allow charges to be laid, as opposed to antisocial behaviors that do not include violence or minor acts of aggression (e.g., hair pulling) (Kropp et al., 1999).

In research on adults and adolescents, the presence of previous violent behavior is understandably the single best predictor of future violence (Farrington, 1991; Kohlberg et al., 1972; Mossman, 1994; Parker and Ascher, 1987; Tolan et al., 1995). The risk of future violence grows incrementally in relation to the number of past episodes of violence.

The frequency, severity and recency of past violent behavior should be taken into account in determining the possible future risks. Some data also suggest that the relationship between past and future violence is greater in the years immediately following the latest violent episode, but, with time, this risk appears to decrease (White et al., 1990).

The assessors must consider the age of the child when violent behavior first appeared as the risk of future violence increases with the early onset of these acts (especially before age 14) (see Farrington, 1991; Thornberry, Huizinga, and Loeber, 1995; Tolan and Thomas, 1995).

25. History of non-violent crimes

Adolescents who have committed non-violent crimes are at a higher level of risk of future violence than those who have not engaged in such behavior (Farrington, 1989; Lipsey and Derzon, 1998; Patterson and Yoerger, 1993). The early onset (before age 14) of antisocial behavior, such as theft, property destruction and drug trafficking, is related, at least for males, with subsequent violent behavior (Hawkins et al., 1998).

A high rate of deviant acts during adolescence can be considered statistically normative; the compiler must consider it for the final evaluation.

26. General behavioral problems

This item concerns a large group of antisocial behaviors that includes, for example, cruelty to animals and people, sexual promiscuity or irresponsible sexual practices, prostitution, gambling, fraud, violations of rules, disruptive behavior in class and truancy.

27. Peer delinquency

Affiliation with delinquent peers is a risk factor for violent juvenile delinquency. Aggressive boys tend to associate with others in real antisocial networks (Cairns et al., 1988). This process is often described as the "second step" of a sequence that begins with the social rejection of an aggressive child by his peers and ends with the later association with deviant peers. Deviant peer groups also appear to influence kids who do not already have a history of aggression or antisocial behavior, at an age when for young people still struggling to find their identities, affiliation with such groups can be very seductive. Even youth with brothers and sisters who are criminals are at increased risk of future violent behavior (Farrington, 1989; Maguin et al., 1995)

28. Use of substances

Use of substances means the use of alcohol and drugs, both legal and illegal, in ways that cause problems with health or with a primary area of life (work, studies, relationships, friendships). There is a strong association between drug use and the occurrence of violent and antisocial behavior. Youth who use substances are 20 times more likely to develop antisocial behaviors (Lipsey and Derzon, 1998). This is especially true for those who start to use substances in early adolescence, but the predictive value decreases in late adolescence when the use of substances can be considered as almost normal. The use of substances can have an effect both of disorganization and organization of identity or temporary disorganization. This is a problem that needs to be addressed on a case-by-case basis because when the drug culture and culture of drug-related crime have become an integral part of the young person's identity, this stabilizes the pattern of deviant behaviors (De Leo, 1990).

VI – Protection domain

The term *protective* refers to those factors that contrast with the effects of risk factors. These factors are protective because they act to limit the risk and outcomes of the vulnerability. Coie et al. (1993) hypothesize that protective factors could operate in one or more of the following ways:

- Directly by decreasing the problems and difficulties.
- Interacting with risk factors to decrease the negative effect (buffer effect).

- Encouraging new possibilities and alternatives for the child.
- Promoting individual well-being and self-esteem.

The presence of one or more risk factors does mean that the youth will, with certainty, repeat the same violent acts or deviant behaviors. Certainly there are risk factors that increase the likelihood that violence will occur, but there are also other factors related to individual and the context that may reduce the negative impact of a risk factor. These are the protective behaviors. They mitigate the impact of other risk factors and, in some circumstances, may be helpful in choosing a treatment or planning an intervention, thus facilitating decreasing the risk of recurrence.

Obviously, the absence of risk, in itself, can be considered a protective factor, but when we refer to the protective factors, we refer to factors that are positive and therefore are noted for their presence rather than by their absence. The following are protective factors related to the domain of protection:

29. Presence of social and familiar support.
30. Presence of strong relationship and bonds.
31. Presence of prosocial involvement.
32. Presence of resilient personality traits.

29. Presence of social and familial support

The absence of supportive social relationships can decrease significantly the ability of youth to reduce risk and, instead, increase the potential for exposure to very dangerous situations (Estroff and Zimmer, 1994; Estroff et al., 1994). Hostile relations and/or conflicts may increase the risk of violence. In a sample of young African Americans, the presence of social support from relatives was positively related to anger management in children in high-risk urban environments (Stevenson, 1998). Similarly, positive family relationships were associated with less violent behavior (Rodney et al., 1999). In a prospective study of preschool-age children, those who received more support were also those with the lowest rate of aggression. Similarly, boys who perceive themselves as "hopeless" may feel that family and friends give them little support and thus be more likely to express anger through illegal and aggressive activities (Kashani et al., 1997).

30. Presence of strong relationships and bonds

One of the most important factors that can mitigate against the possible occurrence of violent behavior is the presence of important and warm relationships with adults who encourage and recognize skills and demonstrate a sympathetic and positive relationship (Fitzpatrick, 1997; Pollack, 1998, 2000, Stouthamer-Loeber et al., 1993).

31. Presence of prosocial involvement

Prosocial behavior refers to socially valued behavior, such as being helpful and cooperative, being capable of negotiation, recognizing the feelings of others, and participating in prosocial activities and membership in prosocial peer groups (groups not involved in deviant activities).

Bandura et al. (2001) emphasize that adolescents who related prosocially to others and who eschewed moral disengagement were disinclined to engage in angering and retaliative rumination. Ruminative affectivity was both concurrently and longitudinally linked to transgressive conduct (p. 133). A study by Molinengo et al. (2005) evaluated how individual resources such as the degree of involvement in activities and social engagement in sports or beliefs about their own abilities have both a direct and an indirect mediation effect on an environmental condition of high vulnerability.

32. Presence of resilient personality traits

Resilience is critical as a protective factor. Resilience is characterized by the ability to achieve positive results even in adverse conditions. The first conceptualization of resilience was proposed by Block with an ego resiliency model that accounts for the ability of people to interact effectively with the environment (Block and Block, 1980). In the literature, resilience has three aspects: (1) personality/temperament, (2) family factors, and (3) social support (Garmezy, 1993). Defined as resilient are those children who show high self-esteem, self-efficacy, ability to solve problems, self-discipline, high maturity, empathy and adaptability (Born et al., 1997; Rutter, 1985).

An Italian longitudinal study (Caprara et al., 2003) showed the predictive role of ego resiliency for some dimensions of wellness and illness in adolescents. In the former case, the ego resiliency correlates positively with sociability, prosociability and self-esteem. The latter reveals a negative correlation between ego resiliency and psychological tendencies, both the internalizing (anxiety disorders and depression) and the externalizing (antisocial and aggressive behavior) types.

References

Apter, A., Gothelf, D., Orbach, I., Weizman, R., Ratzoni, G., Ahreven, D., and Tyano, S. (1995). Correlation of suicidal and violent behavior in different diagnostic categories in hospitalized adolescent patients. *Journal of the American Academy of Child and Adolescent Psychiatry*, 34(7), 912–18.

Augimeri, L., Koegl, C., Webster, C. D., and Levene, K. (2001). Early Assessment Risk List for Boys (EARL-20B), Version 2. Toronto: Earlscourt Child and Family Centre.

Baker, R., and Mednick, B. (1984). *Influences on human development: A longitudinal perspective*. Boston, MA: Kluwer-Nijhoff.

Baldry, A. C., and Farrington, D. P. (2000). Bullies and delinquents: Personal characteristics and parental styles. *Journal of Community and Applied Social Psychology*, 10, 17–31.

Baldry, A. C., and Farrington, D. P. (2005). Protective factors as moderators of risk factors in adolescent bullying. *Social Psychology of Education*, 8, 263–84.

Bandura, A., Caprara, G. V., Barbaranelli, C., Pastorelli, C., and Regalia, C. (2001). Sociocognitive self-regulatory mechanisms governing transgressive behavior. *Journal of Personality and Social Psychology*, 51, 125–35.

Barkley, R. A., Fischer, M., Edelbrock, C. S., and Smallish, L. (1990). The adolescent outcome of hyperactive children diagnosed by research criteria: I. An 8-year prospective follow-up study. *Journal of the American Academy of Child and Adolescent Psychiatry*, 29, 546–57.

Battle, A., Battle, M., and Tolley, E. (1993). Potential for suicide and aggression in delinquents at juvenile court in a southern city. *Suicide and Life-Threatening Behaviour*, 23(3), 230–44.

Block, J. H., and Block, J. (1980). The role of ego-control and ego-resiliency in the organization of behaviour. In W. A. Collins (ed.). *The Minnesota symposia on child psychology*. (Vol. 13, 39–101) Hillsdale, NJ: Erlbaum.

Bonino, S. (2004). Famiglie e rischio in adolescenza (Families and risk in adolescence). *Psicologia Clinica dello Sviluppo*, 2, 235–8.

Born, M., Chevalier, V., and Humblet, I. (1997). Resilience, desistence and delinquent career of adolescent offenders. *Journal of Adolescence*, 20, 679–94.

Borum, R., Bartel, P., and Forth, A. (2000). *Manual for the Structured Assessment for Violence Risk in Youth (SAVRY): Consultation Edition*. Tampa, FL: Louis de la Parte Florida Mental Health Institute, University of South Florida.

Brennan, P., Mednick, S. A., Raine, A. (1997) Biosocial interactions and violence. In A. Raine, P. A. Brennan, D. Farrington, S. A. Mednick (eds). *Biosocial bases of violence*. New York, NY: Plenum Publishing (pp. 163–74).

Brewer, D. D., Hawkins, J. D., Catalano, R. F., and Neckerman, H. J. (1995). Preventing serious, violent, and chronic juvenile offending: A review of evaluations of selected strategies in childhood, adolescence, and the community. In J. C. Howell, B. Krisberg, J. D. Hawkins, and J. J. Wilson (eds). *Sourcebook on serious, violent, and chronic juvenile offenders*. Thousand Oaks, CA: Sage Publications (pp. 61–141).

Bursik, R. J. Jr., and Grasmick, G. H. (1993) *Neighbourhoods and crime: The dimensions of effective community control.* New York: Lexington Books.

Cairns, R. B., Cairns, B. D., Neckerman, H. J., Gest, S. D., and Gariepy, J. L. (1988). Social networks and aggressive behaviour: Peer support or peer rejection. *Developmental Psychology*, 24, 815–26.

Caprara, G. V., Fratte, A., and Steca, P. (2002). Determinanti personali del benessere nell'adolescenza: Indicatori e predittori. *Psicologia Clinica dello Sviluppo*, 6, 203–33.

Caprara, M. G., Steca, P., and De Leo, G. (2003). La misura dell'ego_resiliency [Ego_resiliency measurement]. *Ricerche di Psicologia*, 26, 7–23.

Caravita, S., Fabio, R. A. (2006). Il DDAI come fattore di rischio dei comportamenti prevaricanti in classe: uno studio pilota. *Difficoltà di Apprendimento*, 11(3), 329–46.

Carey, G., and Goldman, D. (1997). The genetics of antisocial behavior. In D. M. Stoff and J. Breiling (eds). *Handbook of antisocial behavior*. New York, NY: Wiley (pp. 243–54).

Catalano, R. F., and Hawkins, J. D. (1996). The social development model: A theory of antisocial behaviour. In D. Hawkins (ed.). *Delinquency and crime: Current theories*. New York, NY: Cambridge University Press (pp. 149–97).

Christian, R., Frick, P., Hill, N., Tyler, L., and Frazer, D. (1997). Psychopathy and conduct problems in children: II. Implications for subtyping children with conduct problems. *American Academy of Child and Adolescent Psychiatry*, 36, 233–41.

Cohen, D. and Strayer, J. (1996). Empathy in conduct-disordered and comparison youth. *Developmental Psychology*, 32, 988–98.

Coie, J. D., Watt, N. F., West, S. G., Hawkins, J. D., Asarnow, J. R., Markman, H. J., Ramey, S. L., Shure, M. B., and Long, B. (1993). The science of prevention: A conceptual framework and some directions for a national research program. *American Psychologist*, 48 (10), 1013–22.

Conry, J., and Fast, D. K. (2000). *Fetal alcohol syndrome and the criminal justice system.* Vancouver, BC: British Columbia Fetal Alcohol Syndrome Resource Society.

Corrado R.R. (2002). An introduction to risk/needs case management instrument for children and youth at risk for violence: The Crackow instrument. In R. R. Corrado, R. Roesch, S. Hart, and J. K. Gierowsk (eds) *Multi-problem violent youth: A foundation for comparative research on needs, interventions and outcomes*. Amsterdam: IOS Press (pp. 295–302).

De Leo, G.(1990) La devianza minorile, Roma: Nuova Italia scientifica.

Dembo, R., Williams, L., Wothke, W., Schneider, J., and Brown, C. H. (1992). The role of family factors, physical abuse and sexual victimization experiences in high-risk youths' alcohol and other drug use and delinquency: A longitudinal model. *Violence and Victims*, 7, 245–66.

Denno, D. W. (1990). *Biology and violence: From birth to adulthood.* Cambridge, UK: Cambridge University Press.

Di Blasio P., Camisasca, E., Procaccia, R.(2007) Fattori di mediazione dell'esperienza traumatica nei bambini maltrattati. *Maltrattamento e Abuso All'infanzia*, 9(2), 33–60.

Durant, R. H., Cadenhead, C., Pendergrast, R. A., Slavens, G., and Linder, C. W. (1994). Factors associated with the use of violence among urban Black adolescents. *American Journal of Public Health*, 84, 612–17.

Eisenberg, N., and Strayer, J. (1987). Critical issues in the study of empathy. In N. Eisenberg and J. Strayer (eds). *Empathy and its development.* Cambridge, UK: Cambridge University Press (pp. 3–16).

Elliott, D. S., Huizinga, D., and Menard, S. (1989). *Multiple problem youth: Delinquency, substance use, and mental health problems.* New York: Springer-Verlag.

Ellis, P. L. (1982). Empathy: A factor in antisocial behavior. *Journal of Abnormal Child Psychology*, 10, 123–34.

Endler, N. S., and Parker, J. D. A. (1990). Multidimensional assessment of coping: A critical evaluation. *Journal of Personality and Social Psychology*, 58(5), 844–54.

Erickson, M. E., Sroufe, L. A., and Egeland, B. (1985). The relationship between quality of attachment and behavior problems in preschool in a high-risk sample. *Monographs of the Society for Research in Child Development*, 50(1,2), 147–66.

Esbensen, F. and Huizinga, D. (1991). Juvenile victimization and delinquency. *Youth and Society,* 22(2) 202–28.

Estroff, S. E., and Zimmer, C. (1994). Social networks, social support and violence among persons with severe, persistent mental illness. In J. Monahan and H. J. Steadman (eds). *Violence and mental disorder: Developments in risk assessment.* Chicago: University of Chicago Press (pp. 259–95).

Estroff, S, E., Zimmer, C., Lachicotte, W. S., and Beniot, G. (1994). The influence of social networks and social support on violence by persons with serious mental illness. *Hospital Community Psychiatry*, 45(7), 669–79.

Farrington, D. (1989). Early predictors of adolescent aggression and adult violence. *Violence and Victims*, 4, 79–100.

Farrington, D. (1991). Childhood aggression and adult violence: Early precursors and later life outcomes. In D. Pepler and K. Rubin (eds). *The development and treatment of childhood aggression.* Hillsdale, NJ: Erlbaum (pp. 5–29).

Farrington, D. P. (2002). Multiple risk factors for multiple problem violent boys. In R. R. Corrado, R. Roesch, S. D. Hart, and J. K. Gierowski (eds). *Multi-problem violent youth: A foundation for comparative research on needs, interventions and outcomes.* Amsterdam: IOS Press (pp. 23–4).

Fergusson, D. M., and Woodward, L. J. (1999). Maternal age and educational and psychosocial outcomes in early adulthood. *Journal of Child Psychology and Psychiatry*, 40, 479–89.

Fitzpatrick, K. M. (1997). Fighting among America's youth: A risk and protective factors approach. *Journal of Health and Social Behavior*, 38, 131–48.

Frick, P. J. (1998). Conduct disorders. In T. H. Ollendick and M. Hersen (eds). *Handbook of child psychopathology*, 3rd edition. New York: Plenum (pp. 213–37).

Frick, P. J., and Ellis, M. L. (1999). Callous-unemotional traits and subtypes of conduct disorder. *Clinical Child and Family Psychology Review*, 2, 149–68.

Frick, P. J., and Hare, R. D. (2001). *The Antisocial Process Screening Device.* Toronto, Ont.: Multi-Health Systems.

Frick, P. J., Bodin, S. D., and Barry, C. T. (2000). Psychopathic traits and conduct problems in community and clinic-referred samples of children: Further development of the Psychopathy Screening Device. *Psychological Assessment*, 12, 382–93.

Frick, P. J., O'Brien, B. S., Wootton, J. M., and McBurnett, K. (1994). Psychopathy and conduct problems in children. *Journal of Abnormal Psychology*, 103, 700–7.

Garmezy, N. 1993. Children in poverty: Resilience despite risk. *Psychiatry*, 56, 127–36.

Garrison,C. Z., McKeown,R. E., Valois,R. F. and Vincent, M. L.(1993) Aggression, substance use, and suicidal behaviors in high school students. *American Journal of Public Health*, 83, 179–84.

Giannotta, F., Molinar, R., Rabaglietti, E., Roggero, A., and Ciairano, S.(2005). Emozioni, contesti relazionali e benessere psicosociale in adolescenza: Uno studio longitudinale (Emotions, relational contexts and psychosocial well-being in adolescence: A longitudinal study). *Psicologia Clinica dello Sviluppo*, 3, 399–414.

Gini, G., Albiero, P., and Benelli, B. (2005). Relazione tra bullismo, empatia ed autoefficacia percepita in un campione diadolescenti (Relations between bullying, empathy, and perceived self-efficacy in adolescents). *Psicologia Clinica dello Sviluppo*, *9*, 461–476.

Gorman-Smith, D., Tolan, P. H., Zelli, A., and Huesmann, L. R. (1996). The relation of family functioning to violence among inner-city minority youths. *Journal of Family Psychology*, 10, 115–29.

Hare, R. (1993). *Without conscience.* New York: Pocket Books.

Hare, R. D., and Hart, S. D. (1992). Psychopathy, mental disorder, and crime. In S. Hodgins (ed.). *Mental disorder and crime.* Newbury Park, CA: Sage Publications (pp. 104–15).

Hart, S. D. (2001). Assessing and managing violence risk. In K. S. Douglas, C. D. Webster, and, S. D. Hart (eds). *HRC-20 Violence Risk Management Companion Guide*, Burnaby: British Columbia (pp. 13–25).

Hawkins, J. D., Catalano, R. F., and Miller, J. Y. (1992). Risk and protective factors for alcohol and other drug problems in adolescence and early adulthood: Implications for substance abuse prevention. *Psychological Bulletin* 112, 64–105.

Hawkins, J. D., Herrenkohl, T., Farrington, D. P., Brewer, D., Catalano, R. F., and Harachi, T. W. (1998). A review of predictors of youth violence. In R. Loeber and D. P. Farrington (eds). *Serious and violent juvenile offenders: Risk factors and successful interventions.* Thousand Oaks, CA: Sage Publications (pp. 106–46).

Hirschi, T. (1969). *Causes of delinquency.* Berkeley, CA: University of California Press.

Hodgins, S. (1992) Mental disorder, intellectual deficiency, and crime: Evidence from a birth cohort. *Archives of General Psychiatry,* 49(6), 476–83.

Hodgins, S., Kratzer, L., and McNeil, T. F. (2001). Obstetric complications, parenting, and risk of criminal behavior. *Archives of General Psychiatry,* 58, 746–52.

Holahan, C. J., and Moos, R. H. (1986). Personality, coping, and family resources in stress resistance: A longitudinal analysis. *Journal of Personality and Social Psychology*, 51, 389–95.

Hollander, E. and Stein, D. (1995). *Impulsivity and aggression*. Toronto, Ont.: Wiley.

Iani, L., De Leo, G., Ciurla, A. (2002). Violent offenders with mental health problems: The Italian youth study. In R. Corrado, R. Roesch, S. Hart, J. K. Gierowsk (eds). *Multi-problem violent youth: A foundation for comparative research on needs, interventions and outcomes*. Amsterdam: IOS Press (pp. 265–74)

Kashani, J. H., Suarez, L., Allan, W. D., and Reid, J. C. (1997). Hopelessness in inpatient youths: A closer look at behavior, emotional expression, and social support. *Journal of the American Academy of Child and Adolescent Psychiatry*, 36, 1625–31.

Kohlberg, L., LaCrosse. J., and Ricke, D. (1972) The predictability of adult mental health from child behavior. In B. Wolman (ed.). *Handbook of child psychopathology*. New York: McGraw-Hill (pp. 1217–84).

Kropp, P., Hart, S., Webster, C., and Eaves, D. (1995). *Manual for the Spousal Assault Risk Assessment Guide.* (3rd ed.). Toronto, Ont.: Multi-Health Systems.

Kumpulainen, K., Rasanen, E., Henttonen, I., et al. (1998). Bullying and psychiatric symptoms among elementary school-age children. *Child Abuse & Neglect,* (22), 705–17.

Laub, J. H., and Lauritsen, J. L. (1998). The interdependence of school violence with neighborhood and family conditions. In D. S. Elliott, H. A. Beatrix, and K. R. Williams (eds). *Violence in American schools: A new perspective*. New York: Cambridge University Press (pp. 127–55).

Lipman, E. L., Offord, D. R., and Dooley, M. (1996). What do we know about children from single-mother families? Questions and answers from the National Longitudinal Survey of Children and Youth. *Growing up in Canada: National Longitudinal Survey of Children and Youth* (Cat. no. 89-550-MPE, no. 1). Ottawa: Minister of Industry (pp. 83–91).

Lipman, E. L., Boyle, M., Dooley, M. and Offord, D. (1998). What about children in lone mother families? Paper presented at the conference on "Investing in Children", National Research Conference, Canada.

Lipsey, M. W., Derzon, J. H.(1998). Predictors of violent or serious delinquency in adolescence and early adulthood: A synthesis of longitudinal research. In R. Loeber and D. P. Farrington (eds). *Serious and violent juvenile offenders: Risk factors and successful interventions.* Thousand Oaks, CA : Sage Publications (pp. 86–105).

Litt, S. M. (1972). Proceedings of the Annual Convention of the American Psychological Association, Vol. 7(Pt. 1), 239–40.

Loeber, R., Green, S. M., Keenan, K., and Lahey, B. B. (1995). Which boys will fare worse? Early predictors of the onset of conduct disorder in a six-year longitudinal study. *Journal of the American Academy of Child and Adolescent Psychiatry*, 34, 499–509.

Maguin, E. and Loeber, R. (1996). Academic performance and delinquency. In M. Tonry (ed.). *Crime and justice: A review of research*, Vol. 20. Chicago, IL: University of Chicago Press (pp. 145–264).

Maguin, E., Hawkins, J., Catalano, R., Hill, K., Abbott, R., and Herrenkhol, T. (1995). Risk factors measured at three ages for violence at age 17–18. Paper presented at the American Society of Criminology, Boston.

Mannuzza, S., Klein, R., Konig, P., Giampino, T. (1989). Hyperactive boys almost grown up: IV. Criminality and its relationship to psychiatric status. *Archives of General Psychiatry*, 46, 1073–9.

Marta, E., Lanz, M., Manzi, C., Tagliabue, S., Pozzi, M., and Bertoni, A. (2004). La relazione genitori – adolescenti: Un predittore della devianza? (Relationship between parents and adolescents: A predictor of future criminal behavior?) *Psicologia Clinica dello Sviluppo*, 8, 269–88.

McCord, J., and Ensminger, M. (1995). Path-ways from aggressive childhood to criminality. Paper presented at the American Society of Criminology, Boston, MA.

Menesini, E. (2005) Fattori di protezione e promozione del benessere in preadolescenza e adolescenza (Protective factors and promoting of well-being in infancy and adolescence). *Psicologia Clinica dello Sviluppo*, 3, 377–84.

Menesini, E. and Fonzi, A. (2005). Strategie di coping e caratteristiche di resilienza in adolescenza (Coping strategies and resilience characteristics in adolescence). *Psicologia Clinica dello Sviluppo*, 3, 437–56.

Moffitt, T. (1993). "Life course persistent" and "adolescence limited" antisocial behavior: A developmental taxonomy. *Psychological Review*, 100, 674–701.

Molinengo, G., Bonino, S., Miceli, R. and Ciairano, S. (2005). Il ruolo diretto e indiretto delle risorse individuali e ambientali nel contrastare il rischio di adolescenza (The direct and indirect role of environmental and individual resources to counter the risk of adolescence). *Psicologia Clinica dello Sviluppo*, 3, 385–98.

Morash, M. and Rucker, L. (1989). An exploratory study of the connection of mother's age at child-bearing to her children's delinquency in four data sets. *Crime and Delinquency*, 35, 45–93.

Morris L., Sallybanks J., Willis K., Makkai, T. (2003) Sport, physical activity and antisocial behaviour in youth. *Trends and Issues in Crime and Criminal Justice* 249. Canberra, Australia: Australian Institute of Criminology.

Mossman, D. (1994). Assessing predictions of violence: Being accurate about accuracy. *Journal of Consulting and Clinical Psychology*, 62, 783–92.

Osgood, D. W., and Chambers, J. M. (2000). Social disorganization outside the metropolis: An analysis of rural youth violence. *Criminology*, 38, 81–115.

Parker, J. and Asher, S. (1987). Peer relations and later personal adjustment: Are low-accepted children at risk? *Psychological Bulletin*, 102 (2), 357–89.

Patterson, G. R., and Yoerger, K. (1993). Developmental models for delinquent behavior. In S. G. Hodgins (ed.). *Mental disorder and crime*. Thousand Oaks, CA: Sage Publications (pp. 140–72).

Patterson, G. R., Reid, J. B., and Dishion, T. J. (1992). *A social learning approach: Vol. IV. Antisocial boys*. Eugene, OR: Castalia.

Plomin, R. P., Owen, M. J., and McGuffin, P. (1994). The genetic basis of complex human behaviours. *Science*, 264, 1733–79.

Pollack, W. (1998). *Real boys: Rescuing our sons from the myths of boyhood*. New York: Henry Holt.

Pollack, W. S. (2000). *Real boys' voices*. New York: Random House.

Pozzoli, T. and Gini, G. (2006). Comportamenti aggressivi e rifiuto sociale in bambini con disturbo da deficit d'attenzione e iperattività (Aggression and social rejection in children with ADHD). *Psicologia dell'Educazione e della Formazione*, 8, 313 – 33.

Prentky, R. A. and Righthand, S.(2003). *Juvenile Sex Offender Assessment Protocol–II (J-SOAP-II) manual*. Justice Resource Institute, Bridgewater, MA.

Reiss, A. J., Jr., and Roth, J. A. (eds) (1993). *Understanding and preventing violence: Panel on the understanding and control of violent behavior*. Washington, DC: National Academy Press.

Reppucci, N. D., Fried, C. S., and Schmidt, M. G. (2002). A preliminary conceptual framework for the prevention and management of multi-problem youth. In R. Corrado,

R. Roesch, and S. Hart (eds). *Multi-problem violent youth: A foundation for comparative research on needs, interventions and outcomes*. Amsterdam: IOS Press (pp. 116–29).

Rodney, H. E., Tachia, H. R., and Rodney, L. W. (1999). The home environment and delinquency: A study of African American adolescents. *Families in Society*, 80(6), 551–9.

Rutter, M. (1985). Resilience in the face of adversity: Protective factors and resistance to psychiatric disorder. *British Journal of Psychiatry*, 147, 598–611.

Rutter, M. (1987). Psychosocial resilience and protective mechanisms. *American Journal of Orthopsychiatry* 57(3), 316–31.

Rutter, M., Giller, H. and Hagell, A. (1998). *Antisocial behavior by young people*. Cambridge, UK: Cambridge University Press.

Sampson, R. J., and Lauritsen, J. L. (1994). Violent victimization and offending: Individual, situational, and community-level risk factors. In A. J. Reiss, K. A. Miczek, and J. A. Roth (eds). *Understanding and preventing violence. Volume 3: Social influences*. Washington DC: National Academy Press (pp. 1–114).

Sattersfield, J., Hoppe, C., and Schell, A. (1982). A prospective study of delinquency in 110 adolescent boys with attention – deficit disorder and 88 normal adolescent boys. *American Journal of Psychiatry*, 139. 795–8.

Seiffge-Krenke, I. (1993). Coping behaviour in normal and clinical samples: More similarities than differences. *Journal of Adolescence*, 19, 285–303.

Singer, M. I., Anglin, T. M., Song, L., and Lunghofer, L. (1995). Adolescents' exposure to violence and associated symptoms of psychological trauma. *Journal of the American Medical Association*, 273, 477–82.

Stevenson, O. (1998). *Neglected children: Issues and dilemmas*. Oxford, UK: Blackwell Science.

Stouthamer-Loeber, M., Loeber, R., Farrington, D. P., Zhang, Q., van Kammen, W., and Maguin, E. (1993). The double edge of protective and risk factors for delinquency: Interrelations and developmental patterns. *Development and Psychopathology*, 5, 683–701.

Surgeon General of the United States (2001). *Youth violence: A report of the Surgeon General*. Rockville, MD: US Department of Health and Human Services, Centers for Disease Control and Prevention.

Thornberry, T. P., Huizinga, D., and Loeber, R. (1995). The prevention of serious delinquency and violence: Implications from the program of research on the causes and correlates of delinquency. In J. C. Howell, B. Krisberg, J. D. Hawkins, and J. J. Wilson (eds). *Sourcebook on serious, violent, and chronic juvenile offenders*. Thousand Oaks, CA: Sage Publications (pp. 213–38).

Tolan, P. H., Guerra, N. G., and Kendall, P. C. (1995). A developmental perspective on antisocial behavior in children and adolescents: Toward a unified risk and intervention framework. *Journal of Consulting and Clinical Psychology*, 63, 579–84.

Tolan, P. H., and Thomas, P. (1995). The implications of age of onset for delinquency risk: II. Longitudinal data. *Journal of Abnormal Child Psychology*, 23, 157–81.

Unnever, J. D. and Cornell, D. (2003). Bullying, self-control, and ADHD. *Journal of Interpersonal Violence*, 18, 129–47.

Webster, C. and Jackson, M. (1997). *Impulsivity: Theory, assessment, and treatment*. New York, NY: Guilford.

White, J. L., Moffitt, T. E., and Silva, P. A. (1989). A prospective replication of the protective effects of IQ in subjects at high risk for juvenile delinquency. *Journal of Consulting and Clinical Psychology*, 57, 719–24.

White, J., Moffitt, T. E., Earls, F., Robins, L. N., and Silva, P. A. (1990). How early can we tell? Preschool predictors of boys' conduct disorder and delinquency. *Criminology*, 28, 507–33.

White, J., Moffitt, T., Caspi, A., Bartusch, D., Jeglum, D., Needles, D., and Stouthamer-Loeber, M. (1994). Measuring impulsivity and examining its relationship to delinquency. *Journal of Abnormal Psychology*, 103, 192–205.

Widom, C. S. (1989a). Does violence beget violence? A critical examination of the literature. *Psychological Bulletin,* 106 (1), 3–28.

7 The EARN project in Italy

A. C. Baldry and C. Porcaro

Juvenile delinquency seems to be a critical problem in our society. Young violent offenders harm both their victims and themselves, at the same time increasing the risk of becoming, as adults, "life course persistent offender[s]" (Moffitt, 1993). Research has identified a number of factors that put children and youth at risk for involvement in future violence. Admittedly, there is no absolute consensus regarding the most salient risk factors for youth violence (Corrado, 2002) or the most useful factors to predict recidivism. The European Assessment of Risks/Needs in Juvenile Violent Offenders (EARN in JVO) is a structured professional assessment checklist (Kropp et al., 1999) based on the CRAKOW (Corrado, 2002) and SAVRY tools (Borum et al., 2000), and has been adapted to Italian social, cultural and legal contexts. The EARN toolkit was used for the risk assessment of juvenile violent offenders who had committed crimes over a six-month period. Afterwards, a six-month follow-up was conducted in order to establish any recidivism rate.

Objectives

The following were the objectives of the study:

1. To understand which factors are better predictors of recidivism.
2. To evaluate the predictiveness of the tool's domains (1. Enviromental, 2. Individual, 3. Familial, 4. Intervention, 5. Externalized behaviors, 6. Protection) at the bivariate level.
3. To evaluate the general predictiveness of the tool compared to different types of scoring (1. Rater's final evaluation, 2. Risk factor score, 3. Critical factor score).
4. To evaluate whether a structured assessment approach could improve the efficacy of professionals in implementing interventions to decrease recidivism rates. Therefore the recidivism rates of two groups of juvenile offenders are compared. With the first group (experimental) practitioners used the EARN approach for six months; with the second group (control) no structured risk assessment was conducted. Recidivism was evaluated after a six-month follow-up.

Method

Participants

Experimental group. The experimental sample consisted of 296 juveniles with a mean age of 16.83 years at the time of the assessment (Standard deviation (*SD*) = 1.14, Range = 14 to 18). Table 7.1 presents the sample characteristics: the juveniles are all males; the large majority, Italian; the level of education a low-medium for their age, with 14.2% not completing junior high school and barely knowing how to read. The majority had past criminal records and, at the time of the assessment, had been charged with robbery (44.9%), violence and aggression (29.4%), threats and harassment (11.4%), sexual aggression (6.5%) and murder (5.3%). Table 7.2 shows the recidivism rate of the experimental group after six months (n = 173), and also the type of intervention implemented by juvenile justice personnel.

Control group. The control group was selected to have characteristics similar to the experimental group. The control sample consisted of 209 juveniles with a mean age of 16.81 years at the time of the assessment (*SD* = 1.26, Range = 14 to 18). Table 7.1 presents the sample characteristics: the juveniles are all males, a large majority are Italians and have a medium level of education for their age; 46.1% have past criminal records and, at the time of the assessment, the following percentages had been charged with robbery (31%), violence and aggression (22%),

Table 7.1 Sample characteristics

Sample characteristics	*% Experimental (n = 294)*	*% Control (n =209)*
Gender		
Male	100	100
Ethnic origin		
Italian	80.7	84.3
East Europe	9.4	8.0
North Africa	7.4	4.3
Other	2.5	3.4
Education		
Junior school or less	14.2	7.9
Junior high school	70.5	67.4
High school	15.3	24.8
Past criminal records		
Yes	54.4	46.1
Present offence		
Robbery	44.9	31.0
Violence and aggression	29.4	22.0
Threats and harassment	11.4	19.4
Sexual aggression	6.5	11.2
Murder	5.3	5.4
Other	2.4	11.0

Table 7.2 Follow-up (six months)

	% Experimental (n =173)	*% Control (n =110)*
Recidivism	19.6	23.5
Robbery*	59	63.3
Violence and aggression*	13.8	6.7
Threats and harassment*	6.9	–
Sexual aggression*	–	–
Murder*	–	–
Other*	20.3	30
Intervention		
Psychological support	50.3	37.3
Addiction centre	13.3	7.3
Job placement	32.8	14.5
House of correction/community	23.7	14.5
Sport/prosocial activities	17.2	25.5
Tutoring	26.9	44.5
Job training	13.8	25.5
School placement	25.7	45.5
Mediation	9.2	14.7

Note: *percentages are referred to recidivist.

threats and harassment (19.4%), sexual aggression (11.2%) and murder (5.4%). Table 7.2 shows the recidivism rate of the control group after six months (n = 110), and also the type of intervention implemented by juvenile justice personnel.

Procedure

Experimental group. A sample of practitioners in the Italian juvenile justice services was selected by the Department of Juvenile Justice, Ministry of Justice, to use the EARN toolkit with 249 juveniles who had committed a violent crime in Italy. For the purpose of this research, *violent crimes* refers to any type of crime in which violent behavior is present, including crimes against propriety such as robbery.

All the raters (social workers, trainers, psychologists) of the sample were trained in coding the EARN and had a booklet guide to aid the assessment. Each youth was evaluated by the operator responsible for the case in that district. The cases came from 17 selected juvenile justice districts (CGM): Ancona, Bologna, Bolzano, Caltanissetta, Catania, Catanzaro, Genova, L'Aquila, Napoli, Perugia, Potenza, Reggio Calabria, Roma, Salerno, Sassari, Torino and Trento. Data were collected during a six-month period in 2007 and 2008. Follow-up was conducted after another six months to establish any recidivism rate.

Control group. A sample of practitioners (social workers, trainers, psychologists) in the Italian juvenile justice who were selected by the Department of Juvenile Justice, Ministry of Justice, collected socio-demographic characteristics, criminal records, and treatment programs used for 209 juveniles who had committed a violent crime in Italy. The cases came from 12 juvenile justice districts (CGM): Bari, Brescia, Cagliari, Campobasso, Firenze, Lecce, Messina, Milano, Palermo, Taranto, Trieste, Venezia. The districts were selected to compare similar groups of juvenile offenders in the experimental and control groups. Data were collected during a six-month period in 2007 and 2008. Follow-up was conducted six months later to establish any recidivism rates.

Privacy

Data collection was authorized by the Department of Juvenile Justice, Ministry of Justice, and performed by practitioners participating in the project. Anonymity was maintained for all participants in the research, the database was protected, and in the raw data a numeric code was substituted for names and addresses.

The tool

The EARN in JVO is a 32-item, evaluator-completed checklist designed to assist the systematic review of risk factors that have been identified in the professional literature as associated with adolescent violent re-offending. EARN is divided into six domains (five of risk: Environmental, Individual, Familial, Intervention, Externalized behavior; one of Protection). Items are scored on a three-point scale in which 0 indicates the absence of the risk factor; 1 indicates some evidence that the factor is present; 2 indicates clear evidence of the presence of the risk factor or that the risk factor is present in a greater frequency. Items are coded as *critical* (*yes* or *no*) if the presence of the factor per se highly increases the level of risk.

Table 7.3 shows the prevalence of the factors in the sample. The picture of youth delinquency in Italy accords with the literature (Farrington, 2004) and seems to be characterized by juveniles of low socio-economic status who live in unorganized communities; who have low or absent school performance; who seem to have difficulty coping with life events and controlling their impulsiveness; who are not able to understand others and others' feelings; whose parents are not able to monitor and to support their development; who have a history of antisocial behaviors, particularly connected with peer delinquency and previously failed interventions; whose participation and efforts in proposed programs of intervention is low; and who seem to have moderate levels of social and familial support but who are not involved in prosocial activities.

Table 7.4 shows the final evaluation of the recidivism risk assessed by the operator responsible for each case.

Missing data

The not negligible amount of missing data could be a limitation of the present study; there are several reasons to explain the lack of data. Because the EARN approach is a new way to evaluate and manage juvenile violent behaviors, practitioners of the juvenile justice system had difficulties changing their method of work and

Table 7.3 Prevalence of the factors (n =294)

	FACTOR	*% Not present*	*% Partially present*	*% Present*	*% Insufficient information*	*% Critical*
ENVIROMENTAL	1. Maternal substance abuse during pregnancy	47.1	7.6	3.8	41.5	1.4
	2. Low SES	33.9	30.1	33.2	2.7	14.6
	3. Community disorganization	27.7	26.0	40.4	5.8	27.2
	4. School environment	30.4	32.8	20.8	16.0	9.2
INDIVIDUAL	5. Birth deficiency	28.9	3.8	3.8	63.6	1.0
	6. Poor school functioning	19.9	27.8	48.1	4.1	26.5
	7. Poor coping ability	25.1	34.0	34.7	6.2	26.2
	8. Impulsivity/risk-taking	23.9	28.7	42.6	4.8	30.3
	9. Low empathy/lack of remorse	27.1	30.5	36.6	5.8	22.8
	10. ADHD symptoms	39.3	26.9	17.6	16.2	9.2
	11 Mental disease	55.6	14.6	9.0	20.8	7.5
FAMILIAL	12. Parental history of mental disease	62.0	1.4	3.8	32.8	2.4
	13. Maternal teenage pregnancy	38.2	27.6	13.4	20.8	2.7
	14. Early caregiver disruption	63.7	12.1	13.1	11.1	10.5
	15. Frequent changes of caregivers	65.3	10.7	14.8	9.3	6.5
	16. Family structure	45.7	21.1	29.4	3.8	7.1
	17. Ineffective parenting	29.3	30.7	32.1	7.9	25.9
	18. Family conflict-domestic violence	55.4	13.1	11.4	20.1	8.5
	19. Parental antisocial practices/attitudes	55.5	6.5	20.9	17.1	9.5
INTERVENTION	20. Failure of previous intervention	36.2	23.6	34.3	5.9	8.2
	21. Poor familial response to intervention	47.5	22.0	25.2	5.3	11.9
	22. Poor youth's response to intervention	41.6	25.6	30.2	2.5	18.4
	23. Inaccessibility to intervention	46.0	23.2	13.4	17.4	6.5
EXTERNALIZED	24. History of violence and aggression	40.5	14.6	23.7	21.2	11.9
	25. General offending	55.5	12.2	11.4	20.9	3.1
	26. General behavioral problem	41.0	15.9	24.7	18.5	13.9
	27. Peer delinquency	32.4	17.4	42.0	8.2	15.3
	28. Use of substances	53.9	8.9	18.6	18.6	7.8

Table 7.4 Final evaluation of the level of recidivism risk (n = 294)

% Low	*% Medium*	*% High*	*% Missing*
29.9	38.4	26.2	5.4

finding different sources of information to assess dimensions like medical condition or prenatal deficiencies. Moreover, much of this information is protected by privacy laws.

Another problem was assessing past criminal behaviors not reported in criminal records; social workers in the juvenile justice system could not report this type of crime. The large mortality of the sample (40%) in a six-months follow-up is due to their leaving the juvenile justice system because, for example, they came of age or their intervention ended or changed.

Results

Factor predictiveness

In order to evaluate which factors are better predictors of recidivism, odds ratio were calculated for any factor included in the instrument (see Table 7.5). *Odds ratio* is a measure of effect size, describing the strength of association between two binary data values. In the analysis, factors were turned into dichotomic variables and protective factors were rotated. At the bivariate level, 25 factors were significant predictors of recidivism, and the better predictors appear to be poor school functioning, impulsivity/risk taking, history of violence, poor response to intervention and history of general behavioral problems.

Other socio-demographic characteristics were included in the analysis (see Table 7.6). Level of education and ethnicity were not predictive of recidivism, whereas past criminal records was a good predictor of future delinquency.

The extent of confidence interval that measures the probability that a population parameter will fall between two set values seems to be large for a portion of the factors analyzed and could reflect, for those factors, the need to collect more data, so data interpretation requires same caution.

Domain predictiveness

The second aim of the present study was to evaluate the predictiveness of the domains proposed in the instrument. Each domain represents a particular dimension of risk that showed a significant relation with recidivism in the literature (see, inter alia, Corrado, 2002); therefore, domains according to Borum et al. (2000) are not intended as "scales".

Internal consistency was evaluated (see Table 7.7) and some items are deleted (1, 5, 13) to improve reliability.

Table 7.5 Bivariate analysis for juvenile recidivism (six months) (n = 163)

	FACTOR	*% of Assessor reporting*	*% Insufficient information*	*Odds*	*Lb*	*Ub*
ENVIROMENTAL	1. Maternal substance abuse during pregnancy	9.2	27.4	2.77^{+}	0.81	9.42
	2. Low SES	62	1.8	4.93**	1.62	14.90
	3. Community disorganization	61.3	5.5	3.44*	1.24	9.58
	4. School environment	47.2	15.3	1.72	0.72	4.18
INDIVIDUAL	5. Birth deficiency	7.4	57.1	2.04	0.45	9.20
	6. Poor school functioning	76.1	1.8	11.67**	1.53	88.73
	7. Poor coping ability	69.9	2.5	3.10*	1.01	9.43
	8. Impulsivity/risk-taking	70.6	2.5	14.12*	1.86	107.22
	9. Low empathy/lack of remorse	66.3	2.5	3.94*	1.30	11.94
	10. ADHD symptoms	42.3	14.1	3.31*	1.29	8.51
	11. Mental disease	24.5	16.0	2.93*	1.18	7.26
FAMILIAL	12. Parental history of mental disease	4.9	28.2	0.66	0.08	5.70
	13. Maternal teenage pregnancy	7.1	27	0.61	0.23	1.55
	14. Early caregiver disruption	22.7	9.2	3.43**	1.44	8.17
	15. Frequent changes of caregivers	29.4	9.2	3.68**	1.53	8.82
	16. Family structure	49.7	2.5	0.64	0.29	1.41
	17. Ineffective parenting	60.1	5.5	4.60*	1.51	14.0
	18. Family conflict–domestic violence	21.5	16.6	2.19^{+}	0.87	5.47
	19. Parental antisocial practices/attitudes	27.6	14.6	2.78*	1.18	6.58
INTERVENTION	20. Failure of previous intervention	55.8	15.5	3.98**	1.29	12.24
	21. Poor familial response to intervention	42.9	7.0	2.94*	1.23	7.02
	22. Poor youth's response to intervention	48.5	5.5	6.48**	2.33	18.04
	23. Inaccessibility to intervention	30.1	18.4	1.77	0.74	4.27

EXTERNALIZED	24.	History of violence and aggression	38.7	20.9	8.31**	2.67	25.90
	25.	General offending	23.9	28.2	4.29**	1.65	11.15
	26.	General behavioral problem	40.5	18.4	16.25**	3.64	72.63
	27.	Peer delinquency	58.3	5.0	3.21**	1.23	8.39
	28.	Use of substances	24.5	22.1	2.37^{+}	0.94	5.97
PROTECTION	29.	Absence of social and familiar support	11.7	1.8	2.97^{+}	0.97	7.56
	30.	Absence of strong relationship and bonds	10.4	3.0	4.33**	1.52	12.37
	31.	Absence of prosocial involvement	52.8	6.1	2.54*	1.05	6.13
	32.	Absence of resilient personality traits	21.5	4.3	1.82	0.76	4.28

Note: $^{+}p < 0.10$; $*p < 0.05$; $**p < 0.01$; all factors are dichotomic.

Table 7.6 Bivariate analysis for juvenile recidivism (6 months) (n = 163)

	% of Assessor reporting this Factor	*% Insufficient information*	*Odds*	*Lb*	*Ub*
Age (scale)	–	5	0.91	0.58	1.44
Nationality (Italian–Not)	72%	11	1.52	0.57	4.05
Education		11			
Junior High School or less vs High School			2.64	0.67	8.65
Junior High School vs High School			0.69	0.22	2.14
Past Criminal Record (No–Yes)	48%	21	**10.47****	2.35	46.6

Note: $**p < 0.01$

Table 7.7 EARN internal consistency

Domain	_	*Item*
Environmental	0.66	3
Individual	0.81	6
Familial	0.71	7
Intervention	0.66	4
Externalized behaviors	0.78	5
Protective	0.68	4
EARN total score	0.84	29

Predictive accuracy was tested using receiver operating characteristic (ROC), an analysis that assesses prediction accuracy by comparing the correct prediction rate (true positive, sensitivity) with the wrong prediction rate (false negative, 1-specificity). The random guess is represented by an area below the curve (AUC) of 0.50; perfect prediction is 1 (Swets, 1996). The analysis in Table 7.8 shows that all the domains are significant predictors of recidivism, but, according to Hosmer and Lemshow's (2000) recommendations, only Individual Domain and Externalized Domain are predictors acceptably accurate to predict short-term, general recidivism. At this point, it is not possible to define a cut-off score (a reliable score that discriminates between recidivist and not recidivist).

Tool predictiveness

In order to estimate the prediction accuracy of the EARN, a ROC analysis was conducted to compare three different scores: the professional evaluation based on the tool (EARN Final Evaluation), the additive score of all EARN factors (EARN Total Score) and the additive score of all the critical factors (EARN Critical Score). The comparison (see Table 7.9) showed that the EARN Final Evaluation seems to be the better predictor of future risk of recidivism.

Table 7.8 ROC analysis – domains; state variable: recidivism

	r^{pbs}	*AUC*	*SE*	*Upper bound*	*Lower bound*
Environmental domain	0.21**	0.64*	0.054	0.54	0.74
Individual domain	0.30**	0.70**	0.045	0.61	0.79
Familial domain	0.16*	0.62*	0.056	0.51	0.73
Intervention domain	0.26*	0.69**	0.048	0.60	0.79
Externalized behaviors domain	0.31**	0.72***	0.047	0.63	0.81
Protective domain (rotate)	0.27**	0.69*	0.055	0.58	0.79

Note: *p <0.05; **p <0.01; ***p <0.001.

Table 7.9 ROC analysis – critical score, total score, final evaluation; state variable: recidivism = yes

	r^{pbs}	*AUC*	*SE*	*Upper bound*	*Lower bound*
EARN critical score	0.27**	0.68*	0.057	0.58	0.79
EARN total score	0.32**	0.72***	0.046	0.63	0.81
EARN final evaluation	0.35**	0.75***	0.047	0.66	0.84

Note: *$p < 0.05$; **$p < 0.01$; ***$p < 0.001$

EARN effect on recidivism

The last objective of this study was to evaluate whether a structured assessment approach could improve the effectiveness of professionals implementing interventions to decrease recidivism rates. In this study the recidivism rates of two groups of juvenile offenders were compared. With the experimental group practitioners used the EARN approach for six months; with the control group no structured risk assessment was conducted. Recidivism was evaluated after a six-month follow-up.

In order to understand if the use of the EARN toolkit, per se, could differentiate the recidivism rate of the two groups of juvenile offenders, a simple crosstab analysis was conducted (see Figure 7.1 and Table 7.10). The analysis did not show significant differences between the two groups.

Discussion

The results of this study show that the EARN approach appears to be a promising new comprehensive instrument for risk assessment.

- The risk factors poor school functioning (Enviromental), impulsivity risk taking (Individual), history of violence, history of general behavioral problems (Exter-

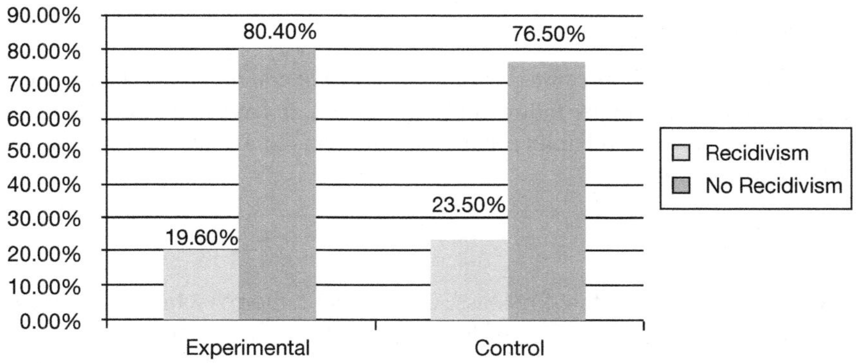

Figure 7.1 Bar chart of recidivism rate (experimental vs. control)

Table 7.10 Crosstabulation

	Not recidivism	*Recidvism*	
Control group	52	16	Frequency
	–0.3	0.5	Std. residual
Experimental group	131	32	Frequency
	0.2	–0.3	Std. residual

Note: $Chi^2(1) = 0.44$, $p > 0.05$

nalized Behaviors), poor youth's response to intervention (Intervention), appear to be better predictors at the bivariate level of brief recidivism (six months).

- Regarding the domains proposed, individual risk factors and externalized behavior risk factors seem to be good predictors according to to Hosmer and Lemshow's (2000) recommendations, but all the domains in the assessment are valid, informative and significant.
- The EARN accuracy in prediction is rather good, in particular the rater's final evaluation, because, given the practitioners' professional expertise, the rater's final evaluation could include all the dimensions proposed by the EARN approach (risk factors, protective factors and critical dimensions).
- The EARN approach seems not to improve the effectiveness of professionals in designing interventions to decrease recidivism rates. However, the short follow-up (six months), the not negligible mortality of the sample (41% Experimental; 46% Control) and the small percentage of the follow-up sample who recidivated (19.6% Experimental; 23% Control) suggests the need to evaluate these results with caution. More studies are necessary, but we hypothesize that it would likely be useless to adapt the EARN approach to the programs currently being implemented in the juvenile justice system. In order to effect a significant improvement in recidivism rates, it would be necessary to develop new individualized programs specifically tailored to the risk/needs analysis proposed by the EARN tool.

Avenue for future research

This study has some limitations. In future research it could be important to study larger samples with longer follow-up (1 to 3 years), to have more raters per case to evaluate inter-rater reliability and more measures to evaluate concurrent and criterion reliability.

Policy implications

Risk assessment. Structured risk assessment could improve clinical judgments by assisting professionals to consider both additional factors and these factors' interactions in their evaluations, as well as encouraging them to investigate in new directions (according to the domain proposed), outside their usual methods of work.

Development of a reliable and predictive risk assessment approach like the EARN, requires that specialized training for practitioners be provided and that practitioners have access to all the different sources of information (archival data, local social services data, police data about the offender and his family) necessary for a multi-dimensional structured assessment.

Risk management. Using structured assessment tools like the EARN has the potential of improving the effectiveness of risk management strategies and reducing the incidence of recidivism. Such tools assist professionals to identify relative risk factors that contribute to criminal behavior and to develop and implement interventions designed to address the impact of those factors on the subject. With a view to preventing and reducing recidivism, it is important to develop a risk management plan that will minimize the circumstances, the risk factors that influenced the choice of violence, and maximize protective factors. When assessing risk, we must take into account the types of risk factors present and contextualize them; they could be static or dynamic, and their influence could be significant for some children but not for others.

Intervention

Intervention is an essential component of the prevention and management of juvenile delinquency. Intervention programs for juvenile offenders should be specifically tailored to the risk dimension evaluated in order to have a positive effect on the recidivism rate. To optimize the EARN approach and to decrease youth offenders' recidivism rates, the juvenile justice system should, according to Andrews et al. (2006), integrate systematic intervention and monitoring with the assessment in one unique circular process (assessment–intervention–monitoring–assessment).

Bibliography

Andrews, D. A., Bonta, J., and Wormith, S. J. (2006). The recent past and near future of risk and/or need assessment. *Crime and Delinquency*, 52, 7–27.

Augimeri, L., Koegl, C. J., Webster, C. D., and Levene, K. (2001). *The Early Assessment Risk List for Boys (EARL-20B) – Version 2.* Toronto: Earlscourt Child and Family Centre.

Baldry, A. C. and Farrington, D. P. (2005). Protective factors as moderators of risk factors in adolescent bullying. *Social Psychology of Education*, 8, 263–84.

Borum, R., Bartel, P., and Forth, A. (2000). Manual for the Structured Assessment for Violence Risk in Youth (SAVRY): Consultation Edition. Tampa, FL: Louis de la Parte Florida Mental Health Institute, University of South Florida.

Corrado R. R. (2002). An introduction to risk/needs case management instrument for children and youth at risk for violence: The Crackow instrument. In R. R. Corrado, R. Roesch, S. Hart, J. K. Gierowsk (eds) *Multi-problem Violent Youth: A Foundation for Comparative Research on Needs, Interventions and Outcomes*. Amsterdam: IOS Press (pp. 295–302).

Farrington, D. (1989). Early predictors of adolescent aggression and adult violence. *Violence and Victims,* 4, 79–100.

Farrington, D. (1991). Childhood aggression and adult violence: Early precursors and later life outcomes. In D. Pepler and K. Rubin (eds) *The Development and Treatment of Childhood Aggression.* Hillsdale, NJ: Erlbaum (pp. 5–29).

Farrington, D. P. (2002). Multiple risk factors for multiple problem violent boys. In R. R. Corrado, R. Roesch, S. Hart, J.K. Gierowsk (eds) *Multi-problem Violent Youth: A Foundation for Comparative Research on Needs, Interventions and Outcomes.* Amsterdam: IOS Press (pp. 23–34).

Hosmer, D.W. and Lemeshow, S. (2000) *Applied Logistic Regression.* 2nd edn. New York, NY: Wiley.

Kemshall, H. (2001). *Risk Assessment and Management of Known Sexual and Violent Offenders: A Review of Current Issues.* London: Home Office.

Kropp, P., Hart, S. D., Webster, C., and Eaves, D. (1999). *Spousal Assault Risk Assessment Guide User's Manual.* Toronto, Canada: Multi-Health Systems, Inc. and BC Institute Against Family Violence.

Moffitt, T. (1993). "Life course persistent" and "adolescence limited" antisocial behavior: A developmental taxonomy. *Psychological Review*, 100, 674–701.

Swets, J. A. (1996). *Signal Detection Theory and Roc Analysis In Psychology and Diagnostics.* Mahwah, NJ: Lawrence Erlbaum.

8 The EARN project in Cyprus

A. Kapardis and G. Poyiadjis

Research into childhood risk factors and risk-focused prevention may have a history of only a few decades, but a great deal of knowledge now exists, especially concerning evidence-based, risk-focused delinquency prevention. As Welsh and Farrington (2007) put it, "Convincing research evidence exists to support a policy of saving children from a life of crime by intervening early in childhood to tackle key risk factors" (p. 801). Tonry and Farrington (1995, p. 603) distinguished four main prevention strategies, namely:

(1) *Developmental prevention* (interventions aimed at preventing an individual's potential for criminal behaviour by focusing on risk and protective factors).
(2) *Community prevention* (interventions that impact on offending by focusing, for example, on the family, peers, and social norms).
(3) *Situational prevention* (making offending more difficult and riskier and reducing opportunities for crime).
(4) *Criminal justice prevention* (prevention through policing, sentences imposed, and custodial institutions — the criminal justice system itself).

Nowadays, the terms *developmental prevention* and *risk-focused prevention* are synonymous (Farrington, 2007, p. 603).

Risk assessment refers to identifying the risk and protective factors in childhood and adolescence that predict later offending. Although a great deal is known about risk factors for delinquency that are associated with the individual, the family, and an individual's broader social environment, such as the school and local community, "Disappointingly less is known about protective factors against offending, but recent empirical research provides some important insights" (Welsh and Farrington, 2007, p. 801). Farrington (2007), in his discussion of the literature, identifies some well-established early childhood risk factors that predict delinquent behaviour: impulsivity, attention problems, low school achievement, inadequate parental supervision, conflict between the parents, having a young mother, having an antisocial parent, belonging to a large-size family, low family income and coming from a broken family (p. 601).

As mentioned in Chapter 4, there has been little research into childhood and adolescence risk factors in Cyprus (see Steketee et al., 2008). In 2006 and 2009

(Kapardis, 2010), in the context of implementing the *Communities That Care* delinquency prevention programme, in November 2010 one of the present authors (Andreas Kapardis) carried out a survey of 495 and 519 junior secondary school children aged 12 to 15, respectively, in a Nicosia suburb and identified the following risk factors at the level of the *individual* (smoking, consuming alcohol, drug use, low self-esteem, belonging to a gang and having been arrested by the police); *the family* (another family member takes drugs, erratic monitoring of children by parents, lack of clear rules regarding substances of addiction, parental conflict); *school* (low scholastic achievement, hating going to school, playing truant, carrying a knife to school, lack of personal contact with any teacher, having been expelled from school); and *local community* (where a youth does not feel he or she belongs, lacks constructive leisure time activities, where drugs are easy to obtain, where fights are frequent). The risk factors identified by the two same-school surveys support the ISRD-2 findings (see Steketee et al., 2008) concerning the importance for antisocial behaviour prevention of a strong bond between adolescents and their family, school, and neighbourhood, as well as a number of characteristics at the level of the individual that predispose towards delinquent behaviour, its maintenance and intensity.

As documented in Chapter 4, there has been no proper study of risk assessment among juveniles in Cyprus using the EARN instrument. The EARN instrument aids in identifying a broad range of risk and protective factors in juveniles, knowledge that can be utilized by police, youth workers, social workers, school counsellors and drug rehabilitation centres. One merit of the EARN instrument used in the study reported below is that it approaches the issue of delinquency risk assessment in a comprehensive way. It is easy to administer and score even by non-specialists in forensic psychology.

Method

The findings reported below were obtained in two surveys, namely an archival study of police "crime files" (i.e., police investigation and prosecution files) on convicted juveniles and a survey of a control group comprising pupils from a private school in Nicosia who had not come to the attention of the police.

Participants

Archival group. Data were coded for analysis from the criminal files kept by the police concerning 50 young offenders (males, 14 to 17 years of age) who had been evaluated by the Juvenile Delinquency Committee, prosecuted and convicted for their crimes by a juvenile court judge. The age distribution was as follows: 12 aged 14 years; 27 aged 15 years; five aged 16 years; and six aged 17 years old. Files were surveyed at the following police stations in the greater Nicosia district: Paphos Gate police station in the city centre, Lakatamia, Kokkinotrimithia and Nisou in the suburbs.

Control group. 67 students attending a private secondary school, 14 to 17 years old, who had not come to the attention of the police and were living in the Nicosia district (city centre and suburbs) comprised the control group. The age distribution was as follows: 24 aged 14 (9M, 15F), 31 aged 15 (15M, 16F), 6 aged 16 (3M, 3F) and, finally, 6 aged 17 (5M and 1F). Thus, 52% were female and 48% males. The fact that over half of the control group were females (known to have lower delinquency rates than males of the same age) means that they provided a good test of the discriminability of the EARN instrument.

Materials

For the purpose of the current study, the EARN questionnaire was used, translated into Greek (see Appendix B). The structure and content of the original EARN questionnaire in English was retained when information was collected from the archival group by the researchers. The EARN questionnaire was adapted for use with the control group by excluding 11 questions (numbers 1, 5, 11, 12, 13, 19, 21, 22, 23, 25, and 26) that were not applicable. (See Appendix C for shortened questionnaire and Appendix D regarding how the questions in the shortened EARN questionnaire correspond to the questions in the full questionnaire.)

The presence of a risk factor was assessed on a three-point scale: *not present, probably or partially present,* or *present*. An overall assessment was also made to determine, on a scale of 1 to100, an overall score of how "critical" the presence of a risk factor was. A risk factor with an overall score of 40 or more is considered as being "present". The critical score values are 0–40 (*probably or partially present*), 41–60 (*present*), 61–100 (*critical*).

Procedure

For the archival group, the collection of data was carried out at the police stations concerned with the permission of the chief of the Cyprus police. In order to comply with Cyprus's data protection legislation, a police officer who was responsible for the archives of each police station was assigned to the project and assisted the researchers to obtain the information needed from a file in order to complete the EARN questionnaire anonymously. In order to comply with data protection legislation in Cyprus, the researchers did not read the criminal files themselves. It should also be noted that the police files included a social enquiry report on the delinquent and his family that provided a great deal of information concerning the family itself, its socio-economic status, and the history of contact with the police and social services. All the information was then stored in an external hard drive, as an Excel file and encrypted with password-protected access.

For the control group, the data collection was performed after permission from the headmaster of the private secondary school concerned was obtained and the pupils had signed a consent form. The questionnaire used was the modified EARN questionnaire translated into Greek (Appendix C). The participants completed the questionnaire during one of their school periods. All the information was then stored in an external hard drive, encrypted with password-protected access, as an Excel file.

Aim of the study

To identify the presence and intensity of risk factors in the archival and control group and to consider policy implications arising from the study.

Results

Official delinquents and risk factors: a profile

Confirming the findings reported by many studies of delinquents (see Farrington, 1997), the following risk factors are present among official delinquents in Cyprus: being a young male, 15 years old, from a large-size (4+ members), low socio-economic status family characterized by persistent intra-familial conflict; having committed offences against property with friends in groups of two or three; lacking the ability to handle stressful situations and being unable to adjust in situations under stress caused by external environmental factors; having shown very low interest and performing poorly in school; and, finally, not participating in structured extracurricular activities and living in a community where such activities are not available. We see that risk factors exist at the level of the individual, the school, the family and the local community.

Comparison of the presence of risk and protective factors between groups

If we look at Table 8.1, we see that, in contrast to the archival group, the control group is not, on the one hand, characterized by such risk factors as poor coping ability, impulsivity/risk taking, low empathy/lack of remorse, ineffective parenting, a previous history of violence and aggression, or exhibiting a general behavioural problem. On the other hand, the control group enjoys a number of *protective factors*: possessing a resilient personality, enjoying the presence of social and familial support, having strong attachments and bonds to their families and school, and participating in prosocial activities.

What is of particular interest is that although, as Table 8.1 shows, there is some evidence of a few risk factors (poor coping ability, impulsivity, low empathy and use of illegal addictive substances) present to a lesser degree among the control group, the impact of those factors is reduced by the beneficial effects of the few crucial protective factors mentioned above at the level of the individual, the family, the school and the local community; namely, the presence of social and familiar support, strong attachments and bonds to the family and the school, involvement in prosocial activities outside school, and, finally, possession of resilient personality traits. Future research should explore delinquency risk and protective factors in Cyprus as a function of a juvenile's gender.

Table 8.1 The presence of risk factors and the intensity of the presence in the archival and control groups*

Question number	*Missing information*		*Not present*		*Probably or partially present*		*Present*		*Critical*	
	Archival	*Control*	*Archival*	*Control*	*Archival*	*Control*	*Archival*	*Control*	*Archival*	*Control*
1	100	100								
2		4.5	28.0	74.6	14.0	20.9	18.0		40.0	
3		3.0	31.9	71.6	10.6	17.9	14.9	6.0	42.6	1.5
4			43.2	83.6	5.4	13.4	5.4	3.0	45.9	
5	78.0	100	8.0		2.0		12.0			
6			18.4	92.5	4.1	6.0	14.3	1.5	63.3	
7			6.0	64.2	4.0	26.9	30.0	9.0	60.0	
8			16.0	49.3	2.0	38.8	26.0	11.9	56.0	
9			28.0	82.1	4.0	9.0	28.0	9.0	40.0	
10	78.0		6.0	79.1	10.0	16.4		4.5	6.0	
11	85.7	100	4.1		8.2		2.0			
12		100	76.2		4.8		9.5		9.5	
13		100	91.7				8.3			
14			83.0	98.5	10.6	1.5	4.3		2.1	
15		4.5	66.7	89.6	6.3	6.0	2.1		25.0	
16			50.0	77.6	22.0	19.4	8.0	3.0	20.0	
17			28.0	65.7	22.0	28.4	24.0	6.0	26.0	
18		1.5	32.7	86.6		1.5	14.3	9.0	53.1	1.5
19		100	48.0		10.0		4.0		38.0	
20			62.5	98.5	2.1	1.5	16.7		18.8	
21		100	69.4		6.1		2.0		22.4	
22		100	28.0		26.0		16.0		30.0	

Table 8.1 Continued

Question number	*Missing information*		*Not present*		*Probably or partially present*		*Present*		*Critical*	
	Archival	*Control*	*Archival*	*Control*	*Archival*	*Control*	*Archival*	*Control*	*Archival*	*Control*
23		100			94.0		6.0			
24			12.8	71.6	17.0	25.4	19.1	3.0	51.1	
25		100	14.6		20.8		18.8		45.8	
26		100	12.5		18.8		14.6		54.2	
27		16.4	28.0	71.6		4.5	18.0	7.5	54.0	
28		7.5	57.1	61.2	28.6	22.4	12.2	9.0	2.0	
29		4.5	36.0	1.5	10.0	4.5	12.0	89.6	42.0	
30			36.0	1.5	10.0	11.9	14.0	86.6	40.0	
31			20.8	1.5	10.4	22.4	16.7	76.1	52.1	
32			18.0	1.5	16.0	11.9	14.0	86.6	52.0	

Notes: Risk and protective factors: 1. Maternal substance use during pregnancy, 2. Low socio-economic status, 3. Community disorganization, 4. School environment, 5. Obstetrical complications/birth deficiency, 6. Poor school functioning, 7. Poor coping ability, 8. Impulsivity/risk taking, 9. Low empathy/lack of remorse, 10. Attention deficit/hyperactivity difficulties, 11. Mental illness, 12. Parental history of mental illness, 13. Teenage pregnancy, 14. Early caregiver disruption, 15. Frequent changes of caregivers, 16. Mono/multi parental family structure, 17. Ineffective parenting, 18. Family conflicts, 19. Parental antisocial practices/attitudes, 20. Previous intervention, 21. Poor familial response to intervention, 22. Poor youth's response to intervention, 23. Inaccessibility to intervention, 24. History of violence and aggression, 25. General offending, 26. General behavioural problem, 27. Peer delinquency, 28. Use of substances, 29. Presence of social and familial support, 30. Strong attachments and bonds, 31. Pro-social involvement, 32. Resilient personality traits.

* The critical score values are 0–40 (*probably* or *partially present*), 41–60 (*present*), 61–100 (*critical*).

Note: *Risk factors in dotted lines have likely always been present, but take on new meaning as others accumulate.

Policy implications

Police. On the basis of the findings obtained and the extensive discussions the researchers were able to have with Cyprus police personnel in the course of the study, it can be argued that there is a visible lack of specialized departments for recruiting and training professionals such as psychologists, criminologists and sociologists in the police service. The need for these kinds of trained specialists in dealing with youth and, in particular, with young people under the age of 14 cannot be over-emphasized. Police stations situated in the outskirts of cities are inadequately staffed to deal with the youth in the surrounding areas. Also, owing to the fact that the Cypriot society remains a small community where the family bond is still very strong, there is some undesirable outside interference by relatives in police handling of juvenile delinquents. The reader should note in this context that there is still a noticeable lack of a long-term national strategy in how to best deal with young offenders.

The courts. The most important issue regarding the current system is the lack of a permanent specialist juvenile court in conjunction with the lack of a safe and well-staffed reformatory institution for convicted offenders under the age of 18.

Department of Social Services. As with the police, the number one problem facing the Department of Social Services in the Republic of Cyprus is that it is understaffed and lacks personnel who have specialized training in dealing with juvenile delinquents, whether for preparing the social enquiry reports for the Juvenile Delinquency Committee and the courts or for supervising juveniles on probation orders or on probation with community service conditions. In addition, the social enquiry reports (SERs) the department provides fail to address some basic issues such as juvenile delinquency risk assessment – let alone prevention strategies. Instead, the SERs merely provide information on the socio-economic conditions of a family. Making the situation even worse, these SERs are provided with excessive delays (up to 2.5 years in certain cases), thus, to a large extent, defeating the purpose of the whole exercise.

The Juvenile Delinquency Committee. Examination of the time that the Juvenile Delinquency Committee takes to assess a case before it and then to make its recommendation to the attorney general about the disposal of a case reveals that (a) the committee has to process a tremendous work load, (b) it does not meet as frequently as it should, and (c) the information before it (as provided in the police investigation file and the SER by the Department of Social Services) cannot be considered sufficient for arriving at an informed and satisfactory decision. An evaluation of the functioning of this committee is long overdue.

Conclusions

Without ignoring the limitations of survey research with self-administered structured questionnaires and of horizontal delinquency surveys as opposed to longitudinal studies (see Farrington, 1997), it can be argued that the EARN project in Cyprus has (a) demonstrated the utility of the EARN instrument in juvenile delinquency risk assessment, (b) made possible the comparison and contrast between the archival and the control groups of adolescents, (c) yielded useful findings that are in agreement with the international empirical literature on risk and protective factors for delinquency and, finally, (d) facilitated formulation of a number of policy recommendations.

References

Farrington, D. P. (1997). Human development and criminal careers. In M. Maguire, R. Morgan and R. Reiner (eds), *The Oxford Handbook of Criminology*, 2nd edition. Oxford: Oxford University Press.

Farrington, D. P. (2007). Childhood risk factors and risk-focused prevention. In M. Maguire, R. Morgan, and R. Reiner (eds), *The Oxford Handbook of Criminology,* 4th edition. Oxford: Oxford University Press (pp. 602–40).

Kapardis, A. (2010). Implementing 'Communities That Care' delinquency intervention programme in Nicosia, Cyprus. Paper presented at the CTC Session, European Forum for Urban Security, International Congress Center, Berlin, May 9–12.

Steketee, M., Moll, M., and Kapardis, A. (2008). *Delinquency in six EU member states.* Netherlands, Utrecht: Verwey-Jonker Instituut.

Tonry, M. and Farrington, D.P. (1995). Strategic approaches to crime prevention. In M. Tonry and D. P. Farrington (eds), *Building a safer society: Strategic approaches to crime prevention.* Chicago: University of Chicago Press (pp. 1–20).

Welsh, B. and Farrington, D. P. (2007). Save children from a life of crime. *Criminology and Public Policy, 6*(4), 801–10.

Appendix A: EARN in JVO questionnaire

E.A.R.N. IN JVO EUROPEAN ASSESSMENT OF RISK/NEEDS IN JUVENILE VIOLENT OFFENDERS		
ID Number: ____________________		
Filled by: ____________________	**Signature:** ____________________	**Date:** ____________________

Innformation:	**Scoring:**
☐ Interview with the youth ☐ Interview with the staff ☐ Criminal records ☐ Other __________________________	***N*** = Not Present ***P*** = Probably/Partially Present ***Y*** = Present – = Omit, insufficient information

Enviromental Domain	**Scoring**	**Critical Factor?**
1. Maternal Substance Abuse During Pregnancy ☐ Cigarettes ☐ Alcohol ☐ Drugs ☐ Other (specify____________________________)	☐ **N** ☐ **P** ☐ **Y** ☐ –	☐
2. Low SES	☐ **N** ☐ **P** ☐ **Y** ☐ –	☐
3. Community Disorganization ☐ No structured social activity in the community ☐ Easy access todrugs and weapons ☐ Many adults involved in illegal activities in the community ☐ Many illegal immigrants ☐ Other (specify____________________________)	☐ **N** ☐ **P** ☐ **Y** ☐ –	☐
4.Negative School Environment ☐ Low teacher/students ratio ☐ Low involvement of the community in the school activities ☐ High levels of violence and conflicts (eg, bullying) ☐ Other (specify____________________________)	☐ **N** ☐ **P** ☐ **Y** ☐ –	☐
Other Considerations:		

Individual Domain	**Scoring**	**Critical Factor?**
5. Birth Deficiency Report the list of complications and the relative period (pregnancy/birth/first few days of birth) Consider things like: ☐ Maternal health impairment (eg, malnutrition, infections, age 35 and over) ☐ Childbirth with the aid of forceps ☐ Umbilical cord prolapse ☐ Pre-eclampsia (hypertensive syndrome in pregnancy) ☐ Premature birth or caesarean ☐ Long-term labor ☐ Temporary interruption of the flow of oxygen to the brain ☐ Abnormal body weight ☐ Disability or chronic illness have been identified during the prenatal ☐ Other (specify____________________)	☐ **N** ☐ **P** ☐ **Y** ☐ –	☐
6. Poor School Functioning Consider things like: ☐ Poor school performance ☐ Poor commitment and interest ☐ Lack of links with the school ☐ Other (specify____________________)	☐ **N** ☐ **P** ☐ **Y** ☐ –	☐
7. Poor Coping Ability Consider things like: ☐ Poor ability to cope with stressful events ☐ Low self-esteem ☐ Other (specify____________________)	☐ **N** ☐ **P** ☐ **Y** ☐ –	☐
8. Impulsivity/Risk Taking Consider things like: ☐ Emotional and behavioral instability ☐ A marked fluctuations in mood or behavior ☐ A tendency to act without thinking ☐ Difficulty in staying alert and compounds especially when under pressure ☐ Other (specify ____________________)	☐ **N** ☐ **P** ☐ **Y** ☐ –	☐
9. Low Empathy/Lack Of Remorse Consider things like: ☐ Poor consideration for the feelings and welfare of others ☐ Tendency to express emotions in a superficial, insincere and inappropriate way ☐ Refusal to accept responsibility for their actions and tendency to blame others ☐ Tendency to minimize the harmful effects of their behavior ☐ Other (specify____________________)	☐ **N** ☐ **P** ☐ **Y** ☐ –	☐

10. ADHD Symptoms Consider things like: ☐ Problems with concentration ☐ Extreme restlessness ☐ Hyperactivity and impulsivity Other (specify________________________)	☐ **N** ☐ **P** ☐ **Y** ☐ –	☐
11. Mental Disease Consider and report in detail elements such as: ☐ History of cognitive/mental insuficiency ☐ History of conduct disorder, oppositional/defiant or other childhood disorders ☐ History of threats, ideation or attempted suicide or self-injury ☐ History of psychiatric pharmacological interventions and/or psychotherapeutic ☐ Any warning signs of serious mental illness (psychosis, depression, etc.) ☐ Possible antecedents of personality disorder (such as chronic anger, impulsivity, etc.) ☐ Other (specify________________________)	☐ **N** ☐ **P** ☐ **Y** ☐ –	☐
Other Considerations:		

Familial Domain	**Scoring**	**Critical Factor?**
12. Parental History Of Mental Disease Report the list of disorders in each biological parent	☐ **N** ☐ **P** ☐ **Y** ☐ –	☐
13. Maternal Teenage Pregnancy Report the mother's age at birth of the child	☐ **>25** ☐ **20-24** ☐ **20** ☐ –	☐
14. Early Caregiver Disruption	☐ **N** ☐ **P** ☐ **Y** ☐ –	☐
15. Frequent Changes Of Caregivers	☐ **N** ☐ **P** ☐ **Y** ☐ –	☐

16. Family Structure (Mon/Multiparental)	☐ **N** ☐ **P** ☐ **Y** ☐ **–**	☐
17. Ineffective Parenting Consider things like: ☐ Parents who do not express warmth and consistency with their children ☐ Parents who are not involved in the lives of children ☐ Parents who adopt a style of education too coercive or permissive ☐ Other (specify________________________)	☐ **N** ☐ **P** ☐ **Y** ☐ **–**	☐
18. Parental Antisocial Practices/Attitudes Indicate whether the parents were involved in crime and antisocial behavior even though these have not led to a complaint or an arrest	☐ **N** ☐ **P** ☐ **Y** ☐ **–**	☐
19. Family Conflict/Domestic Violence Indicate if there is frequent exposure to family conflicts and domestic violence and/or direct physical or sexual abuse:	☐ **N** ☐ **P** ☐ **Y** ☐ **–**	☐
Other Considerations:		

Intervention Domain	**Scoring**	**Critical Factor?**
20. Failure Of Previous Intervention Fill in the grid bringing the type of intervention, duration, objectives, if it came to a conclusion, the results achieved etc.	☐ **N** ☐ **P** ☐ **Y** ☐ **–**	☐

Type	Intervention	Date/Duration	Objectives	Results
Medical				
Parental				
Familial				
Youth				
School				
Civil Justice				
Criminal Justice				
Community				
Other				

21. Poor Familial Response To Intervention Assess the availability to accept parental interventions on the family unit (if applicable) and the involvement and encouragement in supporting the intervention on the child Consider things like: ☐ Do not encourage the young to participate in programs ☐ Do not keep in touch with providers of services ☐ Having a low involvement in treatment plan ☐ Inability to accept the problems of the child ☐ Other (specify_________________________)	☐ **N** ☐ **P** ☐ **Y** ☐ –	☐
22. Poor Youth's Response To Intervention Assess the willingness and motivation of the child to participate in the intervention Indicate such predominant elements as: ☐ Anxiety ☐ Capacity of insight ☐ Awareness of their own problems ☐ Interest for change ☐ Strong relationship with practitioners ☐ Hope to have a benefit ☐ Other (please specify ________________________)	☐ **N** ☐ **P** ☐ **Y** ☐ –	☐
23. Inaccessibility To Intervention Consider the resources in the area other than the proposed plan for that particular individual and the risk factors identified Also consider the level of integration reached by mutual services that deal with the implementation of the plan	☐ **N** ☐ **P** ☐ **Y** ☐ –	☐

Other Considerations:

Externalized Behaviors Domain Includes all behaviors and antisocial behavior exibit by the juvenile even if they did not result in a report	**Scoring**	**Critical Factor?**
24. History Of Violence And Aggression Fill in the grid indicating violent behaviors and the age at which they occurred the first time, the frequency with which they occur and contexts in which they occur (home, school, community, neighborhood, etc.):	☐ **N** ☐ **P** ☐ **Y** ☐ –	☐

Behaviors	Age	Frequency	Contest	Other

25. General Offending Fill in the grid describing behaviors, frequency and contexts in which the offense was committed, indicate the age at which these behaviors occurred the first time	☐ **N** ☐ **P** ☐ **Y** ☐ **–**	☐

Behaviors	Age	Frequency	Contest	Other

26. General Behavioral Problem Fill the grid describing the variety, frequency and severity of behavioral problems exhibited by individuals as well as the various environments in which they occurred (school, home, community, etc.) Consider things like: 1. Cruelty to animals and people 2. Sexual promiscuity or irresponsible sexual practices 3. Cheating/deceiving, 4. Serious violations of rules 5. Disruptive behavior in class/truancy, 6. Runaways 7. Other (please specify ______________________)	☐ **N** ☐ **P** ☐ **Y** ☐ **–**	☐

Behaviours	Age	Frequency	Contest	Other

27. Peer Delinquency Report if the child is associated or has been associated with other deviant peers in perpetrating antisocial acts Note:	☐ **N** ☐ **P** ☐ **Y** ☐ **–**	☐
28. Use Of Substances Fill the grid reporting the list of substances, frequency of use, the age when the addiction started, if the use of the substance had a role in past violent behavior	☐ **N** ☐ **P** ☐ **Y** ☐ **–**	☐

Substance	Frequency	Type of Assumption	Age	Violence Related To Drug Abuse

Other Considerations:

Protection Domain	Scoring	Critical Factor?
29. Social And Familiar Support Evaluate the presence of parents, caregivers, or other adults to offer emotional support, help and guidance	☐ **N** ☐ **P** ☐ **Y** ☐ –	☐
30. Strong Relationships And Bonds Evaluate the presence of solid and stable emotional relationships with adults (family, teachers or others) that identify and encourage the skills of the child and transmit affection and acceptance	☐ **N** ☐ **P** ☐ **Y** ☐ –	☐
31. Prosocial Involvement Evaluate whether the child participates in socially valued activities and/or prosocial friendship groups (groups not involved in deviant activities) Consider things like: ☐ Involvement in activities including cooperation and conflict management (volunteer, parish activities, etc.) ☐ Involvement in socially positive activities (organized sports, groups, clubs etc.) ☐ Other (specify____________________________)	☐ **N** ☐ **P** ☐ **Y** ☐ –	☐
32. Resilient Personality Traits Consider elements such as: ☐ Average I.Q. ☐ Ability to develop thoughtful solutions to conflicts and problems ☐ Adaptability to changes ☐ Ability to calm themselves or to be reassured by the others in stressful situations ☐ Realistic and positive self-esteem ☐ Other (specify____________________________)	☐ **N** ☐ **P** ☐ **Y** ☐ –	☐

Other Considerations:
FINAL EVLUATION OF RISK Risk of Recidivism ☐ LOW ☐ MEDIUM ☐ HIGH
© Baldry & Kapardis (2012). EU Daphne project. No unauthorized reproduction. www.sara-cesvis.org

Appendix B: EARN in JVO questionnaire translated into Greek and used in the archival study

ΠΕΡΙΒΑΛΛΟΝΤΙΚΟΙ ΠΑΡΑΓΟΝΤΕΣ Βιολογικοί και κοινωνικοί παράγοντες όπως εξάγονται από το περιβάλλον που ζει ο νεαρός	Σοβαρότητα	Κίνδυνος
1.Χρηση ουσιών από την μητέρα κατά τη διάρκεια της εγκυμοσύνης □ Τσιγάρα □ Αλκοόλ □ Ναρκωτικά □ Άλλο______________ Να συμπληρωθεί αν υπάρχει έστω και ένας από τους προαναφερθέντες παράγοντες	□ N □ P □ Y □ -	□
2. Χαμηλό Κοινωνικό-Οικονομικό επίπεδο της οικογένειας.	□ N □ P □ Y □ -	□
3. Κοινοτική αποδιοργάνωση Λάβετε υπόψη στοιχεία όπως : □ Απουσία δομημένων δραστηριοτήτων □ Πρόσβαση σε όπλα □ Πρόσβαση σε ναρκωτικά □ Παρουσία ενηλίκων της γειτονιάς που εμπλέκονται σε αντικοινωνική συμπεριφορά και βία □ Παρουσία παράνομων μεταναστών □ Άλλο______________ Να συμπληρωθεί αν υπάρχει έστω και ένας από τους προαναφερθέντες παράγοντες	□ N □ P □ Y □ -	□
4. Σχολικό Περιβάλλον Λάβετε υπόψη παράγοντες όπως : □ Ελλιπής επίβλεψη (αναλογία εκπαιδευτικών προς μαθητές) □ Έλλειψη πόρων και δομημένων δραστηριοτήτων □ Παρουσία βίας και συγκρούσεων σε έντονο βαθμό □ Άλλο______________ Να συμπληρωθεί αν υπάρχει έστω και ένας από τους προαναφερθέντες παράγοντες	□ N □ P □ Y □ -	□
Άλλοι προβληματισμοί		□
ΑΤΟΜΙΚΟΙ ΠΑΡΑΓΟΝΤΕΣ Ατομικές διαφορές που αλληλεπιδρούν με επικίνδυνους περιβαλλοντικούς παράγοντες έτσι ώστε να καθοριστεί αντικοινωνική συμπεριφορά.	Σοβαρότητα	Κίνδυνος

5. Δυσκολίες κατά τη κύηση / Ανεπάρκεια στη γέννα. Περιπλοκές και περίοδοι (κυοφορία / γέννα / βρεφική περίοδος) Λάβετε υπόψη παράγοντες όπως : ☐ Κακή φυσική υγεία κατά τη διάρκεια της κύησης (π.χ. κακή διατροφή, μεταδοτικές ασθένειες) ☐ Εξαγωγή με λαβίδες ☐ Ανάποδη γέννηση ☐ Περίκαμψις ☐ Πρόωρη γέννηση—καισαρική ☐ Γέννα μεγάλης διάρκειας ☐ Έλλειψη οξυγόνου ☐ Πολύ ελαφρύ / βαρύ στη γέννα μωρό ☐ Δυσκολίες ή χρόνιες ασθένειες που διεγνώσθησαν μέχρι το 1° έτος του. ☐ Άλλο_______________ Να συμπληρωθεί αν υπάρχει έστω και ένας από τους προαναφερθέντες παράγοντες	☐ N ☐ P ☐ Y ☐ -	☐
6. Δυσλειτουργία στο Σχολειό Λάβετε υπόψη στοιχεία όπως : ☐ Κακή σχολική απόδοση ☐ Ανεπαρκής δέσμευση και ενδιαφέρον ☐ Κακή δέσμευση προς το σχολειό ☐ Άλλο_______________ Να συμπληρωθεί αν υπάρχει έστω και ένας από τους προαναφερθέντες παράγοντες	☐ N ☐ P ☐ Y ☐ -	☐
7. Δυσκολία αντιμετώπισης καταστάσεων Λάβετε υπόψη στοιχεία όπως : ☐ Κακή δυνατότητα αντιμετώπισης αγχωτικών καταστάσεων ☐ Κακή δυνατότητα προσαρμογής σε αγχωτικές καταστάσεις ☐ Χαμηλή αυτό-υπόληψη. ☐ Άλλο_______________ Να συμπληρωθεί αν υπάρχει έστω και ένας από τους προαναφερθέντες παράγοντες	☐ N ☐ P ☐ Y ☐ -	☐
8. Παρορμητικότητα / Ρίσκα Λάβετε υπόψη στοιχεία όπως : ☐ Ασταθής συμπεριφορά ☐ Κυκλοθυμικές αντιδράσεις ☐ Πράττει χωρίς να σκεφτεί εις βάθος ☐ Ανικανότητα διατήρησης συγκέντρωσης, κυρίως όταν υπό πίεση. ☐ Άλλο_______________ Να συμπληρωθεί αν υπάρχει έστω και ένας από τους προαναφερθέντες παράγοντες	☐ N ☐ P ☐ Y ☐ -	☐
9. Χαμηλή κατανόηση των συναισθημάτων των άλλων ατόμων / Έλλειψη μετάνοιας Λάβετε υπόψη στοιχεία όπως : ☐ Λίγες τύψεις για συναισθήματα που αφορούν άλλους. ☐ Τάση να εκφράζονται οι συγκινήσεις με επιφανειακό και ακατάλληλο τρόπο. ☐ Άρνηση ανάληψης ευθυνών για πράξεις που έγιναν και τάση να φταίξουν άλλους. ☐ Δεν θεωρούν ότι έγινε κάτι σημαντικό, πως είχαν αρνητική συμπεριφορά. ☐ Άλλο_______________ Να συμπληρωθεί αν υπάρχει έστω και ένας από τους προαναφερθέντες παράγοντες	☐ N ☐ P ☐ Y ☐ -	☐

10. Υπερκινητικότητα / Ελλειμματική Προσοχή Παρουσιάστε τη βάση της αξιολόγησης (π.χ. WISC-III) Λάβετε υπόψη στοιχεία όπως : ☐ Προβλήματα προσοχής / συγκέντρωσης ☐ Υπερβολική ανησυχία ☐ Υπερκινητικότητα και αυθορμητισμός ☐ Άλλο______________ Διευκρινίστε, αν η αξιολόγηση είναι ☐ Τελική Αξιολόγηση: Βασισμένη σε προηγούμενες αξιολογήσεις ή η αυτούσια αξιολόγηση ☐ Προσωρινή Αξιολόγηση: Να επιβεβαιωθεί με κλινική διάγνωση Να συμπληρωθεί αν υπάρχει έστω και ένας από τους προαναφερθέντες παράγοντες	☐ N ☐ P ☐ Y ☐ -	☐
11. Ψυχικά νοσήματα Λάβετε υπόψη και παρουσιάστε λεπτομερή στοιχεία όπως : ☐ Ιστορικό γνωστικής και πνευματικής καθυστέρησης ☐ Ιστορικό αντιπαραθετικής προσωπικότητας ή άλλων βρεφικών δυσλειτουργιών. ☐ Ιστορικό προσπάθειας πρόκλησης κακού στον εαυτό του ή απόπειρα αυτοκτονίας ☐ Ιστορικό ψυχιατρικής, φαρμακολογικής ή/και ψυχοθεραπευτικής παρέμβασης ☐ Ενδείξεις για μελλοντικές σοβαρές ψυχικές διαταραχές ☐ Ενδείξεις για μελλοντικές διαταραχές προσωπικότητας Διευκρίνιση, αν η αξιολόγηση είναι ☐ Τελική Αξιολόγηση: Βασισμένη σε προηγούμενες αξιολογήσεις ή η αυτούσια αξιολόγηση ☐ Προσωρινή Αξιολόγηση: Να επιβεβαιωθεί με κλινική διάγνωση Να συμπληρωθεί αν υπάρχει έστω και ένας από τους προαναφερθέντες παράγοντες	☐ N ☐ P ☐ Y ☐ -	☐
Άλλοι προβληματισμοί		☐
ΟΙΚΟΓΕΝΕΙΑΚΟΙ ΠΑΡΑΓΟΝΤΕΣ Συμπεριλαμβάνονται ιδιαιτερότητες, δυναμικές και σχέσεις μεταξύ οικογένειας και παιδιών. Σημ. Αν τα παιδιά δεν έχουν μεγαλώσει με τους βιολογικούς γονείς, να γίνεται προσπάθεια κωδικοποίησης και των ανάδοχων αλλά και βιολογικών γονιών.	Σοβαρότητα	Κίνδυνος
12. Ιστορικό ψυχικής ασθένειας από στους γονείς Παρέχετε λίστα με ασθένειες για κάθε ένα γονιό.	☐ N ☐ P ☐ Y ☐ -	☐
13. Εφηβική εγκυμοσύνη Ηλικία της μητέρας όταν γέννησε το παιδί.	☐ N ☐ P ☐ Y ☐ -	☐

14. Περιγραφή του άτομου που του παρείχε φροντίδα στα πρώτα του χρόνια.	☐ N ☐ P ☐ Y ☐ -	☐
15. Συχνές αλλαγές στο άτομο που του παρείχε φροντίδα στα πρώτα του χρόνια.	☐ N ☐ P ☐ Y ☐ -	☐
16. Μονογονία ή όχι, η οικογενειακή δομή.	☐ N ☐ P ☐ Y ☐ -	☐
17. Ανεπαρκείς γονική φροντίδα Λάβετε υπόψη στοιχεία όπως : ☐ Γονείς που δεν εκφράζουν ζεστασιά και συνοχή στις επαφές τους με τα παιδιά τους ☐ Γονείς που δεν ασχολούνται με τη ζωή των παιδιών τους ☐ Γονείς που είναι υπερβολικά διορθωτικοί ή υπερβολικά επιτρεπτικοί με τα παιδιά τους Να συμπληρωθεί αν υπάρχει έστω και ένας από τους προαναφερθέντες παράγοντες	☐ N ☐ P ☐ Y ☐ -	☐
18. Ενδοοικογενειακές διαμάχες Διευκρινίστε αν ήταν παρών σε οικογενειακές διαμάχες και βία και αν δέχτηκε σωματική βία το ίδιο το παιδί. Λάβετε υπόψη τη σοβαρότητα και τη συχνότητα των συγκρούσεων ή της βίας στο σπίτι.	☐ N ☐ P ☐ Y ☐ -	☐
19. Αντικοινωνικές συμπεριφορές / στάσεις γονέων Παραθέστε αν οι γονείς έχουν εμπλακεί σε εγκληματικές και αντικοινωνικές συμπεριφορές ακόμη και αν δεν έχουν καταγγελθεί ή συλληφθεί.	☐ N ☐ P ☐ Y ☐ -	☐
Άλλοι προβληματισμοί:		☐
ΠΑΡΑΓΟΝΤΕΣ ΠΑΡΕΜΒΑΣΗΣ Συμπεριλάβετε προγράμματα / στρατηγικές που χρησιμοποιηθήκαν για πρόληψη, θεραπεία ή διαχείριση αντικοινωνικής συμπεριφοράς	Σοβαρότητα	Κίνδυνος

20. Προηγούμενες παρεμβάσεις

Παρέχετε στον πινάκα τον τύπο, τη διάρκεια, το στόχο των παρεμβάσεων, καθώς και πληροφορίες για συμπεράσματα και αποτελέσματα.

Τύπος	**Αίτημα**	**Χρόνος / διάρκεια**	**Στόχος**	**Συμπεράσματα / Αποτελέσματα**
Νοσοκομειακού				
Γονείς και οικο ένε α				
Π ιδιού				
Σχολειού				
Δικαιοσύνη				
Κοινότητα				
Άλλο				

☐ N
☐ P
☐ Y
☐ -

☐

21. Αδύνατη αντίδραση της οικογενείας στην παρέμβαση

Λάβετε υπόψη τη γονική προθυμία για προσπάθειες παρόμοιου τύπου.
Λάβετε υπόψη την οικογενειακή στήριξη και συμμέτοχη στην υποστήριξη θεραπειών προς το παιδί.
Λάβετε υπόψη στοιχεία όπως :

- ☐ Μη προτροπή για συμμετοχή σε προγράμματα
- ☐ Όχι επαφές με το γραφείο ευημερίας
- ☐ Να έχει λίγη συμμετοχή στο σχέδιο επεξεργασίας
- ☐ Είναι ανίκανος να δεχθεί τον προβληματισμό του ανηλίκου
- ☐ Άλλο___________________

Να συμπληρωθεί αν υπάρχει έστω και ένας από τους προαναφερθέντες παράγοντες

☐ N
☐ P
☐ Y
☐ -

☐

22. Αδυναμία αφοσίωσης του παιδιού προς την παρέμβαση

Αξιολογήστε τη θέληση και το κίνητρο του για συμμέτοχη σε παρέμβαση

- ☐ Διορατικότητα
- ☐ Κατανόηση του προβλήματος
- ☐ Ενδιαφέρον για αλλαγή
- ☐ Καλές σχέσεις με τους λειτουργούς
- ☐ Ελπίδα για θετικό αποτέλεσμα
- ☐ Άλλο___________________

Να συμπληρωθεί αν υπάρχει έστω και ένας από τους προαναφερθέντες παράγοντες

☐ N
☐ P
☐ Y
☐ -

☐

23. Μη προσβασιμότητα στις Παρεμβάσεις

Αξιολογήστε όλες τις προσφερόμενες υπηρεσίες στην περιοχή σε σχέση με την παρέμβαση και συγκεκριμένους παράγοντες κινδύνων για το παιδί. Λάβετε υπόψη αν οι υπηρεσίες της περιοχής έχουν ενσωματωθεί στο σχεδιασμό της παρέμβασης.

☐ N
☐ P
☐ Y
☐ -

☐

Άλλοι προβληματισμοί:

☐

ΕΞΩΤΕΡΙΚΕΥΟΝΤΑΣ ΣΥΜΠΕΡΙΦΟΡΙΚΟΥΣ ΠΑΡΑΓΟΝΤΕΣ

Να συμπεριληφθούν όλες οι συμπεριφορές και αντικοινωνικές επαφές του παιδιού ακόμη και αν δεν καταγγέλθηκε ή συνελήφθηκε για αυτές.

Σοβαρότητα

Κίνδυνος

24. Ιστορικό βίας και επιθετικότητας.

Συμπληρώστε τον πίνακα σημειώνοντας βίαιες συμπεριφορές, ηλικία κατά την οποία εμφανίστηκαν κάθε πρώτη φορά, συχνότητα και τόπο όπου προέκυψαν αυτές οι συμπεριφορές.

Συμπεριφορά	Ηλικία	Συχνότητα	Τοποθεσία	Άλλο

☐ N
☐ P
☐ Y
☐ -

☐

25. Γενικές Παραβάσεις

Συμπληρώστε τον πίνακα περιγράφοντας συμπεριφορές, συχνότητα και περιεχόμενο κατά τα οποία έγινε για πρώτη φορά το παράπτωμα και αναφέρετε την ηλικία του νεαρού κατά τη κατάσταση αυτή.

Συμπεριφορά	Ηλικία	Συχνότητα	Περιεχόμενο	Άλλο

☐ N
☐ P
☐ Y
☐ -

☐

26. Γενικά Προβλήματα Συμπεριφοράς

Συμπληρώστε τον πίνακα περιγράφοντας το εύρος, τη συχνότητα και τη σοβαρότητα των προβλημάτων συμπεριφοράς όπως παρουσιάστηκαν από το άτομο καθώς και την τοποθεσία όπου παρουσιάστηκαν αυτά τα προβλήματα (σχολείο, σπίτι, κοινότητα).
Λάβετε υπόψη παράγοντες όπως:
1.Βία ενάντια σε άτομα και ζώα, 2.Σεξουαλική Επιπολαιότητα ή ανεύθυνη σεξουαλική δραστηριότητα, 3.Απάτη / Εξαπάτηση 4.Παραβίαση Σοβαρών Κανόνων, 5. Ενοχλητική συμπεριφορά στην τάξη, 6. Εγκατάλειψη σπιτιού. 7. Άλλο (συγκεκριμενοποιείστε)

Τύπος	Συχνότητα	Σοβαρότητα	Τοποθεσία	Άλλο

☐ N
☐ P
☐ Y
☐ -

☐

27. Εγκληματικότητα Συνομηλίκων

Παρουσιάστε αν το νεαρό άτομο σχετίζεται με άλλους παραβάτες συνομηλίκους του που εμπλέκονται σε αντικοινωνικές πράξεις.
Σημειώσεις:

☐ N
☐ P
☐ Y
☐ -

☐

28. Χρήση Ουσιών

Συμπληρώστε τον πίνακα παρέχοντας λίστα με ουσίες, συχνότητα και τρόπους χρήσης, ηλικία έναρξης. Επίσης αναφέρετε αν η χρήση έπαιξε σημαντικό ρόλο σε προηγούμενες βίαιες συμπεριφορές.

Τύπος	Συχνότητα	Τρόπος Χρήσης	Ηλικία έναρξης	Βία

☐ N
☐ P
☐ Y
☐ -

☐

Άλλοι προβληματισμοί:		☐
ΠΑΡΑΓΟΝΤΕΣ ΑΣΦΑΛΕΙΑΣ Συμπεριλάβετε παράγοντες ασφάλειας που θα μπορούσαν να μειώσουν τους κινδύνους	Σοβαρότητα	Κίνδυνος
29. Παρουσία Κοινωνικής και Οικογενειακής υποστήριξης Αξιολογήστε την παρουσία γονιών, ατόμων που παρέχουν φροντίδα και άλλων υπεύθυνων ενήλικων ικανών να παρέχουν συναισθηματική στήριξη, βοήθεια και να καθοδηγήσουν το νεαρό άτομο.	☐ N ☐ P ☐ Y ☐ -	☐
30. Δυνατοί Δεσμοί και Συνδέσεις Αξιολογήστε την παρουσία ζεστών και στοργικών σχέσεων με ενήλικες (μέλη της οικογένειας, δάσκαλους και άλλους ενήλικες), που ενθαρρύνουν και αναγνωρίζουν τις ικανότητες του νέου μεταβιβάζοντας του στοργικότητα και επιδεκτικότητα	☐ N ☐ P ☐ Y ☐ -	☐
31. Θετική Κοινωνική Συμμετοχή. Αξιολογήστε αν το νεαρό άτομο συμμετέχει σε κοινωνικά σημαντικές δραστηριότητες οργανωμένες με θετικές ομάδες συνομηλίκων του (άλλοι συνομήλικοι που να μην είναι παραβάτες αλλά να εμπλέκονται σε δραστηριότητες βοήθειας) Λάβετε υπόψη στοιχεία όπως : ☐ Συμμετοχή σε δραστηριότητες βοήθειας, συνεργατισμού και επίλυσης διαφορών ☐ Συμμετοχή σε κοινωνικά θετικές δραστηριότητες (αθλητισμός, ομάδες συνομηλίκων, λέσχες) και άλλα. Να συμπληρωθεί αν υπάρχει έστω και ένας από τους δυο προαναφερθέντες παράγοντες	☐ N ☐ P ☐ Y ☐ -	☐
32. Ελαστικά Γνωρίσματα Προσωπικότητας Λάβετε υπόψη στοιχεία όπως : ☐ Πάνω από το μέσο όρο νοητική και γνωστική ικανότητα ☐ Δυνατότητα να παράξει στοχαστικές λύσεις σε διαμάχες και προβλήματα ☐ Ανταπόκριση σε τρίτους ☐ Προσαρμοστικότητα σε αλλαγές στο περιβάλλον ☐ Δυνατότητα αυτό-επούλωσης ή δεκτικότητα βοήθειας για επούλωση τραυμάτων από τρίτους μετά από αγχωτικά ή γεγονότα που προκαλούν ένταση. ☐ Υγιής και ρεαλιστική αυτό-υπόληψη. ☐ Άλλο (συγκεκριμενοποιήστε) Να συμπληρωθεί αν υπάρχει έστω και ένας από τους προαναφερθέντες παράγοντες	☐ N ☐ P ☐ Y ☐ -	☐
Άλλοι προβληματισμοί		☐

ΤΕΛΙΚΗ ΑΞΙΟΛΟΓΗΣΗ ΚΙΝΔΥΝΟΥ			
Κίνδυνος για Σοβαρή Αντικοινωνική Συμπεριφορά	ΜΙΚΡΟΣ ☐	ΜΕΤΡΙΟΣ ☐	ΜΕΓΑΛΟΣ ☐
Σε πιο βαθμό θα χρειαστεί να φτάσει η προσπάθεια ή η παρέμβαση για να αποτρέψει τον συγκεκριμένο άτομο από του να εμπλακεί σε σοβαρή αντικοινωνική			

συμπεριφορά ;

Appendix C: Modified EARN in JVO questionnaire used with control group

------------- ΕΡΩΤΗΜΑΤΟΛΟΓΙΟ -------------

Γενικές Πληροφορίες:

DAPHNE, Ευρωπαϊκό Ερευνητικό Πρόγραμμα για Έφηβους. Πανεπιστήμιο Κύπρου, Cambridge University και Napoli (II) University. Το ερωτηματολόγιο αυτό είναι ΑΝΩΝΥΜΟ. Δεν υπάρχουν σωστές ή λάθος απαντήσεις. Παρακαλείστε όπως απαντήσετε σε όλες τις ερωτήσεις.

Αγόρι / Κορίτσι Ηλικία :______

	Ηλικία	Επίπεδο Εκπαίδευσης (*κυκλώστε το κατάλληλο*)
Πατέρας		Κανένα / Δημοτικό / Γυμνάσιο / Λύκειο—Τεχνική / Πανεπιστήμιο
Μητέρα		Κανένα / Δημοτικό / Γυμνάσιο / Λύκειο—Τεχνική / Πανεπιστήμιο

	Πόσα Αδέλφια έχουν
Πατέρας	
Μητέρα	

Έχεις αδέλφια ; Ναι ή Όχι

Αν Ναι πόσα ______ αγόρι/α

______ κορίτσι/α

Οδηγίες:

Κυκλώσετε τη κατάλληλη απάντηση.

Υπάρχουν ερωτήσεις που μπορείτε να κυκλώσετε περισσότερο από μια φορά.

----

1. Η κοινωνικό-οικονομική κατάσταση της οικογένειας σου είναι:1.Χαμηλή, 2.Μέτρια, 3.Εύπορη
2. Έχεις στο σπίτι πρόσβαση σε: 1. Όπλα, 2. Ναρκωτικά
3. Υπάρχουν ενήλικες της γειτονιάς που εμπλέκονται σε αντικοινωνική συμπεριφορά και βία:1.Ναι ή 2.Όχι
4. Υπάρχουν παράνομοι μετανάστες στη γειτονιά σου: 1.Ναι ή 2.Όχι
5. Στο σχολειό η αναλογία εκπαιδευτικών προς μαθητές είναι χειρότερη απ ότι πρέπει:1.Ναι ή 2. Όχι

6. Στο σχολειό υπάρχουν δομημένες δραστηριότητες: 1.Ναι ή 2.Όχι

7. Υπάρχει βία και συγκρούσεις σε έντονο βαθμό στο σχολειό: 1.Ναι ή 2.Όχι

8. Πως κρίνεις τη σχολική σου απόδοση: 1.Καλή ή 2.Όχι καλή

9. Σε ενδιαφέρουν τα μαθήματα σου: 1.Ναι ή 2.Όχι

10. Πως αντιμετωπίζετε αγχωτικές καταστάσεις: 1.Με επιτυχία ή 2. Όχι

11. Προσαρμόζεσαι σε αγχωτικές καταστάσεις: 1.Εύκολα ή 2.Δύσκολα

12. Γενικά η συμπεριφορά σου είναι: 1.Σταθερή ή 2.Όχι

13. Αλλάζεις συχνά χωρίς λόγο διάθεση: 1.Ναι ή 2.Όχι

14. Πόσο πολύ σκέφτεσαι πριν κάνεις μια πράξη: 1.Λίγο, 2.Καθόλου ή 3.Αρκετά

15. Όταν είσαι υπό πίεση μπορείς να είσαι συγκεντρωμένος/η: 1.Ναι ή 2.Όχι

16. Πόσο σε ενδιαφέρουν τα συναισθήματα των άλλων ανθρώπων:
    1.Λίγο, 2.Καθόλου ή 3.Αρκετά

17. Υπάρχει διάγνωση για υπερκινητικότητα / ελλειμματική προσοχή:
    1.Ναι ή 2.Όχι

18. Ποιο άτομο σου παρείχε φροντίδα στα πρώτα σου χρόνια:
    Μητέρα / Πατέρας / Παππούς / Γιαγιά άλλο________

19. Υπήρξαν πολλές αλλαγές στο άτομο/α που σου παρείχε/αν φροντίδα στα πρώτα σου χρόνια:
    1.Ναι ή 2. Όχι

20. Οι γονείς σου έχουν ζεστή σχέση με τα παιδιά τους: 1.Ναι ή 2.Όχι

21. Οι γονείς σου συμπεριφέρονται με τον ίδιο τρόπο τις περισσότερες φορές: 1.Ναι ή 2.Όχι

22. Οι γονείς σου ασχολούνται με τη ζωή των παιδιών τους: 1.Ναι ή 2.Όχι

23. Οι γονείς σου είναι υπερβολικά διορθωτικοί: 1.Ναι ή 2.Όχι

24. Οι γονείς σου είναι υπερβολικά επιτρεπτικοί με τα παιδιά τους: 1.Ναι ή 2.Όχι

25. Οι γονείς σου έρχονται συχνά σε έντονη αντιπαράθεση: 1.Ναι ή 2.Όχι

26. Η οικογένεια σου έχει επαφή με το Γραφείο Ευημερίας: 1.Ναι ή 2.Όχι

27. Τσακώθηκα και κτύπησα κάποιο: συμμαθητή / συγγενή / φίλο / γνωστό μου:
1.Ναι ή 2.Όχι
Αν Ναι σε πια ηλικία έγινε για πρώτη φορά:_________

28. Έχω φίλους μου που προβαίνουν σε αντικοινωνικές πράξεις:
1.Ναι ή 2.Όχι

29.

Έχεις χρησιμοποιήσει πότε:			Αν Ναι σε ποια ηλικία ;
Τσιγάρο	Όχι	Ναι	
Δυνατό ποτό	Όχι	Ναι	
Ελαφριά Ναρκωτικά	Όχι	Ναι	
Σκληρά Ναρκωτικά	Όχι	Ναι	

30. Υπάρχουν άτομα στην οικογένεια σου ή εκτός που γνωρίζεις ότι σε στηρίζουν:
1.Ναι ή 2.Όχι

31. Υπάρχει κάποιος/οι ενήλικας/ες που ενθαρρύνει/ουν και αναγνωρίζει/ουν τις ικανότητες σου:
1.Ναι ή 2.Όχι

32. Ζω και με τους δυο μου γονείς: 1. Ναι ή 2.Όχι
Αν Όχι γιατί: διαζύγιο / σε διάσταση / θάνατος / άλλο

33. Συμμετέχεις σε δραστηριότητες βοήθειας, συνεργατισμού και επίλυσης διαφορών: 1.Ναι ή 2.Όχι

34. Συμμετέχεις σε κοινωνικές δραστηριότητες όπως αθλητικές ομάδες, προσκόπους και άλλα:
α) Ναι ή β) Όχι

———————— **Ευχαριστούμε για τη Συμμέτοχη και το Χρόνο σου** ————————

Αν θέλετε να κάνετε οποιαδήποτε σχόλια για την έρευνα αυτή μπορείτε να χρησιμοποιήσετε το χώρο αυτό ή να στείλετε email στο kapardis@ucy.ac.cy .

____

____

____

____

Appendix D: Corresponding question numbers from short to long version of EARN in JVO questionnaire used in Cyprus

Short Version	*Long Version*	*Short Version*	*Long Version*
1	2	18	14
2	3	19	15
3	3	20	17
4	3	21	17
5	4	22	17
6	4	23	17
7	4	24	17
8	6	25	18
9	6	26	20
10	7	27	24
11	7	28	27
12	8	29	28
13	8	30	29
14	8	31	30
15	8	32	16
16	9	33	31
17	10	34	31

Baldry and Kapardis/RAJVO

Index

For Product Safety Concerns and Information please contact our EU representative GPSR@taylorandfrancis.com Taylor & Francis Verlag GmbH, Kaufingerstraße 24, 80331 München, Germany

Batch number: 10725973

Printed by Printforce, the Netherlands